# METABLOCK

Prepared for the course team by Richard Stevens
and unit authors

**SOCIAL SCIENCES: A THIRD LEVEL COURSE**
**SOCIAL PSYCHOLOGY: DEVELOPMENT, EXPERIENCE**
**AND BEHAVIOUR IN A SOCIAL WORLD**

THE OPEN UNIVERSITY

**Open University Course Team**

Melanie Bayley   *Editor*
Hedy Brown   *Senior lecturer in social psychology*
Rudi Dallos   *Staff tutor, Region 03*
David Graddol   *Research Fellow, School of Education*
Judith Greene   *Professor of psychology*
Jane Henry   *Lecturer in educational technology*
Pam Higgins   *Designer*
Clive Holloway   *BBC producer*
Tom Hunter   *Editor*
Mary John   *Staff tutor, Region 02*
Maggie Lawson   *Project control*
Dorothy Miell   *Lecturer in psychology*
Eleanor Morris   *BBC producer*
Stella Pilsworth   *Liaison librarian*
Ortenz Rose   *Secretary*
Roger J. Sapsford   *Lecturer in research methods*
Varrie Scott   *Course manager*
David Seligman   *BBC executive producer*
Ingrid Slack   *Course manager*
Richard Stevens   *Senior lecturer in psychology*
Kerry Thomas   *Lecturer in psychology, Course team chairperson*
Barbara Thompson   *Staff tutor, Region 01*
Eleanor Thompson   *Project control*
Pat Vasiliou   *Secretary*
Doreen Warwick   *Secretary*
Chris Wooldridge   *Editor*

**External Course Team Member**

Jeannette Murphy   *Polytechnic of North London*

**Consultants**

Charles Antaki   *University of Lancaster*
Glynis M. Breakwell   *University of Surrey*
Steve Duck   *University of Lancaster*
Susan Gregory   *University of Nottingham*
Patrick Humphreys   *London School of Economics*
Kim Plunkett   *University of Aarhus, Denmark*
Harry Procter   *Southwood Hospital, Bridgewater*

**Course Assessor**

Professor Robert Farr   *London School of Economics*

The Open University
Walton Hall, Milton Keynes
MK7 6AA

First published 1984. Reprinted 1989, 1991

Copyright © 1984 The Open University

Designed by the Graphic Design Group of the Open University.

Printed in the United Kingdom by Staples Printers St Albans Limited at The Priory Press.

ISBN 0 7492 0025 1

This text forms part of an Open University course. The complete list of Blocks and Units in the course appears on the back cover.

For general availability of supporting material referred to in this text, please write to Open University Educational Enterprises Limited, 12 Cofferidge Close, Stony Stratford, Milton Keynes, MK11 1BY, the United Kingdom.

Further information on Open University courses may be obtained from the Admissions Office, The Open University, P.O. Box 48, Walton Hall, Milton Keynes, MK7 6AB.
2.2

# CONTENTS

page

**Part I   Introduction and Course Guide**                                5

1.1    The Metablock                                                      5
1.2    D307: Course Plan                                                  5
1.3    Outline of the unit texts                                         6
1.4    Set books                                                         8
1.5    Assessment                                                        8
1.5.1  Tutor-marked assignments                                         9
1.5.2  The examination                                                   9
1.6    Video and audio material                                         9
1.7    The practical project                                            9
1.8    Day schools                                                      10
1.9    Integration Essay                                                10
1.10   Studying social psychology                                      10

**Part II   Vade Mecum**                                                 11
Block 1 – Creating a social world (study weeks 1–5)                     12
Block 2 – Becoming a social being (study weeks 6–8)                     19
Block 3 – Understanding other people and developing relationships (study
            weeks 9–14)                                                 22
Block 4 – Personal worlds (study weeks 15–20)                           29
Block 5 – Attitude theories: ancient and modern (study weeks 21–25)    34
Block 6 – People in groups (study weeks 26–28)                          39
Block 7 – Society, culture and change (study week 29)                   40
            Integration and revision (study weeks 30–32)               41

**Part III   Key issues in social psychology**                          43
Paper 1 – People and perspectives in social psychology                 43
Paper 2 – Making sense of theories in social psychology                60
Paper 3 – Levels of analysis                                            74
Paper 4 – Behaviour and action                                          81
Paper 5 – The significance of meaning                                   85
Paper 6 – Research methods                                              92
Paper 7 – The construction of reality                                  100
Paper 8 – Nomothetic, idiographic and hermeneutic social psychology    109
Paper 9 – A note on assumptions of autonomy and determinism in social
            psychology                                                 122
Paper 10 – A note on the nature of social psychology                   126

**Part IV   Revision exercises**                                        131

# PART I – INTRODUCTION AND COURSE GUIDE

*by Richard Stevens and Kerry Thomas*

## 1.1 The Metablock

The purpose of the Metablock is (i) to help you reflect on the nature of the course as a whole, (ii) to see how each part links with the others and (iii) to draw your attention to some of the major themes which run through it. (The prefix 'meta' indicates a 'higher' level of inquiry.)

The Metablock is divided into four parts:

*Part I: The Course Guide.* The Course Guide sets out how the course is structured, outlines the blocks and the other components of the course and describes how your work will be assessed. The Course Plan, which you should have to hand whilst you read Part I, is the 'centrefold' of the *Assignments Booklet*. You can pull this out and use it for planning your studies alongside Part II of the Metablock. On the back of the Course Plan you will find update notes if these are necessary in any given year.

*Part II: The Vade Mecum.* This is a week-by-week guide to the course – designed as a companion to your studies as you progress through the year. *Vade Mecum* (Latin, literally 'go with me') is an old term for a guide book.

*Part III: Key issues in social psychology.* This section consists of a set of papers, written by course team members, in which major themes arising at various points in the course are taken up. *Many of these issues are controversial and you should be aware that the authors are presenting their own synthesis of the debates and their own viewpoint on certain controversies.* The styles of the papers are varied: some are fairly short, others are more discursive. But each paper takes up an issue (perhaps a definition, or perhaps a much wider topic) and discusses it in greater depth than is possible in the unit text. Each Metablock paper is intended to be self-contained so some overlap between papers is inevitable.

Your depth of understanding of these papers will depend to a large extent on how much of the course you have read. Use the Metablock papers as a resource – whenever you need to – but do not necessarily expect to reap their full benefit on a first reading. The issues discussed will become clearer with re-reading.

*Part IV: Revision exercises.* This is a set of suggested revision strategies or exercises to help you assimilate the work you have covered. You can use these either at the end of the course or after finishing a particular block.

Before you start reading Block 1 you should read the rest of this section of the Metablock. Then read the introduction to Part II – the Vade Mecum and the section on Block 1 (study weeks 1–5). In this way, you will be setting the pattern for reading and consulting the Vade Mecum alongside *every* block and study week.

## 1.2 D307: Course Plan

Turn to the Course Plan which is the centrefold of your *Assignments Booklet*. If you keep this to hand while you read the rest of Part I the structure of the course will fall into place more easily. You will see that there are twenty-two unit texts which leaves ten weeks of the course for other components. Two weeks are allotted to the TMA 04 Project (double TMA) and about two weeks to prepare for the Integration Essay – which will necessarily include some revision. Six weeks, therefore, are available for work on the Metablock and the parts of the Course

Reader and set books not directly referred to in the units. There is, therefore, quite a lot of room for flexibility in the way you study, although TMA cut-off dates will constrain your pattern of work. Be sure to keep to the schedule for choosing the Project option, because you may need to start collecting data, so you need to make sure that you have enough time to do this before the cut-off date. Also, choosing the Project option will be linked, wherever possible, to a day school for which you will need to be fully prepared (i.e. have read through each of the five options – see 1.7 below).

## 1.3 Outline of the unit texts

The basic aim of D307 is to introduce you to *Social Psychology*. By the end of the course we hope that you will have enriched your understanding of:

1 the ways in which people behave and make sense of themselves, make sense of their relationships with others and the social situations they find themselves in; and how they relate to society and culture;

2 the ways in which psychologists have studied and thought about these issues;

3 what kind of knowledge is possible about human social behaviour and experience.

We also hope that you will find some personal relevance in the course: that your study will stimulate your thinking about your own experience and the ways in which you can live your life. It is worth noting that, although this course is relevant to real-life situations, it does not provide prescriptions for behaviour; rather it seeks to give a wider appreciation of the complexities and limitations as well as the uses of psychology.

The first two blocks of the course set up a developmental theme by exploring how an infant becomes a fully *social* being. The context for this development is described in Block 1, *Creating a social world* and in particular in Unit 1, 'The family'.

By starting out like this with a description of a commonplace social institution, which in some form or other is experienced by almost everyone, we ensure that the course takes account of the 'social world as it exists out there' and the roles played by all of us – adults and infants in creating our social worlds. Thus the unit asks 'what is a family?', 'what is its significance and function for adults?', '. . . for infants?', '. . . and for society?', 'to what extent and in what ways is "a family" a pattern of living arrangements common to all humans as a species?', and 'how far is the family a product of society?' Unit 1 also considers the possibility that the problems and pitfalls of family life can be avoided by our own conscious attempts to change the social world as given and create our own version: Thus the unit ends by looking at alternative living and child-rearing arrangements, in particular those of communes and Israeli *kibbutzim*.

The second unit examines the family from a different perspective; it looks at what actually happens in families. By treating a family as a system rather than as a set of individuals it is possible to see how our everyday behaviour in social relationships defines and creates the 'social reality' that we experience.

The final two units of Block 1 examine the different kinds of theoretical and research perspectives which we need to take into account in order to understand how a child evolves into a social being. Unit 3 looks at the role genetic factors play in underpinning social behaviour and experience, while Unit 4 contrasts four major perspectives on the socialization of the child (psychoanalysis, social learning theory, cognitive theories like those of Piaget and symbolic interactionism). Each perspective has its own way of conceptualizing and approaching the issues in question and each is based on a somewhat different set of underlying assumptions about the nature of persons and the ways in which it is best to study them. This discussion provides the foundation for applications of these theories later in the course.

*[handwritten margin notes:]*
Block 1 – how infant becomes a fully social being.

Socialisation of child
① psychoanalysis
② social learning theory
③ cognitive theories
④ symbolic interactionism

6

One of the central aspects of being a person is our consciousness of identity; in other words, your and my awareness that each of us is a particular individual with specific characteristics, a past and a possible future. This is interlinked with a sense of agency; that we can choose and act to bring about certain events. Both of these aspects of 'social being' are premised on the development of meaning, i.e. the capacity to make some kind of sense of, and predictions about, our behaviour and the social world in which we live.

This depends on mastery of language. Block 2, *Becoming a social being*, is concerned with the development of such capacities and skills in the growing child. Unit 5 describes how children acquire language, and Unit 6 shows how language functions in society as a social marker, as a vehicle for expressing social identity and as a means to control relationships. Having demonstrated the power of language, the block concludes in Unit 7 by exploring the *development* of understanding and agency: how a child comes to attribute and communicate meaning in social situations.

Block 3, *Understanding other people and developing relationships*, moves on to explore how adults 'understand' each other and how and why they develop and establish and perhaps end relationships. How do relationships develop? How can we describe what goes on in social interactions and understand how one person forms an impression of another? Why is it that we can easily form relationships with some people and not with others? In tackling this sort of question Block 3 has to deal with problems about appropriate methods and research ethics.

Block 4, *Personal worlds*, focuses on how adults experience the personal and social worlds in which they live. Through glimpsing the experiential worlds of a few very different individuals (i.e. how they experience themselves and the world about them) several descriptive dimensions are drawn out which seem to be intrinsic to the experience of being human. There is, for example, a sense of personal consciousness which is located in time and space. We have a sense of identity, of who we are, and what we have been and may be. We probably feel that we experience some degree of control, albeit small, over the course of events in our lives. We are also aware of our own fragility – that some day we shall have to confront the fact of our own death. The block goes on to explore these dimensions of personal experience. In what ways, for example, can conscious awareness be considered as rooted in our biological nature as human beings and therefore universal to our species? How far is it historically and culturally shaped? In what ways does our sense of being evolve and change as we develop through life to old age?

Although Block 4 attempts to look *directly* at personal and social life as we *experience* it, many social psychologists have focused on *measuring* the ways in which we react to and feel about different aspects of the world in which we live. Thus Block 5, *Attitude theories: ancient and modern*, looks at the ways in which psychologists have studied people's attitudes. The first two units show how different kinds of attitude research (individualistic and personality-related, survey research, experimental studies etc.) have developed over the last sixty years or so and how attitude studies have been influenced by social and political concerns. These are illustrated further in the second half of Block 5 by research on mass communication and 'persuasion', and by a case study of attitude research in the 'real world'. This longitudinal study examines the effects of group membership, family influence and the media on the development of people's political attitudes and on their voting behaviour.

Block 5 emphasizes that many of our beliefs take the form of 'collective representations', i.e. that we hold many of our world views in common with other people. Block 6, *People in groups*, continues this shift from an individual to a social or group level of analysis. It explores the processes involved in the often powerful influence which a group can wield on the behaviour and attitudes of its members. This block covers a wide variety of group-related issues such as leadership, conflict between groups, decision making, identity as a function of

7

group membership, and social behaviour in crowds and riots. It also discusses prejudice and deliberate attempts to influence the behaviour and beliefs of others.

In Block 7 the course concludes by returning to the level of society and culture. Unit 22, 'Social movements and their strategies' discusses social movements, how these emerge and develop and the role they play in changing the society in which we live and hence its influence on individuals' attitudes and behaviour. The block ends with a postscript to the course which uses social and economic change to highlight the influence of culture, social structure and ideology in making possible different patterns of life experience. The continuing spiral whereby individuals create social worlds and are also influenced by these worlds is thus emphasized. Questions about whether there can ever be universal laws in social psychology and the inevitable ethnocentrism of the social psychology created in the Western world are also raised.

## 1.4   Set books

There are two set books and a Course Reader.

1   *Freud and Psychoanalysis* (Stevens, 1983) is intended to serve two functions. The first is to provide an account of psychoanalytic theory which is *one* of the perspectives which run through the course. The second is to serve as a detailed *case study* illustrating some of the problems of investigating social behaviour and experience and questioning what kind of knowledge social psychology can be expected to provide.

*Freud and Psychoanalysis* is used at various points throughout the course and if you want to read one of the set books before the course begins, this is the best one to start with.

2   *How Voters Decide* (Himmelweit, Humphreys and Jaeger, 1984, 2nd edition) provides a detailed study of a research project which was carried out over several years in the United Kingdom and investigates the factors underlying political attitudes and vote choice.

*How Voters Decide* is specifically associated with Block 5 on attitudes and specific guidance will be given there on how to use the book.

3   The Course Reader, *Dialogues and Debates in Social Psychology*, (Murphy, J., John, M. and Brown, H. (eds)), serves a number of purposes. Many of the articles it contains directly support individual units either as set reading or as recommended reading and study time has been allocated for reading these articles alongside the unit texts. However, you will find that the Reader as a whole has a structure which does *not* mirror that of the course. Instead it is organized around a socio-historical approach to social psychological research. We have set aside time, primarily in the second half of the course, for you to study the arguments presented in the Reader. Guidance for your study of the Reader is given in the appropriate sections of Part II of the Metablock. Since the Reader serves more than one purpose, articles will often be referred to on more than one occasion. For instance, while each article plays a role in the structure of the Reader, it may also support and extend a course unit and provide additional material for TMAs and for your 'integration' essay.  The Reader as a whole should also enhance your knowledge of methods and the practical and ethical difficulties of research in social psychology.

## 1.5   Assessment

Your final grade for the course will be based on your tutor-marked assignments (TMAs) and on a three-hour, three-essay question examination. The continuous

8

assessment and the exam each contribute 50 per cent to the total marks for the course.

### 1.5.1   Tutor-marked assignments (50 per cent of total marks for the course)

You will be required to submit essays and a report of your practical project for continuous assessment. Details are given in the *Assignments Booklet.*

### 1.5.2   The examination (50 per cent of total marks for the course)

For the examination, you will have to write essay type answers to three questions and you will have three hours to complete the paper (a specimen exam paper is included in your mailings for this course). The paper is divided into two parts. You have to answer two questions from *Part 1* which will comprise questions based on the unit text material, the set reading and the set books. Although some of the questions will require you to make comparisons or argue across a range of units from different blocks, they will not require extensive integration across the course as a whole, nor will they be directed at wider social psychological issues. This kind of question will be the basis of Part 2 of the examination paper.

You also have to answer one question from Part 2. The questions in Part 2 will be designed to test your knowledge of and ability to integrate the course as a whole, i.e. the threads which tie the course together. For instance, it is possible to draw on material from many units to illustrate how underlying 'models of the person' influence the kind of research techniques that are used; or you could be asked to use the material in the Course Reader together with unit texts to illustrate ethical problems in social psychological research. These are no more than examples of the type and range of integration that Part 2 of the exam paper will assess.

The three examination questions will be weighted equally.

## 1.6   Video and audio material

There are no radio or TV programmes for D307, however *it is essential that you organize access to a video tape recorder (VHS) if you decide to choose either the* Family Observation Project *or the* Mother/Child Interaction Project. The video material for D307 consists of two video programmes of thirty minutes each. The audio tape is associated with the Family Observation Project. If you cannot arrange access to the video material there is an alternative: the video programmes will be available in regional centres.

## 1.7   The practical project

The TMA 04 project is a double TMA. The practice of doing and writing up the project *and* the reading on methods associated with the five options for the project make up the major part of the *methods* teaching for the course. Through your reading and undertaking of this project, you will learn about the advantages and shortcomings of the different research techniques and the relationship between certain research methods and the kind of topic that is being studied. Knowledge of research methods and the wider issues of methodologies will extend your critical evaluation of the research and the theories discussed in the unit texts, the Course Reader and the set books. Thus a knowledge of methodology is essential to D307 and will be part of the material on which you may be examined.

The project is a double TMA. Two weeks are set aside (between study weeks 18 and 20) to do the project, but before then you need to choose which of the options you want to do. Look in the *Assignment Booklet* to check whether all five options listed below are available in a given year:

1  Family Observation Project (associated with Unit 2)

2  Mother/child interaction Project (associated with Unit 7)

3  Kelly Project (associated with Unit 8)

4  Diary Project (associated with Unit 10/11)

5  Interview Project (associated with Block 4)

In order to choose between these options, you will need to study the different methods involved and read about the practical requirements and constraints of each. You will be given time to do this preparatory work in study week 14 as shown in the Course Plan. You are advised to make your choice at that particular time because you need to have read as far as Unit 10/11 in order to appreciate what is involved in the practical work. If you choose the Diary Project associated with Unit 10/11 for example, you will need to collect data for ten minutes per day for four weeks *before* the time set aside to do the project. Therefore, although there *is* flexibility in your timetable you need to choose your project early and before you decide the best two weeks in which to actually carry it out.

## 1.8   Day schools

It is hoped that day schools, half day schools or at least a tutorial can be arranged to precede weeks 3 and 15. The first of these will be an introduction to the course. The second day school will, at least in part, be given over to a discussion of methods and the 'choice' you have to make about options for the Project. Where possible, a third day school will be arranged for later in the study year, mainly for revision.

## 1.9   Integration Essay

For your final TMA you will be asked to submit an 'integration' essay. Although two weeks will be allocated for writing the essay towards the end of the course, you are nevertheless advised to work on this essay throughout the year. A choice of questions is given in the *Assignments Booklet* together with some guidance to help you think in some depth about whatever topic you select. You will be able to draw on relevant material from any part of the course and also, if you wish, from your further reading.

## 1.10   Studying social psychology

Now that you have an impression of the structure and content of the course, a question may occur to you – how is D307 different from or similar to other university courses in social psychology? If you glance at some contemporary textbooks on social psychology you will see that they are likely to include topics like the following: *socialization*; *attitudes* including measurement, survey research, attitude organization and change, prejudice; *social perception*; *interpersonal attraction*; *communication* including both language and non-verbal communication; *social interaction*; *role theories*; *groups* including group dynamics, problem solving, conflicts, leadership and conformity.

You will find that all these topics appear in one way or another in this course. But we have tried to do more than this.

A good deal of space is devoted to exploring the *origins* of social behaviour and experience, in particular the origins of our sense of self-awareness and social being and our construction of our social worlds. We also include consideration of evolutionary and genetic factors (a topic only rarely discussed in social psychology courses). Many texts and courses in social psychology approach the origins of social behaviour and experience from one specific standpoint. Thus, some look at them only in terms of experimental research, others from the viewpoint of a particular theoretical position like 'learning theory' or 'symbolic interactionism'. A special feature of this course is that we adopt what we call a *multiple perspective* approach. We suggest that, as you progress through the course, you try to be especially alert to (and collect notes on) the different theoretical traditions as they appear. Many of these are introduced in Block 1 and are then taken up in greater detail later in the course. The use of different theories will be flagged in the units and in the Vade Mecum.

To help you contrast the scope, different assumptions, values, kinds of explanation offered and models of the person and the world implied by different perspectives, a scheme of ten dimensions for comparing theories is included as the second paper in Part III of the Metablock. You might like to read this through before you begin work on Block 1.

One reason why we have taken a 'multiple perspective' approach is that we take the view that knowledge cannot be regarded as absolute, as something 'out there' which only has to be discovered. Rather, we create knowledge – whether this knowledge is made up of our formal, psychologists' theories or whether it is everyone's everyday knowledge about the world in general. This theme of 'constructivism' runs throughout the course, thus the first block is called *Creating a social world*. In Unit 1, the idea that we construct our realities is introduced; it is developed using Kelly's Personal Construct Theory in Unit 2 where we see how families create their own shared reality, and in Unit 8 which discusses how we construct our unique models of other people, in an attempt to understand them. At the level of psychological enquiry we also take a constructivist view. For example, the set book *Freud and Psychoanalysis* specifically illustrates how psychoanalytic theory can be seen as a construction which emerges from the social context of the time and from the particular pattern of Freud's background and personality. Later in the course, in Block 5, the way that research is created by intellectual and academic fashions and political issues in society is traced in relation to research on attitudes and opinions. This 'sociology of knowledge' approach to social psychological theory and research is also taken up in the Course Reader.

Another strand that runs through the course is that of the *theme* or *debate*. For example, in Block 1, you will be introduced to the argument about whether we can consider ourselves to be entirely determined by factors outside our control (our biology or our experience in the environment) or whether we are, to some extent at least, autonomous creators of our own actions and experience. This is just one major debate which emerges in different guises throughout the course. Other such themes will be flagged as they occur in the units and in the Vade Mecum. Where appropriate, you will be guided to the papers in Part III of the Metablock. There, key issues are discussed with reference to the course as a whole.

# Part II – Vade Mecum

*by Richard Stevens and unit authors*

'Vade Mecum' means literally 'go with me' and is the old name for a guide book. This part of the Metablock acts as a week-by-week guide to the course. It lists what you should be reading, doing or planning for the future if you follow the pattern of study recommended by the course team. There are also brief notes on the scope and purpose of each unit or task and on the issues it raises and its relation to the rest of the course.

We hope that the Vade Mecum will go with you as you progress through the course. We suggest that you read each block synopsis first, to prepare yourself for what is to come, and then read the relevant text. You may find it helpful to re-read the synopses after you have completed the work as some of the comments may then have more meaning for you. The comments should also help revision.

*Study note:*

In the pages which follow, guidance is given as to the appropriate times to read the articles in Part III of the Metablock and in the Course Reader. It is up to you, however, whether you choose to follow this or to read them all in one go. References are made to the Part III papers as and when they are relevant to issues raised in the course. (There is, of course, no need to look up each one every time it is mentioned unless you wish to do so.)

---

## Block 1 – Creating a Social World (Study weeks 1–5)

Block 1 is a heterogeneous set of four units focused on the family and the socialization of the child. It serves two primary functions:

1  to introduce social psychology and its major perspectives, and to introduce the course;

2  to explore how early development and immediate social context and relationships make possible and lay the basis for later patterns of social behaviour and experience.

> STUDY WEEK 1

*To read:*   Metablock Part I
　　　　　 Introduction to Block 1
　　　　　 Unit 1: The family

*Optional:*  Metablock, Part III, Papers 1, 2 and 3
　　　　　 Set book – *Freud and Psychoanalysis*, Chapter 5.

**Unit 1: The family**

*Content: Part I* introduces the diversity of forms which the family may take in this and other societies. Part II then reviews the functions and effects which it serves for adults and children and for society, as these are conceptualized by different perspectives. In Part III we look at alternatives to the pattern of the traditional family – alternative variations on the nuclear family, communes, and *kibbutzim*.

*Purpose:* To act as an introduction to your studies. By reviewing theories about the purpose and nature of the family – one of our society's fundamental institutions – the unit introduces a range of theories about people in society which you will meet throughout the course. It will also raise many issues which are fundamental to social psychology.

*Comment:*

1  The unit offers brief introductory outlines of 'schools' of psychological theory, most of which you will meet again elsewhere in the course: sociobiology, learning theory, the psychodynamic approach (Freud and Erikson), Marxist and other radical psychologies, and humanistic approaches. The sociobiological perspective is developed in Unit 3 where the relevance of genetic and biological factors to *social life* is discussed. Learning theory and symbolic interactionism are taken up in Unit 4, 'Perspectives on socialization', where psychoanalysis is also discussed in addition to in the set book. Humanistic approaches in psychology are focused on in Block 4 – *Personal worlds*.

2   The unit introduces briefly some of the *methods* used by social psychologists and their relative advantages/disadvantages.

3   It emphasizes two important points about the *nature of understanding in social psychology.*

(i) The social reality with which social psychology deals is created or *constructed* rather than existing 'out there' (see Metablock, Part III, Paper 7).

(ii)  It can be analysed at a number of different *levels* (e.g. the experience of the individual, at the level of interacting individuals, in terms of 'society', in terms of the 'species' – see Metablock, Part III, Paper 3) and also from a variety of *perspectives.*

*Study note:* In Unit 1 you are recommended to look at Papers 1–3 of the 'key issues' papers in the Metablock, Part III as they present useful frameworks for looking at the variety of theories which are introduced in the unit. As the issues of 'meaning' and 'the construction of reality' are also raised, you might also like to skim through Papers 5 and 7. Try to become aware at least of the general points which these papers make, but note that there will be time allocated later for more detailed reading.

---

STUDY WEEK 2

---

*To read/do:*   Unit 2: Family processes
Course Reader: article by Haley
*Offprints Booklet:* article by Palazzoli
Metablock, Part III, Paper 4
*Optional:*   Family Observation Project Instructions – see Project Booklet and the *Introduction to the Projects Booklet.*

**Unit 2: Family processes**

*Study note 1:* One of the Project Options for TMA 04 is linked to Unit 2. You may wish to look through the Family Observation Project Instructions at the time you are reading Unit 2. You should certainly return to Unit 2 if you choose to complete this project option.

*Content:* Unit 2 examines what goes on in relations between family members. It introduces a 'systems' approach to studying family interaction and the concepts and techniques used in family therapy. The associated project option for TMA 04 gives you an opportunity to observe and analyse family interactions for yourself.

*Purpose:* Unit 2 is not only a development of Unit 1 in that it deals with the family, but also a contrast because of the level of analysis and approach which it adopts. It is more tightly focused in that, rather than viewing the family as a social institution, it explores what goes on between members of a family. In so doing, it:

(a)   gives us insights into the nature of family and group interactions;

(b)   emphasizes that individuals cannot be regarded in isolation. They exist socially as part of dynamic interacting systems. Much of the 'reality' with which social psychology must deal is created at an 'interpsychic' level, i.e. through the interactions and negotiations *between* people.

*Paper 4* in Part III of the Metablock, which you are asked to read with this unit, briefly clarifies a distinction which is pertinent here – between the concepts of 'behaviour' and 'action'. As you can see, the essential difference is that 'action' is deemed to include the meanings of the behaviour in question.

*Comment:*

1   In contrast with Unit 1, this unit focuses on one perspective – interactional family therapy (derived from systems theory). It also introduces the construct

theory of George Kelly which is discussed in more depth at several points later in the course, especially in Unit 8. Here, however, it is used with a particular social orientation rather than with its usual personal/individual one.

2   The unit touches upon, if only indirectly, a number of key issues which are dealt with in Part III of the Metablock.

(a)   Together with Unit 1, it sensitizes us to (i.e. brings to the forefront) the notion of the different *levels of analysis* which can be used for studying the same topic (the family) (see Metablock, Part III, Paper 3 and Paper 2, Section 9).

(b)   It raises questions about what *form* of *explanation* is most appropriate for social behaviour. In place of cause-effect accounts, it postulates the need to look at the *system* (see Papers 2, 5 and 8).

(c)   By making us aware of how dependent our behaviour and experience are on the others with whom we interact, it raises questions about the degree of *autonomy* we can attribute to our own behaviour and thoughts (see Paper 9).

*Study note 2:* Unless you choose to, there is no need to read the Metablock, Part III papers referred to in depth at this stage – but do try to become aware of the general nature of the issues referred to here.

---

STUDY WEEK 3

---

*To read:*   Unit 3: The relevance of genetic and biological factors to social life.
Course Reader: article by Clarke and Clarke.

*Optional:* Course Reader: articles by Rutter and Madge, and by Kamin.

### Unit 3: The relevance of genetic and biological factors to social life

*Content:* The unit is divided into four sections. (i) The first section raises broad questions about the impact of early experience by focusing on case studies of children who have spent long periods of time cut off from human society. (ii) Section 2 then lays the foundations for understanding biological or genetic factors – looking at the concepts, methods and data of the science of genetics and the concept of heredity. (iii) The third section questions the assumptions that underlie the nature–nurture debate. It draws on material in Section 2 to demonstrate just how complex is the relationship between what we inherit from our parents and what we become within our unique environment. (iv) The unit concludes by examining the way in which evolutionary biologists look at behaviour and development.

*Purpose:* This unit is linked to Units 1 and 2 through its concern with the nature and origin of our social world. However, while Units 1 and 2 take social structure and family dynamics as the organizing principles from which to view the creation of a social world, Unit 3 asks questions about the significance of *biological* factors in human social behaviour.

Its purpose is to stimulate you to think about the role of biology and whether or not there is a clear dividing line between biological and social or environmental factors. The unit encourages you to think of them as *continuously influencing each other in an interactive way*. In order that you understand these issues, you are introduced to key ideas in genetics and evolutionary biology.

*Comment:*

1   Unit 3 bears on several Metablock, Part III issues (i.e. general problems and issues in social psychology).

(a)   Levels of analysis – can behaviour and development be explained solely in terms of heredity or environment? Are nature and nurture two competing or antagonistic forces? Do we need more than just these two levels of analysis to explain behaviour and development? (See Paper 3 and Paper 2, Section 9.) The value of an interdisciplinary approach is emphasized in the view that genetic *and* environmental factors *interact* in their influence on what people become.

(b) The approaches discussed here are *determinist*. We can detect three particular forms – a biological/genetic determinism; environmental determinism; early childhood determinism (the notion of critical periods of development). (See Paper 9.)

(c) The diverse methods of research that social psychologists draw upon, and the question of what counts as evidence (see Paper 6). Note that several *ways of studying* human development from an evolutionary/genetic perspective are set out, for example:

(i) classical or *Mendelian genetics*, which tries to isolate genes and to determine how genes come to express themselves in the development of the organism;

(ii) the statistical method of investigating the interaction of heredity and environment, which compares biologically related individuals to see whether there are family similarities (also known as the *biometric approach*);

(iii) ethology, which involves asking questions about the relationships between behaviour, environment and evolution.

2  The political implications of social research and the problems of applying scientific knowledge are raised here. See the Course Reader article by Clarke and Clarke for a discussion of these issues.

3  This is the only unit in the course where the influence of genetics and biology on social behaviour is directly addressed; although it is implicit in cognitive developmental theories which are explored in Units 4, 5 and 7. Also biological influences on the life cycle are implicit in Unit 2 and in Block 4, and in Block 3 certain biological assumptions are made about the basis of human sociability that echo some of the ideas about evolutionary biology presented here.

*Study note:* You are introduced to genetic studies and processes in order to appreciate the possible implications for understanding social behaviour and experience. You should try to understand them, but you will not be expected to remember, for examination purposes, the technical details of this work.

STUDY WEEK 4

*To read:*   Unit 4: Perspectives on socialization
             Set book: *Freud and Psychoanalysis*, Chapters 3, 4 and 5.

*Optional:*  Course Reader: articles by Hardyment and by Rapoport *et al.*
             Set book: *Freud and Psychoanalysis*, Chapters 2, 6 and 7
             Open University DS262 *Introduction to Psychology*, Unit 3 – I. Slack,
             'Learning and conditioning' (if you have this available).

**Unit 4: Perspectives on socialization**

*Content:* Unit 4 investigates and compares four major models of socialization:

(a)  *Freud's psychodynamic theory* which emphasizes the significance for adult life of childhood experience and emotions.

(b)  *Social learning theory*, derived from behaviourism, which stresses the importance of studying *overt* behaviours and the use of experimental methods.

(c)  *Piaget's cognitive-developmental approach* which puts emphasis on ways in which a child actively constructs his/her understanding of physical and social reality.

(d)  *Symbolic interactionism* which is concerned with the way in which subjective states and meanings are closely interwoven with objective social structures and events; also on the way in which the 'self' is constructed during socialization.

*Purpose:*

(a)  to familiarize you with four major psychological perspectives on socialization which are of central interest to social psychology;

(b)  to show why the study of children is an important topic for social psychology;

(c)  to indicate the ways in which theories may evolve and may influence one another;

(d)  to demonstrate the interplay that exists between theory and research.

*Comment:*

1  This is a particularly crucial unit. Although the theories presented here are focused on human development, they are major psychological perspectives (though by no means the only ones) and they will recur in some form or other throughout the course. The unit lays the foundation for each. The *Freudian* approach of the family has already been outlined in Unit 1. Freudian (and other) psychoanalytic theories will be specifically referred to in Block 4, but the role of unconscious processes more generally will appear in several places (e.g. Unit 15 and Block 6). *Piaget's cognitive developmental approach*, based *within* the child's own world of childhood experience and understanding is taken up again in Unit 5 in the context of language and, more extensively, in Unit 7 – 'The development of understanding'. Unit 7 also picks up concepts similar to those of *Mead*, when discussing the concept of communication, and responses, not to the behaviour of the other person, but to perceptions of his/her intentions and meaning. Block 4 also takes up issues about personal and social meaning, similar to those of symbolic interactionism. Behaviourist *social learning theory*, as such, does not appear again in the course, but references to and versions of behaviourism will recur. You have already met it in Unit 1. A behaviourist view of language development is criticized in Unit 5. In Unit 10/11 some of the theories of relationship, development and maintenance are premised upon notions of what is rewarding and what is punishing; thus factors which may serve to strengthen and weaken relationships are viewed in behaviourist terms. 'Social exchange theory', in particular, comes into this category. In Block 6 the strength of group membership and the rewards and costs of conformity to group norms is discussed in similar terms.

2  Many of the key issues of social psychology are met with in this unit (references below in parentheses refer to papers in Part III of the Metablock).

(a)  In studying the process of socialization, we confront many of the big philosophical questions relating to *autonomy and determinism* (see Papers 9 and 8). What we seek to understand is the extent to which we are shaped or determined by early childhood experiences. Can we escape from the shadow of our past? We encounter some ambiguous answers. At first sight, for example, psychoanalysis, with its emphasis on unconscious forces, biologically-based development and early environmental influence, might seem to support a determinist view. But the essence of psychoanalytic procedures is the possibility of change brought about with the help of insight and awareness.

(b)  Are there any *universals* that characterize human behaviour and experience and which cut across the obvious differences that characterize particular social groups and cultures? In the area of socialization, this question crops up when we consider whether or not there are universal stages that transcend cultures.

(c)  The unit is particularly relevant to any consideration of *the nature of understanding* in social psychology. These four very different accounts of socialization and perspectives on social behaviour make it clear how theories are *constructions* (see Paper 7). The historical material presented should aid you in thinking about the social and intellectual forces which have shaped these theories and also give you some insight into the way in which social concerns may come to be mirrored in social research and conversely how the concepts and preoccupations of researchers may filter through to the general public (see the Course Reader, especially Chapter 5).

The presentation of four very different perspectives raises questions about the extent to which they are compatible and whether they represent mutually exclusive ways of doing psychology (see Paper 2).

3 The unit also raises more specific questions about the nature of social psychology:

(a) Where does the boundary lie between social psychology and other disciplines? Some social psychology courses assume that there are clear separations between social psychology and the rest of psychology, and between social psychology and the other social sciences. In this course we are constantly puzzling over where to draw the line. Hence, the course spills over into biological science, child development, sociology and social philosophy. In this unit we suggest that social psychology requires a developmental approach to social behaviour. What this means is that we believe that we cannot make sense of adult social life without delving back into people's past experience since ways of relating to other human beings and of interpreting social rules have their origins in early experience.

(b) Just as social psychology draws on a wide range of theories, so too it employs a variety of *research strategies and designs*. In this unit we consider how theories have their own preferred methods of research and their own beliefs as to what counts as evidence (see Papers 2 and 6).

(c) What place does the study of *meaning* have in social psychology? (see Paper 5). The behaviourist approach tries to exclude it as far as possible by focusing on overt behaviour; the other three approaches in different ways regard investigating the *meaning* of experience as crucial to their theories.

*Study note:* There is a lot of ground to be covered this week and you are unlikely to have time to look at in any detail the Metablock, Part III papers referred to above. You will be allocated time to read them in more depth later.

STUDY WEEK 5

By now, you have covered a good deal of ground. This week you have the opportunity to consolidate what you have learned so far and to reflect on what you have read and done. You can also extend your awareness of key issues which arise out of the material.

*To do/read:* TMA 01
               Metablock, Part III: especially Papers 1–3
               Set book: *Freud and Psychoanalysis*, Chapter 2
               *Assignments Booklet:*
               Notes for the Integration Essay
*Optional:*    Course Reader: Preface and Chapter 1
               Set book: *Freud and Psychoanalysis*, Chapter 8

1 *TMA 01*
See *Assignments Booklet*

2 *Metablock, Part III: 'Key issues in social psychology'*
The aim of this part of the block is to explore key issues which arise out of the study of social psychology. It deals with issues which apply not only to specific units but also to the course as a whole (which is why they have been put together in the Metablock). You have already been asked to look at some specific papers, but now is the time to look at Part III as a whole and get a general feeling for the issues which are discussed in the papers. The contents of the papers are necessarily abstract and therefore not always easy to grasp at first. There is a 'chicken–egg' problem in their presentation: you need to be alerted to the issues early on so that you can bear them in mind and understand in more depth the material you encounter in the units. However, until you have progressed some

way through the course, it is unlikely that the full implications of the arguments contained in the papers will become clear to you. So, while you are asked to look at all the papers now to find out what they contain, do note that you will be asked to read each in turn in more depth as you progress through the course.

In Block 1 you encountered the diversity of theories and perspectives which are found in social psychology. In order to help you set these in context and to contrast and compare them, it is suggested that this week you read *in depth* Papers 2 and 3 and look at Paper 1, especially the first chart.

*Paper 1: People and perspectives in social psychology.* With the help of a set of charts, this paper illustrates the origins of the various strands of social psychology and its main lines of development up to the present day. Look for the theories and perspectives you have read about so far and try to locate them, especially on Chart 1. You should continue to refer to this paper as you work through the course and again during your revision.

*Paper 2: Making sense of theories in social psychology.* This paper sets out ten dimensions along which social psychology theories differ. After you have read it try to think about the dimensions suggested in relation to the theories mentioned in Block 1.

*Paper 3: Levels of analysis.* This paper consists of a more extended discussion of one of the dimensions introduced in Paper 2. In particular, you should try:

(i) to relate this to the analyses of the family presented in Unit 1;

(ii) to contrast the different approaches to understanding individual behaviour presented in Units 3 and 4.

3 *Set book: 'Freud and Psychoanalysis', Chapter 2 (and Chapter 8, optional)*
Chapter 2 gives a brief account of Freud's life. One of the themes of Block 1 is that theories are constructions, they are created by the theorist and will be influenced by his characteristics and background, they do not just 'emerge' from a study of the subject matter in question. Reading Chapter 2 may help you to appreciate the following:

(i) Freud's ideas did not just emerge as a fully-fledged and unified theory. They evolved and were modified during the course of his lifetime.

(ii) Events and experiences in his life played their part in influencing the pattern of his thinking.

You might like to consider Freud's ideas in the light of his biography. Can you suggest any possible connections? (These issues of the construction of theory and the influence of Freud's background and life on his ideas will be taken up in more detail later in the course. If you want to read further now look at Paper 7 in Part III of this Metablock and Chapter 12 of *Freud and Psychoanalysis*.)

Chapter 8 provides further examples of the way in which theories are initiated and developed. It plots the way that Freud's ideas were extended and modified by his followers. This is optional reading only and you will not be expected to remember the details of the particular theories mentioned. Note, however, that aspects of Fromm's and Erikson's theories will be considered later in Block 4.

4 *The Integration Essay*
For TMA 07 which you have to submit at the end of the course, you will be required to write an essay which rests on the integration of material from across the course. Several topic options are suggested from which you can choose. Although you are not required to write at greater length than usual, we consider that the Integration Essay is a very important part of your coursework. It is a compulsory part of your continuous assessment and time is allocated to writing it at the end of the course. However, you will probably find it easier if you work on it as you progress through the course – taking relevant notes as you go. It is suggested, therefore, that you now read the notes for the *Integration Essay* which you will find in the *Assignments Booklet*. You do not have to *decide* on your option just yet, but we suggest that you do so as soon as you can so that you can begin preparatory work for your essay fairly early on in the course.

5 *Course Reader: 'Dialogues and debates in social psychology' (optional)*
You have already looked at individual articles in the Reader in conjunction with Units 2, 3 and 4 and you will be referred to further papers as you proceed. There will also be time allowed in study weeks 10, 19–21 and 31–32 for you to look at papers in the Reader of more general interest which are not associated with specific units. A study guide to the Reader is given in the Vade Mecum section for study week 10. The Reader focuses on the idea that knowledge is constructed and looks at the way theories and research in social psychology have been influenced by social and political concerns and, in turn, how social psychological ideas permeate the way we think about things in everyday life. You may wish, therefore, to read now at least the Preface to the Reader which will give you a clear idea of what the book is about. You might also like to look at Chapter 1, although at this stage of the course this is entirely optional.

---

## Block 2 – Becoming a Social Being (Study weeks 6–8)

Block 2 consists of three units. These continue the concern of Block 1 with socialization and the development of social being. In Block 2, however, the focus is on 'cognitive' development in the sense of how we come to achieve an awareness of ourselves and the world about us and the capacity to communicate with others.

In looking at language and the development of understanding, the block emphasizes that:

1  we are born into a pre-existing social world with its established conventions and ways of conceptualizing reality;

2  the developing child does not just passively assimilate these established conventions but actively interacts with them and creates his or her own awareness of this social world;

3  the emphasis of the block is therefore *dialectical* in the sense that it shows the complex, continuous interactions and negotiations between individuals and society in the construction of our awareness of ourselves and the social world.

The block serves the *specific* functions of introducing you to a range of contemporary research on language, sociolinguistics and child development. It also serves the *general* functions of:

(a)  showing us something of the complexity of the relationship between self and society;

(b)  emphasizing the significance of *meaning*; that is, what is of interest, both to the social psychologist and in everyday life, is not just our overt behaviours but the meanings which we ascribe to them.

STUDY WEEK 6

*To read:*    Introduction to Block 2

Unit 5: Becoming understood: the development of language

### Unit 5: Becoming understood: the development of language

*Content:* This unit presents different approaches to the study of language development during the first few years of life. The order in which these are discussed follows the historical development of research traditions. First, the study of the grammatical rules and vocabulary that children use (syntactic approach); second, the study of the meanings of children's utterances (semantic approach); and third, the study of what and why the child communicates (pragmatic approach).

*Purpose:*

(a)   to acquaint you with some of the difficulties in trying to interpret children's speech;

(b)   to present theories about how children gain access to their native tongue;

(c)   the unit also shows how the mastery of language facilitates the child's entry into the social community *and* is the result of the child's situation in this community.

*Comment:*

1   The study of language is treated as a specific case study – part of an overall concern in the block with questions about how we become social beings, about how we enter a social world. Clearly, language is only one of the skills required, but a crucial one. This unit is written with an emphasis on cognitive aspects of language acquisition and on the social functions which language serves. In its cognitive emphasis the unit is clearly linked to the Piagetian tradition you will have read about in Unit 4. The *social* aspects of language use and language development are further developed and elaborated in the later units of this block.

2   This unit emphasizes the interaction of biological and social factors in development: on one hand the possible genetic pre-programming of language and the age-related development of cognitive skills, and on the other hand, appropriate and rich social experience.

3   This unit also alerts us to the spiral between our construction of our social world and the need to be already part of a given social community in order to develop the cognitive and social skills required to participate in that process of construction. Language is necessary to social interaction and the development and maintenance of social relationships. But language can only develop fully *given* such a social context.

---

STUDY WEEK 7

---

*To read:*   Unit 6: Language and social identity

## Unit 6: Language and social identity

*Content:* This unit looks at speech behaviour and why it is of particular interest to social psychologists. It considers the way we judge people on the basis of the way they speak. It examines the major social influences on how we talk and looks at the role which language variations play in distinctions of social class and of regional background. It also considers the relevance of language in establishing group identity and in negotiating and maintaining social relationships.

*Purpose:* The purpose of the unit is to widen the focus of our consideration of language by looking at its use in relation to the structure of society. It presents the viewpoint of *sociolinguistics*. This is concerned with the *use* of language, how this is fashioned by social factors, and the implications of the resulting variations for social identity, group cohesion and day-to-day social relationships.

*Comment:*

1   The unit extends our awareness of the *functions* of language, the social aspects of the role which language plays in the organization of thought; its social control functions; its role in the maintenance of relationships, and in marking personal social identity.

2   The unit nicely illustrates a way in which we are shaped by our social environment. The variations of language which we use to express ourselves are shown to be a function of the society in which we grow up and live, the roles we occupy and the groups to which we belong. This picks up a theme which was introduced in Block 1 (Units 1, 2 and 4) and is present throughout much of the course – the

extent to which we are shaped by other people and by social institutions (such as the family). In Block 4 we take up this theme by looking at the way personal worlds depend on social context, and in Block 5 the impact of society, culture and ideology is discussed in relation to people's attitudes. Conformity, obedience and social identity are key topics in Block 6.

3    Since the way we use language serves to establish certain kinds of relationship and at the same time is an important source of information on which other people make personal and social judgements about us, this unit has some relevance to the discussion of relationships in Block 3.

4    Unit 6 emphasizes that social identity is not just a product of child development, it goes on evolving throughout life, depending among other things on the groups with which we associate as adults.

5    The sociolinguistic approach provides further insight into the way in which we construct our social reality. Not only is our language use shaped by the social environment, but we also perceive and classify others in terms of their socially-shaped regional accents, dialects and so on. To the extent that we can deliberately adopt types of speech we have some control over the impressions of our identity we convey to others.

STUDY WEEK 8

*To read:*    Unit 7: The development of understanding
              *Offprints Booklet*: article by Youniss

*Optional:* Mother/child Interaction Project instructions – see Project Booklet
            and the *Introduction to the Projects.*

**Unit 7: The development of understanding**

*Content:* This unit goes beyond language to look at the development of 'understanding'; at research on how children come to be aware of themselves, of other people and the world around them, and to learn appropriate ways of behaving towards others. It argues that children learn how to attribute meanings and learn about the purposiveness of action *through their interactions with others* (particularly those people who look after them). It is because such people act *as if* the child means and intends what she/he does that the child is able to develop meaningful and intentional behaviour and come to appreciate himself or herself as an 'agent' in a social world.

*Purpose:*

(a)    to extend our understanding of the origins of social being by exploring the development of the sense of self and the capacity for meaningful action and the way these originate in early interactions;

(b)    to show by what means empirical research can give us insights, if only partial ones, into this area.

*Comment:*

1    The approach to development presented in this unit is prefigured in ideas you have already encountered:

(i) Piaget's work also investigates the child's constructions of reality. The difference is that greater emphasis is placed in this unit on the importance of *relationships* for this process (not just with parents but also with other children).

(ii) The work of Mead and the symbolic interactionists emphasize both the importance of how we attribute meanings and how these emerge from social interactions.

2    This unit develops our awareness of an important aspect of the *construction of reality* (see Metablock, Paper 7). Like Unit 2, it emphasizes the notion of

*interpsychic* realities: that our construction of the world emerges from negotiations with others, from interaction and *mutual* understanding; it is not just created by an individual nor simply imposed by the social environment. (Note the difference between '*inter*psychic' and '*intra*psychic'. Interpsychic refers to what is happening *between* people – or 'minds' – i.e. interaction; intrapsychic refers to what is happening *within* the mind.) The unit also raises issues about the nature of 'childhood'. In what sense could this be regarded as a social construction, changing from culture to culture and at different historical periods?

3   Another important feature of this unit is its emphasis on the centrality of *meaning* (see Metablock, Paper 5). It makes clear that in order to understand human social behaviour and experience, social psychologists must find some way of studying how we attribute meaning and make sense of our world of experience. This is a theme taken up later in Block 3 *Understanding other people and developing relationships* (see the work of Kelly and also attribution theorists) and in Block 4 *Personal worlds*.

*Study note:*

1   One of the options for the TMA 04 Project is about mother–baby interactions and is associated with Unit 7. When you have completed the unit and it is still fresh in your mind, you might like to have a *quick* look at what this project entails (for further details about the project see Vade Mecum, study week 14 and the *Introduction to the Projects*). Note that even if you decide not to do this option, the associated videotape provides some very useful illustrations of points made in Unit 7.

2   The Youniss article is not easy reading. But, as it discusses the contribution which relationships in childhood make to the emergence of 'self', you may find it amplifies your understanding of the material in Units 4 and 5, and that it also has some relevance to the work on relationships which you will be dealing with in the next block.

---

## Block 3 – Understanding Other People and Developing Relationships (Study weeks 9–14)

*Purpose:*
To present a variety of social psychological research and theories about:

(a)   how we perceive and make sense of other people;

(b)   the development and maintenance of social relationships.

In this block, we shift from the developmental emphasis of the previous two blocks to focus on adult social behaviour. In some sense, though, we find a continuation from the previous block in the theme that the study of social interaction is crucial for any understanding of human social behaviour and experience.

With important exceptions such as Kelly's personal construct theory, the approach adopted in this block is primarily that of *experimental* social psychology.

STUDY WEEK 9

*To read:*   Unit 8: Understanding others I: a personal construct theory account

*Optional: The Kelly Project* and the *Introduction to the Projects* booklet.

### Unit 8: Understanding others I: a personal construct theory account

*Content:* Unit 8 describes and explains Kelly's personal construct theory, especially its application to the way we perceive and interact with other people. It also describes the main method associated with this theory – the repertory grid, which forms the basis of the *Kelly Project* option.

*Purpose:* To introduce you to a widely used perspective on how we make sense of our world, particularly our social world of potential acquaintances and friends. This section also equips you to do the *Kelly Project* (see options for TMA 04 Project).

*Comment:*

1 Although personal construct theory has already been introduced (e.g. Unit 2), it is explained most comprehensively here, and as such serves as a 'resource centre' on this theory as you work through the course. Most direct links, however, are to the remainder of Block 3, to the Kelly project and to Block 4.

2 Personal construct theory relates to three of the issues discussed in the papers of Part III of the Metablock.

(a) It emphasizes the constructed nature of personal experience (see Paper 7).

(b) It implies that individuals have considerable autonomy over the ways in which they construe their worlds (see Paper 9).

(c) It provides one of the strongest examples in the course of an idiographic approach to psychology, i.e. the study of unique individuals with the aim of giving in-depth understanding (see Paper 8).

*Study note:* As the *Kelly Project* option ties in closely with this unit, you may like to read the instructions for this while the unit is fresh in your mind.

> STUDY WEEK 10

*To read:*   Unit 9: Understanding others II: the approach of attribution theory
            Postscript to Units 8 and 9
            *Offprints Booklet:* article by Lalljee.

**Unit 9: Understanding others II: the approach of attribution theory**

*Content:* This unit traces the development of three models constructed by experimental social psychologists to account for how and why people try to explain other people's actions – what they do and why.

*Purpose:*

(a)  to introduce a theory of how we make sense of other people which contrasts with personal construct theory presented in Unit 8;

(b)  to examine the points of similarity and difference between attribution theory and personal construct theory;

(c)  to provide detailed examples of traditional experimental social psychology and to assess some of the strengths and weaknesses of this approach.

*Comment:*

1 The experimental social psychology tradition, and, in particular the 'cognitive' approach of attribution theories presented here, does not have strong links with many of the other units, most of which present rather different perspectives on the explanation of social behaviour. The closest cross links are with Unit 10/11 and the experimental tradition of attitude research described in Unit 16. There is a direct correspondence between attribution theories' explanation of ordinary observers' explanations of other people's behaviour and social psychologists' explanations and predictions of behaviour discussed in Unit 16.

2 The unit deals with material which follows a *nomothetic* view of human behaviour, i.e. one attempting to establish general 'laws' to explain how ordinary people account for the behaviour of those around them (see Paper 8).

3 The critique of attribution theories in Lalljee's paper has two especially interesting implications.

(a) He stresses the need to view attributions in the wider context of the language and communication history of the individuals concerned. He directs attention to the emergence of meaning in the social interactions (both present and past) between explainer and 'explainee'. This links attribution processes to the interactional perspective presented in Units 2 and 7.

(b) His critique points out that the whole approach to the study of attribution processes may well be culture bound. Making sense of other people's behaviour in cause–effect terms and distinguishing between people as sources of action in contrast to an inanimate world may well be exclusive to our own culture. This relates to the issue (see Metablock, Paper 10) of how far social psychology is essentially localized in its theories and explanations and how far it can purport to explain human social behaviour in universal terms.

---

STUDY WEEK 11

---

This week is allocated to completing TMA 02 and to consolidating your understanding of the more general implications which Block 2 and Units 8 and 9 raise.

*To do/read:*  TMA 02
Metablock, Part III, Paper 5
Set book: *Freud and Psychoanalysis*, Chapters 9 and 11
Course Reader: Preface and Chapter 1

*Optional:*  Course Reader: Chapter 2.

1 *TMA 02*
see *Assignments Booklet*.

2 *Metablock, Paper 5*
One of the general themes to emerge from Block 2 and Units 8 and 9 was the significance of *meaning* in human social behaviour and experience. Paper 5 examines:

(a) what 'meaning' means;

(b) the need for social psychology to study meaning;

(c) the problems this poses for the study of social psychology.

3 *Set book: 'Freud and Psychoanalysis', Chapters 9 and 11*
These two chapters develop this theme of the need to study meanings and the problems this poses.

*Chapter 9* (pp. 85–90) argues that one of the primary values of psychoanalysis is the tools it offers us for interpreting meaning.

*Chapter 11* (pp. 117–27) relates to the discussion in Metablock, Paper 5 and should be read in conjunction with it. It emphasizes the significance of meaning, explores something of its nature and argues that this may imply that the traditional aims and methods of the natural sciences are inappropriate for investigating meanings. Although the discussion is geared to psychoanalysis, it has more general relevance also to social psychology.

4 *Course Reader: Preface, Chapter 1 (Chapter 2 optional)*
More time will be devoted to the Reader later, however it would be helpful if, by the end of this week, you had familiarized yourself with its structure and purpose. You will then get some idea of the Reader's function in relation to the course as a whole, so that you are ready to start working through it whenever you have the time, and so that its themes can begin to inform your reading of the unit text.

*Content:* From the list of contents and the Preface, you will be aware that the reader is in five sections, the arguments in each chapter being exemplified or amplified by the selected readings.

*Chapter 1: The legacy of the past.* This chapter traces the history of the liberal tradition in social psychology, the radical challenge to that tradition and the response of mainstream psychology. Note that, as the opening of the chapter indicates, this is a very *selective* look at the history of social psychology which focuses on a particular aspect of the way in which early social psychologists responded to some of the social issues of the day.

*Chapter 2: The perilous past from social research to social intervention.* To illustrate the problems of social research in a controversial, political area, this chapter focuses on a case study of the school desegregation debate in the USA.

*Chapter 3: The social role of 'the man of knowledge'.* This chapter examines how far our knowledge can be considered to be independent of the society in which it is generated. It looks at the role of psychologists in relation to society; in particular, whether they represent a means of maintaining existing traditions and to what extent they can act as catalysts for change.

*Chapter 4: Psychologists in action.* This chapter moves the discussion of the previous chapter to a more concrete plane by examining research reports which illustrate the different roles which research psychologists play in relation to society: from independent expert to advisor to other professions, from commercial consultant to agent for social change.

*Chapter 5: Psychology in the popular imagination.* This chapter examines the way certain psychological findings and theories have been taken up by the population at large and have come to shape popular beliefs.

*Chapter 6: The Epilogue.* The Reader concludes not by drawing pat conclusions but by acknowledging the dilemmas and debates which are intrinsic to social psychology. How far are the kind of problems on which social psychology may be brought to bear an intrinsic part of what it is to be human and as such admit of no solution?

*Purpose of the Reader:* To demonstrate the extent to which social psychological research arises out of the real world and the extent to which social psychology, in turn, may influence the world. This theme is also evident in the course, particularly in Blocks 5, 6 and 7.

*Comment:*

1 The Reader emphasizes a theme which runs throughout the course − that knowledge is always constructed and that there cannot be only one final version of the truth (see Metablock, Paper 7). The questions one may wish to ask and the answers research will uncover always reflect the social contexts which have given rise to them. This, of course, also means that social psychological findings and insights are likely to be bound to a particular time, place and culture, and may need to be revised in the light of new experiences or changed contexts. What always matters in social psychology is the *interpretation* one puts on experimental or other research findings.

2 The Reader also emphasizes the complex inter-relationship between social psychological research and theory, and the social and political context in which it is carried out. Almost all social psychologists, operating as they do in a social context, tend to focus on the issues which are seen by them (or society in general) as problematic − issues such as authoritarianism, conformity, poverty, loneliness, under-achievement, old age, race relations and a host of others. Not only are social psychologists drawn to such 'problems' − whether they are perceived as personal or social problems − they tend to study them with a view to remedying them through intervention, or by getting politicians or others to intervene. This, of course, in itself poses problems for social psychology as a science. Are we in too much of a hurry to apply localized and timebound knowledge and do we pay

too little attention to developing a firmer theoretical base for our discipline? Having got as far as you have in your course, you will be aware of the fact that we have many divergent and limited theories, but overall 'meta' theories which could encompass this piecemeal knowledge are much more problematic.

*Preface and Chapter 1.* If you have not already done so, now is a good time to read the Preface and Chapter 1. Note that, as mentioned in the *Contents* section above, Chapter 1 looks only at a highly selective segment of the history of social psychology.

Although the articles in *Chapter 2* may be considered as optional reading, it is worth reading the editorial sections at least because they illustrate well the general problem which confronts attempts to bring psychological research to bear on political issues.

---

STUDY WEEKS 12–13

---

*To read:* Unit 10/11: Developing relationships

*Optional:* Course Reader: article by Argyle
*The Diary Project* and *Introduction to the Projects* booklet.

## Unit 10/11: Developing relationships

*Content:* This double unit introduces a number of theories about how personal relationships develop, are maintained and how they decline. It considers the nature of and role of communication in this process and the methodological and ethical problems which can arise when the social psychologist is studying relationships.

*Purpose:*

(a) to show how experimental social psychologists have formulated questions about relationships and the kind of research they have carried out;

(b) to allow you to assess the usefulness of the experimental approach in investigating areas of complex social behaviour;

(c) to show not only the methodological difficulties involved in investigating a topic like social relationships, but also that there are ethical problems.

*Comment:*

1  There are some direct links between this unit and your previous work on the course. The work of the social exchange theorists, for example, is similar in its assumptions to learning theory (see Unit 4), and the dramaturgical analysis of social interaction to symbolic interactionism (see also Unit 4). Relationships have been focused on in the interactional approaches presented in Units 2 and 7. You might like to contrast the approach and treatment of social interaction there with that presented here. Freudian theory also has relevance to relationships in that they may be coloured by unconscious motivations, and by residues of past conflicts (see, for example, *Freud and Psychoanalysis*, Chapter 5).

2  Most of the studies discussed in Unit 10/11 adopt a nomothetic approach (see Metablock, Paper 8). They assume that the general approach of the natural sciences, especially the experimental testing of hypotheses, is the best way to investigate relationships. This is, of course, but one approach to social relationships and the critique by Hinde suggests an alternative: he argues that, at least at this 'early stage' of relationship research, ethological methods and 'inductive' data collection are more appropriate than formal experiments.

3  As you might expect, given the emphasis on experimental method, there is a strong determinist flavour in the theories presented (see Metablock, Paper 9).

Thus the work on personality and its relevance to forming relationships suggests the possible role of biological factors, and the work on 'field of eligibles' implies environmental determination. There is a counterbalance however: both exchange theory and dramaturgical theories suggest that people have some autonomous control in the management of their relationships, although this would seem to depend on the degree of self-awareness which they have of their strategies and behaviours.

*Study note:* One of the options for the TMA 04 Project (the *Diary Project*) also deals extensively with material discussed in this part of Block 3. If you choose not to do this project, you may nonetheless find it useful to read the *Diary Project* to extend your understanding of material presented in the block.

---

STUDY WEEK 14

---

This week is largely given over to learning about *research methods* in social psychology and to choosing your option for the TMA 04 Project.

*To read/do:*   Metablock, Part III, Papers 6 and 8
*Introduction to the Projects* booklet (for TMA 04 see also the *Assignments Booklet*)
Materials for the TMA 04 Project, options 1–5
Set book: *Freud and Psychoanalysis*, Chapter 10

1 *Metablock, Part III, Papers 6 and 8*
*Paper 6* provides a general introduction to research methods in social psychology. It is essential to read this before choosing your option for the Project.

*Paper 8* takes up a basic distinction between different approaches in social psychology of which we saw examples in Block 3.

(i) The *nomothetic*: those approaches which aim at formulating laws to explain behaviour in general.

(ii) The *idiographic*: those which aim to provide an intensive in-depth understanding of an individual or event.

(iii) It also contrasts a nomothetic with a *hermeneutic* approach (i.e. one which focuses on interpreting the *meaning* of actions and experiences). The hermeneutic approach is illustrated by much of the work of Kelly and in Block 4 which follows. Although Freud set out with nomothetic aims, it could be argued (see set book *Freud and Psychoanalysis*) that his achievement is primarily in the hermeneutic area. These different approaches are also related to the question of determinism.

2 *Choosing your project for TMA 04*
Two weeks are allocated later to allow you to *do* the project, however it is advisable that you choose the option you intend to do now since the *Diary Project* requires you to start collecting data from study week 15. One of your main tasks this week is to review the options and to make your choice. This process of choosin the project is a crucial part of the way methods are taught in this course. Deciding which option you wish to do, the particular method, and the practical constraints involved will focus your attention on the differences between methodologies. Reference has already been made to three of the options in connection with units you have already read and you may have looked at the instructions then.

1  Family Observation Project (Unit 2)

2  Mother/child Interaction Project (Unit 7).

3  Kelly's Personal Construct Project (Exploring Personal Worlds) (Unit 8).

4  Diary Project (Unit 10/11).

There is one further option which is associated with Block 4 –

5 Interview Project.

*Purpose of the project*

The project is the main vehicle in the course for teaching you about research methods in social psychology. Its purpose is to:

(a) give you an idea of a range of research methods used and their relative advantages/disadvantages. This will be accomplished by reading the booklet *Introduction to the Projects* and by reading *all* of the options in order to make your choice, and the associated Metablock reading about methods (Paper 6);

(b) give you an in-depth experience of social–psychological research with the method of your choice;

(c) deepen your understanding of that part of the course with which your chosen option is associated.

*Procedure:* At this stage, you should read:

(a) The *Introduction to the Projects* booklet, which outlines each option, its basic method and its practical requirements. This booklet tells you how much of each project booklet to scan to get a feel for its contents.

(b) Once you have made at least a preliminary choice, note what you will need to set up or do and when you will need to do it.

*Study note:* The project is allocated two weeks' work and forms a substantial part of your assessment. Do bear in mind that its purpose is not just to carry out your own research investigation, but to familiarize you with methods of research in social psychology. By the time you have begun work on your project you should be able to:

(a) make comparisons between the five options in terms of the methods they offer, the advantages and disadvantages of these methods, the different kinds of data that will be generated and the kinds of answers to particular kinds of questions that can be achieved;

(b) give an outline of the aims and methods of the four options you have rejected;

(c) relate all five options to the varieties of social psychology described in Paper 8 of the Metablock;

(d) distinguish between hypothetico–deductive and inductive research models and the methods described in Paper 6.

3 *'Freud and Psychoanalysis', Chapter 10*

A major perspective presented in Block 3 is *experimental* social psychology, but the work of Kelly stresses the need for meaning. It was suggested in the Metablock reading (Paper 5) associated with Block 2 that it is difficult to bring orthodox scientific methods to bear in investigating meaning or propositions which are based on a hermeneutic approach. Chapter 10 explores this issue in relation to psychonalysis. How far is it possible to formulate Freud's theory in terms of testable hypotheses? The chapter reviews experiments and other research designed to test the theory. In particular, it discusses the formidable problems which lie in the way of such undertakings, considers the reasons why this is so and raises the question as to whether such attempts are misconceived.

It is useful to read this now since the arguments put forward can be extended to social psychology in general. You might like to think about the questions raised in relation to the research on relationships with others which you have just studied. The discussion of how hypotheses are formulated on the basis of a theory and then put to the test should also deepen your understanding of the research process in social psychology.

## Block 4 – Personal Worlds (Study weeks 15–20)

Although our interest remains focused on adults, in Block 4 we introduce a very different kind of approach to that of Unit 10/11. Here, the emphasis is not on the development of explanatory laws by means of experiments, but on analysing the nature of subjective experience. What does it feel like to be an individual human being in a social world? We shall look at ways of making sense of this experience and how it changes as we develop throughout life.

---

STUDY WEEK 15

---

*To read:* Introduction to Block 4: Personal worlds
Unit 12: The experience of being a person
Set book: *Freud and Psychoanalysis*, Chapter 8 (pp. 71–3).

*Optional:* Begin collecting data for Diary Project if you have chosen this option.

### Unit 12: The experience of being a person

*Content: Part I* of Unit 12 attempts to describe what is meant by 'personal worlds'. With the help of examples, it suggests thirteen features which characterize our experience of being an individual person. It also discusses the methodological difficulties involved in investigating subjective experience.

*Part II* explores four aspects/problems of human existence: the flow of time, the need to choose, to find some meaning in life and to create some kind of identity.

*Purpose:*

(a)   to stimulate you to reflect on your own experience of being a person;

(b)   to emphasize the importance for psychology of exploring such issues and the difficulties in doing so.

*Comment:*

1   *Perspectives introduced.* There are few, if any, psychological theories which deal adequately with the issues which this unit attempts to tackle. It does not, therefore, offer an exposition of any particular theories or research studies. We might consider the approach adopted in the unit as being essentially *phenomenological* in that it takes an 'inside' perspective (see Metablock, Paper 2) and focuses on analysing subjective experience. It is also *existential* in that it is concerned with fundamental issues which arise from the nature of our experience of existence. In addition, two neo-Freudian versions of psychoanalytic theory are touched upon. One is Fromm's notion of existential dichotomies (though this owes as much, if not more, to existential philosophy as it does to psychoanalysis). The other is Erikson's concept of identity which draws on several psychoanalytic ideas such as introjection and identification. Assagioli's *psychosynthesis* theory is briefly referred to in respect of his analysis of will and the technique of disidentification. There is some reference also to *labelling theory* in considering how identity is mutually created through the interaction between an individual and the society in which he or she lives.

Once again, the use of theory in this unit demonstrates the fragmentary nature of so much of psychological theorizing. What is designated as a theory is often really more a perspective – a way of looking at things, or a cluster of ideas related to a specific phenomenon.

2   *Relation to rest of the course.* The most significant link with the earlier part of the course is with Unit 7. There notions central to this unit (like agency, meaningfulness and awareness of self) are discussed in relation to how they develop in the child and how they are constructed through social interactions.

Links with other parts of the course are relatively sparse and tenuous because this particular unit, as indicated above, does not attempt to work specifically from prevailing theoretical or research traditions. One reason for this is that, while theories can illuminate, they can also obscure important characteristics of the subject matter under discussion because they look at it in a particular way. Sometimes, as here, the concepts and approaches which theories provide just do not easily accommodate the existential experience which we want to look at. (For example, almost all psychological theories are premised on a determinist concept of human beings. Because of this they cannot conceptualize a subjective 'reality' like 'willing' which rests on the assumption of an active autonomous agent.) So you are encouraged, at least in beginning your work on the block, to investigate personal worlds by looking directly at the experience of yourself and of other people.

The phenomenological perspective has been encountered earlier in the course. Both symbolic interactionism, which was introduced in Unit 4, and Kelly's personal construct theory, discussed in the previous block, could be considered as forms of the phenomenological approach. Like these approaches, this block is concerned with how people construe and make sense of their life situations. However, concepts from these theories have not been drawn on specifically (except briefly in discussing the work of George Kelly in Unit 13).

3   This unit is particularly relevant to two of the key issues considered in the Metablock:

(a)  It emphasizes most strongly the constructed nature of our personal and social experience (see Paper 7).

(b)   The unit focuses on the human capacity for autonomy rather than adopting the determinist perspective of more traditional psychology (Papers 8 and 9). Autonomy may be seen as evidenced by our ability to initiate actions, think about things in different ways, reflect on what we are and play some role in creating what we will be. Several of the features suggested as inherent characteristics of our personal experience imply such capability (e.g. agency, multiplicity, reflexiveness and the search for meaning). The scope we have for autonomy is further suggested in the discussion of at least three of the problems of human existence (creating one's own identity, the need to make choices and the search for meaningfulness in life).

> STUDY WEEK 16

*To read:*   Unit 13: Making sense of subjective experience

*Optional:* Set book: *Freud and Psychoanalysis*, Chapter 1.

**Unit 13: Making sense of subjective experience**

*Content:* The first part of the unit discusses psychological theories which try to make sense of subjective experience. Each adopts a different perspective and level of analysis:

(a)  Emphasis on *social construction.* Goffman's 'frame analysis' emphasizes the way our awareness is framed by conventions provided by our society.

(b)  Emphasis on *individual awareness.* The approach of Jaynes and Romanyshyn explain the intangibility of subjective experience by stressing its *metaphorical* nature. The role of *fantasy* in subjective experience is also discussed.

(c)  Emphasis on *unconscious meaning.* The implications of psychoanalysis for making sense of subjective experience.

*Part II* looks at the *origins* of subjective experience:

(a)  The way consciousness is rooted in biological structures and evolutionary development (e.g. Crook and Humphreys).

(b) The way the nature of conscious awareness may have changed over historical time (e.g. Jaynes).

(c) The impact on individual consciousness of different forms of social and economic organization, in particular the effects of living in a technological society (e.g. Berger *et al.*).

*Purpose:*

(a) to stimulate your thinking about and to deepen your understanding of the nature of subjective experience by examining it from a number of perspectives;

(b) to show the difficulties which lie in the way of any effective conceptualization and investigation of subjective experience.

*Comment:*

1 *Perspectives included.* Several very different perspectives on subjective experience are discussed here.

We can identify three approaches of a phenomenological kind (i.e. at the level of analysis of subjective experience): the 'metaphor' theory of Jaynes and Romanyshyn, personal construct theory and James' stream of consciousness.

Two others (the approach of Berger *et al.* and Goffman's frame analysis) combine phenomenological concerns (how we make sense of the world) with an emphasis on the way such awareness is socially constructed.

Psychoanalysis is also used to stress the unconscious aspects of subjective experience, and an evolutionary perspective to explain the origins of personal identity, self-awareness and agency.

2 Most of the perspectives discussed here have been introduced in some form earlier in the course. Thus the notion of the social construction of reality was first introduced in relation to the family (Unit 1) and subsequently in relation to childhood (see Unit 7 and Metablock, Paper 7). Frame analysis has its roots in symbolic interactionism (Unit 4). Psychoanalysis is dealt with in Unit 4 and the set book; Personal Construct Theory is discussed in Unit 8. Evolutionary theory was discussed in Unit 3 and it is brought in here as one *possible* factor which helps us to understand the origins of a sense of personal identity and of our capacities for agency and reflexiveness. It is interesting to compare this approach with the analysis put forward in Unit 7. There, their origins were traced in the development of the individual. (The two approaches are, of course, quite compatible with each other.) The only approach used here which has not been introduced before is the idea of consciousness as a metaphorical reality (Jaynes and Romanyshyn).

3 This unit has special relevance to Metablock issues of the nature of understanding in social psychology (Papers 7 and 10) and autonomy and determinism (Paper 9 and also Paper 8).

(a) The range of different conceptualizations of subjective experience illustrates the way social–psychological theories and descriptions (like those of any other discipline) are essentially constructions. The approaches presented differ in the facets of subjective experience which they try to explain and draw attention to (e.g. social structuring of consciousness, the fluid quality of subjective awareness, the shaping of consciousness by evolution). They differ also in the primary concepts they bring to bear. Taken together, they emphasize the value of a multiple perspective approach in illuminating different aspects of a given subject-matter. They warn also against reductionism. It is not possible to understand consciousness properly if it is reduced to one level (e.g. conscious awareness or physiological functioning) and studied at that level alone. But the unit also throws into relief the problems of satisfactorily relating one approach to another. Because they use different concepts and focus on different aspects, they are not easily integrated together.

(b) Although much of the unit deals with approaches which seem *determinist* in their implications (e.g. evolutionary theory, psychoanalysis and social construction approaches) there are some theories (e.g. personal construct theory and the idea of consciousness as a metaphorical reality) which emphasize the individual's role in *creating* his or her own experience. Is it any coincidence that the theories which emphasize autonomy are at the level of analysis of individual consciousness?

4   One important theme which emerges from the contrast of the varied approaches presented in the unit is the importance of *integration*. There are many factors which contribute to human experience. Thus, it is suggested that individual awareness is the outcome of a complex and continuous process of interaction between biological and social influences during the course of an individual's life history. This echoes the emphasis placed on the *interaction* of the biological and the social in Unit 3 and the notion of the 'individual as integrator' presented specifically in Chapter 1 of the set book *Freud and Psychoanalysis*. This is quite difficult reading but if you have not looked at it yet you might like to do so now.

---

STUDY WEEK 17

---

*To read:*   Unit 14: Development and change in personal life

Set book: *Freud and Psychoanalysis*, Chapter 8 (pp. 76–8) and Chapter 14 (pp. 143–8)

*Optional:*   Course Reader: article by Sarason in the Epilogue.

**Unit 14: Development and change in personal life**

*Content:*

The first part of the unit looks at studies of the *life cycle*, in particular:

1   Erikson's conception of ego development in terms of eight phases (the eight ages of man).

2   Levinson's *et al.* study of forty men at different stages in their adult lives.

The second part serves as a conclusion to the block, in particular:

1   It suggests that the study of personal worlds is focused on *meaning* and it discusses why this is such an intractable subject-matter for a scientific psychology.

2   It considers the inevitable limitations to any understanding of personal worlds.

3   It looks at the implications of the analyses of personal worlds presented here for the ways in which we might lead our lives, emphasizing that psychology should be concerned, as we all are as individuals, with what is possible as well as with why things are as they are.

*Purpose:*

(a)   to encourage you to think about the way our experience of life changes as we grow older;

(b)   to present some of the ideas and research of psychologists on this issue;

(c)   to take up, in the light of the discussion in the block, questions about the nature of social psychology and the kind of understanding we can expect it to provide.

*Comment:*

1   The unit emphasizes that the nature of being a person and the salient features of our personal worlds and the existential problems we confront continue to develop and change as we grow through life.

2   Although the research and ideas about development through adult life presented here are thought-provoking, both the empirical base on which they rest

and their generalizability to the population at large are limited. In terms of the distinction made in Paper 2 of the Metablock (dimension 5), their differentiating power is high but their testability weak. So these accounts of adult development can only be considered as interesting ways of looking at our lives, to be tested for their value against our own experience. However, Part II of the unit suggests that this may be the only kind of understanding we can expect social psychology to provide in this kind of area. Because of its very nature, more definitive and generalizable forms of understanding of our experience of existence and the pattern of our lives may not be feasible.

3   The discussion in the unit has relevance to several Metablock themes.

(i) Unit 14, reflecting on the block as a whole, comes down firmly in favour of the need for a hermeneutic rather than a nomothetic approach in investigating personal worlds (see Papers 5 and 8).

(ii) It also bears on the whole issue of the *construction of knowledge* (see Paper 7) and argues that there is no one definitive account of the pattern of the person's life or experience which is the 'right' one. Like other subject-matter in social psychology, it can be conceptualized and made sense of in different ways.

(iii) In arguing for psychology to deal with the *possible* as well as explaining things as they *are*, the unit emphasizes, by implication, the autonomy of people – their own capacity to play some part in initiating events and creating what they are (see Paper 9). It also supports the idea of social psychology as a 'moral' rather than a natural science (see Paper 10).

*Course Reader: Article by Sarason* (optional). This optional reading is a little long-winded but is relevant here in that Sarason raises questions about the nature of social psychological understanding particularly in the applied field. He suggests that it is inappropriate to look for solutions to human problems in the same way as we seek answers to problems in the physical and technological world. Whereas the latter may permit agreed solutions, many of the problems we face in personal and social life stem from the conditions of human existence. They do not necessarily permit generally agreed and established answers. We may only be able to find answers of a creative and individual rather than a universal kind.

---

STUDY WEEKS 18–20

---

These three weeks are allocated for completing TMA 03, carrying out and writing up the Project for TMA 04, and for further reading.

*To do/read:*   TMA 03, Project TMA 04 (including video for Family Observation Project and Mother/Child Interaction Project, if chosen)
Metablock, Part III, Papers 7 and 9
Set book: *Freud and Psychoanalysis*, Chapter 12

*Optional:*     Course Reader: Chapter 3.

### 1   TMA 03

This is an essay for which you have a choice of options based on the work of Blocks 3 and 4. For further details see the *Assignments Booklet*.

### 2   Project TMA 04

Two weeks are likely to be needed for working on and completing the project for TMA 04. (See study week 14, the *Assignments Booklet* and the *Introduction to the Projects* booklet for further details about this.)

### 3   Metablock, Set book and Course Reader

This period is also for reading and reflection on Metablock issues and for further work on one of the set books and the Course Reader.

(i) *Metablock, Part III, Paper 7 – The construction of reality*
This paper takes up a theme which has been running through the course but which received particular emphasis in Block 4. It argues not only that the way individuals experience their world is a construction or creation but also that the conventions and modes of thought of our society, and what is often considered to be 'objective knowledge', are constructions.

(ii) *Set book: 'Freud and Psychoanalysis', Chapter 12*
The very different forms which social psychological theories about a similar subject-matter can take, illustrate how such theories are constructions. We can sometimes also trace their origins in the background and characteristics of the theorist. Chapter 12 attempts to do this in relation to Freud. Although admittedly speculative, it again provides an illustration of the theme of Paper 7 by showing how a theory may be a reflection of the theorist as much as the subject-matter theorized about.

(iii) *Metablock, Part III, Paper 9 – A note on assumptions of autonomy and determinism in social psychology*
Several of the concepts and ideas presented in Block 4 (e.g. agency, reflexiveness, choice, search for meaning) imply a notion of persons as having scope for autonomy. However, elsewhere in the course, you have encountered theories and research which work from the very different assumption that human behaviour is essentially determined – the product of factors outside an individual's control. This controversy is examined in this paper and some possible ways of helping to resolve it are discussed. This is a good point in the course to direct your attention to this issue. (You might also like to have another look at the relevant parts of Paper 8.)

(iv) *Course Reader: Chapter 3 (optional)*
Although this chapter is optional reading, it does raise some thought-provoking and interesting issues. It is essentially concerned with the role of psychologists in relation to society. How might social research be used by policy makers and others and can psychologists remain neutral in this matter? The chapter discusses both how far research itself can ever be considered to be value-free and what the consequences of research may be. It raises questions both about how psychology may be used to maintain the existing social order and how it may be used to bring about change. Chapter 3 also considers the problems that can arise because of the different goals sought by researchers and policy makers; researchers, on the one hand, are likely to be concerned with understanding, which may involve pursuing and even extending the full complexity of an issue rather than supplying definitive and often simple, solutions which policy makers require. Policy makers, on the other hand, seek to supply easy answers. As Block 5 is concerned at least in part with the interrelationships between research programmes on attitudes and societal/historical trends, and social control and policy, this is useful preparatory reading.

---

## Block 5 – Attitude Theories: Ancient and Modern (Study weeks 21–25)

*Purpose:*

(a) to trace the historical development of social-psychological research on people's attitudes;

(b) using attitude research as an illustration, to consider how political and social concerns, and world events, can influence the course of research in social psychology;

(c) to present a branch of social psychology which seeks generalizations relating people's representations of the world and their behaviour to elements of the social structure and economic and political events;

(d)  to illustrate the nomothetic approach to social psychology by a detailed longitudinal study of political attitudes and voting behaviour conducted in the UK during the 60s and 70s.

---

STUDY WEEK 21

*To read:*  Introduction to Block 5
Unit 15: Individuals and their attitudes
Course Reader: Extracts from Smith, Bruner and White

*Optional:*  Metablock, Part III, Paper 8.

### Unit 15: Individuals and their attitudes

*Content:* The unit initially takes an individualistic approach to attitudes by looking at the functions they serve for individuals and the relation between attitudes/opinions and personality. The study of prejudice enables the unit to move from an individualistic to a more social viewpoint in that prejudiced attitudes are explained at the level of individual cognitive styles and personality *and* in terms of the social and economic climate and current political ideologies. The unit concludes with a discussion of collective representations of the world in a Durkheimian sense, and an outline of more recent French work on social representations.

*Purpose:*

The unit has three main aims:

(a)  to introduce attitude theory and research and its terminology;

(b)  to make the reader aware of the part played by one's attitudes in everyday life;

(c)  to use some of the research on prejudice to illustrate that attitude theory can contribute to understanding people's representations of the world and their behaviour at both an individualistic and at a social level.

*Comment:*

1  *Links with other parts of the course*

(i) Although the idea of attitudes has already appeared in the course (e.g. in the discussion of socialization; and similarity of attitudes in interpersonal attraction), this unit lays the foundations for a rigorous approach to attitude theory and research.

(ii) The discussion of the way in which individuals build their unique models of their worlds, in terms of beliefs and feelings (attitudes), is closely related to the personal words of Unit 12. There are similarities also to the 'personal constructs' of Kelly's theory though these are conceptualized in a rather different, bipolar similarity/difference form.

(iii) The later parts of the unit shift away from an individualistic perspective toward the idea that people's consciousness is not only deeply affected by their experience of the social world, but that consciousness may reflect the structure of society. People in a given culture may well have many areas of similarity in the way they internally represent and 'construct' their social worlds. This then echoes earlier discussion in the course which emphasized the social construction of consciousness (see especially the work of Berger *et al.* in Unit 13).

2  At several points this unit bears on important general issues in social psychology (see particularly Metablock, Paper 8, also Papers 4 and 6).

(i) The research described in Unit 15 illustrates both idiographic and nomothetic approaches to social psychology. The depth interviews and projective tests described in Smith, Bruner and White and in Adorno *et al.*'s study of the authoritarian personality are idiographic, in-depth approaches. These contrast with the formalized questionnaires that were also part of the Authoritarian Personality study and aimed at making generalizations about people's upbringing and their adult constellations of beliefs and feelings, their prejudiced behaviour and political ideologies.

(ii) The two approaches to method described in (i) above tend to correspond with the two views of attitudes which are fuel for the autonomy/determinism debate (see Papers 8 and 9): to the extent that individuals construct models of their unique worlds in such a way as to facilitate their perceptions, understanding, and behaviour in those worlds, then perhaps these can be seen as *chosen* and active coping strategies (although of course they may be adaptive, but not consciously chosen). However, the findings of the authoritarian personality study tend to imply that people's attitudes are *determined* by their early environment and the kind of socialization to which they have been exposed.

---

STUDY WEEK 22

*To read:*   Unit 16: Attitudes and behaviour

*Optional:* Metablock, Part III, Paper 4.

### Unit 16: Attitudes and behaviour

*Content:* Unit 16 traces the history of the concept of attitude in social psychology. Several branches of research are outlined together with the 'models of the person' on which they are based. Most of the research is in the experimental tradition. Several studies are described in detail together with an evaluation of the techniques used to *measure* attitudes and behaviour, and the logic of the experimental designs which explore the relationship between people's attitudes and what they actually do.

*Purpose:*

(a)   to present changing 'fashions' in attitude research;

(b)   to examine the status of the assumption that there is a simple causal relationship between people's attitudes and their behaviour;

(c)   to evaluate methods of measuring attitudes and how these relate to different aspects and definitions of 'attitude';

(d)   to explore relations between beliefs, feelings and behaviour.

*Comment:*

1   There is an implicit assumption in many places throughout the course, that what people *do* is related, in a fairly simple way, to their internal representations of the world. Unit 16 is where this assumption is made explicit, and where research directed specifically at the nature of the relationship is described and evaluated. A nomothetic approach to the problem (whether through experimentation or surveys) tends to focus on the possibility of a causal relationship. In Part 2 attitudes are studied as *causes* of behaviour; but Part 3 suggests that behaviour *causes* attitudes. The final part of the unit suggests that a much more complex relationship is likely; and that exploration of feedback loops between people's representations of the world – in terms of beliefs *and* feelings – needs to build on idiographic and hermeneutic versions of social psychology.

2   In Unit 16, and at other places in Block 5, the authors tend to switch back and forth between the terms 'behaviour' and 'action'. Sometimes 'behaviour' is used just as in ordinary language (what people do), and sometimes loosely as a term which emcompasses *both* 'behaviour' *and* 'action'. These points are discussed in Paper 4 of Part III of the Metablock. This suggests that psychologists tend to use 'behaviour' within a nomothetic and perhaps deterministic view of psychology, and to use 'action' when approaching the subject matter from a more idiographic,

individualistic and hermeneutic standpoint. You might like to look back to Paper 4 and to check this idea as you read through the unit (and the rest of the block).

3   Note that any discussion of *causes* of behaviour skates on rather thin philosophical 'ice'. The idea of cause and effect is inextricably bound up with a nomothetic approach. Once we try to understand what a single individual does intentionally and meaningfully in terms of her/his beliefs and feelings then we are, strictly, outside the usual scientific domain of cause and effect – because each instance of beliefs, feelings and action that we explore is 'unique'. Paper 8 discusses this further.

---

STUDY WEEKS 23 and 24

---

*To read:*   Unit 17/18: Changing attitudes
             Set Book: *How Voters Decide*, Chapters 1, 4, 9, 10, 12

*Optional:* Set Book: *How Voters Decide*, Chapters 3, 6, 7, 8, 14

### Unit 17/18: Changing attitudes

*Content:* The first part of this double unit describes studies of attitude change and persuasion. It picks up on one of the strands of attitude research that was mentioned, but not developed, in Unit 16. As in Unit 16, the wider historical and social context of the studies is discussed. Changes in the political scene, primarily in the USA, led to the demise of attitude research aimed at understanding and producing changes in 'public opinion'; these had depended on a *consensus* about the 'correctness' (morally and politically) of the end product of such techniques. The unit then takes up another 'real world' aspect of attitude research – people's political beliefs and voting patterns – one where 'consensus' has never been applicable. Clearly, if a social scientist wants to understand how people are socialized into particular party political groupings then it is *differences* between what they believe and feel and how they vote that are important. This second part of the unit describes three models which try to account for such variance, focusing in depth on a British longitudinal study which is the topic of the set book *How Voters Decide*.

*Purpose:*

(a)   to describe and evaluate research on persuasive communications and attitude change;

(b)   to describe three models of vote choice and discuss the evidence (in its historical context) for each;

(c)   to present a longitudinal study of political attitudes and vote choice in Britain;

(d)   to discuss the methodology of longitudinal studies in general and *How Voters Decide* in particular; and to illustrate the kind of statistical techniques that can be used, in conjunction with survey data, to test complex models of the determinants of political attitudes and voting behaviour.

*Comment:*

1   This is the place in the course where you are asked to consider, in some depth, the methods of collecting and analysing large scale survey data. You are not expected to have any knowledge of statistics – the analyses and graphs are described in a way that gives an intuitive grasp of the search for *patterns* in the data which is the essence of the nomothetic approach.

2   The variety of social psychology that is described in Unit 17/18 is nomothetic and societal. It searches for general laws: exploring and testing models of persuasion and of vote choice. The emphasis is on cause and effect and on the search for

determining influences. The research is societal because it relates people's representations of the world to 'external' variables, such as social class, world events and 'real' changes in the structure of society, in economic conditions and political issues.

3   Note that the collective representations of political issues described at the end of Unit 17/18 are rather different from those discussed earlier in the block (e.g. Durkheim, Moscovici). Here they are *re-structured* by statistical procedures and primarily based on the researchers' view of what the issues were rather than an empirical investigation of how *voters* themselves view the political scene.

4   It is worth noting that the Yale programme of *experimental* research provided an important training ground for many key social psychologists. Also, the programme illustrates interesting developmental trends: from a purely empirical orientation designed to answer practical questions to a search for theory; from a mechanistic view in the earlier stages to an explicit recognition of the need for cognitive theory in later work by Rosenberg. This can be seen as another example of the move from *passive* to *active* models of the person seen in other parts of the block. Such a trend can be seen *within* the experimental tradition (e.g. in cognitive dissonance studies studied in Unit 16).

*Study note:*

The set reading from *How Voters Decide* is introduced in the text of Unit 17/18. Try to read these chapters alongside the unit. Several other chapters are highly recommended; if you do not have time for these (or for all the set chapters) you will be able to use part of the next study week to catch up and/or further extend your reading of the set book.

---

STUDY WEEK 25

---

*Reading and Review*

*To read:*   Set book: *How Voters Decide*, Chapters 1, 4, 9, 10, 12
         Course Reader: Chapter 4
         Set book: *Freud and Psychoanalysis*, Chapter 13 (pp. 134–9)

*Optional:*  Set book: *How Voters Decide*, Chapters 3, 6, 7, 8, 14
         Metablock, Part IV, Revision Exercises.

1   *How Voters Decide*

The reading guide to this book is in Part 3 of Unit 17/18. If you have not yet read the set chapters try to do so now while the issues are still fresh in your mind. This would also be a good time to read the recommended chapters and any remaining chapters that interest you.

2   *Course Reader: Chapter 4 – Psychologists in action*

This chapter looks at the activities of psychologists in relation to a variety of social issues from cigarette smoking to a doctor's consultation, giving a selection of examples of the way in which political, social and theoretical concerns are interwoven in the work of applied social psychologists. You have already been referred to five of the articles as set or optional reading for earlier blocks (*Smith, Bruner and White*; *Clarke and Clarke*; Rutter and Madge; Argyle; *Hayley*). Four others (*Milgram*; Savin; Zimbardo; *Reicher*) are related to the next block (articles in italics are set reading). At this stage you might like to read the editorial linking sections throughout Chapter 4 which set the articles in context and discuss points which arise from them. You may also choose to read or re-read some or all of the articles which are mentioned above.

Chapter 4 raises a number of general issues including:

(a)   The importance of the social, political, historical and geographical context in determining the research undertaken and in limiting its application and generalization to other contexts (see Metablock, Paper 7).

(b)   Research itself cannot solve policy problems, but can clear the ground for informed discussion and clarify the problems that need to be faced (see Paper 6).

(c)   Problems tend to increase in complexity and extensiveness as they come under closer inspection.

(d)   For the psychologists working in 'real world' experimentation there are problems which concern ethics and value systems. A discussion between Savin and Zimbardo shows up these difficulties.

(e)   The shift of the focus away from individuals to the whole system of relationships of which the person is a part (Hayley paper) (see also Metablock, Paper 3).

(f)   A model for psychology that takes account of social and personal structures as well as dynamic relationships between them is proposed by the brief extract from Llewelyn and Kelly – a model of a dialectical psychology. This argument relates to issues raised in Paper 10.

3   *'Freud and Psychoanalysis', Chapter 13*

This brief chapter is worth looking at here for two reasons:

(a)   Block 5 has moved us from individualistic concerns to social and collective representations. Chapter 13 briefly reviews Freud's theories about society (in contrast to his theories about the individual).

(b)   A major theme of the block and the Course Reader has been the close interlinking between social psychological ideas and research and attitudes and concerns in society. Chapter 13 comments not just on the moral implications of psychoanalysis, but on the influence which psychoanalysis may have had on contemporary attitudes and behaviours.

---

## Block 6 – People in Groups (Study weeks 26–28)

*To read:*   Block 6: People in groups
Course Reader: articles by Reicher and Milgram (in Chapter 4)

*Optional:* Course Reader: articles by Savin and Zimbardo (in Chapter 4); Chapter 5 (editorial) and articles by Watson; Ehrenreich and English

*To do:*   Select your option and begin work on TMA 06.

### Unit 19/20/21: People in groups

*Content:* The block is concerned with the antecedents, nature and outcomes of the interaction of people in groups, from small transient laboratory groups to crowds. It is structured in five main sections:

(a)   The first part looks at ways in which groups have been studied both in the laboratory and in real-life situations, including studies of group pressure and conformity.

(b)   The second part considers social control in groups from decision making and leadership to political indoctrination and 'brainwashing'.

(c)   The third part discusses intergroup relations, taking up the issues of prejudice, conflict and group identity.

(d)   The fourth part looks at crowd behaviour.

(e)   The block concludes by taking up ethical concerns and the implications of research on groups for social psychology in general.

*Purpose:* to review social psychological research on the behaviour of people in group situations.

*Comment:*

1   This block follows naturally from much that has been discussed earlier in the course. Social interaction in groups may well involve many of the processes (like self-disclosure, reciprocity, etc.) discussed in the context of relationships in Block 3. The source of identity in group memberships was briefly referred to in Block 4 and the discussion of prejudice here relates to the research on the authoritarian personality in Block 5.

2   One interesting aspect of the study of people in groups is to follow the changing foci of research in this field. They can be seen to have developed from two interlaced strands:

(i) the influence of the social context and what appears 'problematic' in this context, and hence becomes a focus of research, (i.e. *applied* research); and

(ii) 'internal' developments and progress within the discipline and hence how phenomena are studied and explained (i.e. '*pure*' research).

These two traditions of research – the 'applied' and the 'pure' – also reflect some broad differences in methodology. Thus, the applied social psychologist tends to engage in *field* research of contemporary concerns and the theoretician tends to use *laboratory* experiments.

However, in this block you will find that, whilst one or other approach may dominate at a given period, many issues have been most fruitfully explored by using both laboratory *and* field methods of research. Indeed, the applied researcher will, on occasions, be able to contribute to theoretical knowledge and the 'pure' researcher to the greater understanding of pressing social issues.

Whilst the tensions between the applied and the theoretical, the field and the laboratory work, stand out very clearly in the area of the study of groups, they can be detected in many areas of social psychology. It is because of this that the *Reader* highlights these debates and dialogues and the implications they have for the discipline and for the theorist and practitioner of social psychology.

3   One issue discussed in the Metablock which is particularly relevant to this block is *level of analysis* (see Paper 3). Group research shows more clearly than most topic areas in social psychology how research can be directed at different levels, from that which focuses on the reactions of individuals to that which looks at groups in sociological terms.

4   Research on groups also throws into particular relief the ethical issues which may arise in social psychological research.

*Course Reader: Chapter 5 – Psychology in the popular imagination* (optional)

This chapter is concerned with a particular view of psychology – the way it is perceived by the public at large. In other words, to use a concept introduced in Block 5, this chapter explores social representations of psychology. What kind of psychological research tends to filter through to the public and what distortions occur in this process?

By the time you have finished Block 6 you will have been referred to five of the articles in this chapter as optional reading (Hardyman; Rapoport *et al.*; Ehrenreich and English; Watson; Kamin). It is therefore a good idea to read the editorial section of this chapter along with the articles listed above at least so that they can be set in context and in relation to the general issues which they raise.

## Block 7 – Society, Culture and Change (Study week 29)

*Purpose:* To continue the move towards societal concerns begun in Blocks 5 and 6 and end the course by considering some social psychological aspects of social change (Unit 22) and the interactions between change at a societal and personal level (Postscript).

*To read:* Unit 22: Social movements and their strategies
Postscript

*To do:* Complete and submit TMA 06. This is an essay based on the work of Blocks 5 and/or 6 (see *Assignments Booklet*)

### Unit 22: Social movements and their strategies

*Content:* The final unit of the course develops the societal level of analysis introduced in Blocks 5 and 6 by looking at the development of social movements and the strategies they adopt to achieve their aims.

*Purpose:*

(a)   to increase your understanding of social movements including their origins, the strategies they adopt, the roles individual members play and the implications for individuals of their membership;

(b)   to round off the course by considering social psychological processes which bring about *change*.

*Comment:* Several ideas put forward in the unit pick up on topics and theories presented earlier in the course. For example, social movements can provide a potent source of individual identity and social identity; and the rhetoric of social movements is related to sociolinguistic issues raised in Unit 6. Attitude change is clearly highly relevant to the study of social movements.

*Postscript*

*Content:* The postscript questions the universality of the social psychology created in the Western World. The impact of culture is illustrated by considering the relation between social and economic *change* and ideology in a culture very different from our own.

*Purpose:*

(a)   to question the culture-bound assumptions of Western social psychology;

(b)   to question the possibility of universals in social psychology;

(c)   to show how the study of *change* at a societal level can contribute to our understanding at other levels of analysis of social psychological processes such as those described in the course as a whole.

## Integration and revision

These final three weeks of the course are allocated for you to complete your Integration Essay (TMA 07) and to review and revise the course material in preparation for the examination.

*To do/read:*   TMA 07 (Integration Essay)
Metablock, Part III, Paper 10, *A note on the nature of social psychology.*

*Optional:*   Course Reader: Epilogue
Metablock, Part IV – revision exercises
Vade Mecum

1   *Integration Essay* (TMA 07). By now you should have extensive notes on the option you have selected. You are asked to write them up as a TMA and submit it as soon as possible (see *Assignments Booklet* for cut-off date).

2 *Metablock, Paper 10.* It is suggested that you read Metablock, Paper 10 at this point. It offers some comment on the nature of social psychology as seen through this course.

3 *Course Reader: Epilogue.* This reviews the themes of the Reader and looks ahead to the ways in which social psychology may develop in the future. It also acknowledges that it is not possible to tie up all the loose ends. The various dialogues, debates and controversies which we have encountered are intrinsic to social psychology and part and parcel of any attempt to apply it to the problems of society. The Epilogue emphasizes the need for social psychologists to take a socio-historical perspective both to the issues they study and to their own discipline as well. This concluding chapter bears on the issue of what kinds of knowledge and solutions are possible in social psychology. Many of the problems which we confront as individuals and as societies may be seen as part of what it is to be human. The notion of solutions in a sense of definitive answers does not apply. The chapter also raises the question of how far a scientific methodology is appropriate for the subject-matter and questions with which social psychology deals.

4 *Metablock, Part IV: Revision exercises.* If you have not already done so, it would be helpful now to begin work on the exercises given here which are designed to help you with your revision. You may also find that going back over the Vade Mecum gives you a useful overview of the course.

All that remains for your guide to say now is – the best of luck with your exam and for your future explorations in social psychology.

# PART III – KEY ISSUES IN SOCIAL PSYCHOLOGY

## Introduction

The ten papers in Part III of the Metablock deal with general issues about the nature of social psychology and the kind of understanding which it is possible for it to provide. The issues discussed include ways of distinguishing between social psychological theories, the use of different methods, autonomy and determinism, and the constructed nature of our understanding. Some of these papers deal with controversial topics on which there is by no means agreement among social psychologists themselves. Inevitably these, to some extent, reflect the viewpoints of their authors. You should bear this in mind as you read through the papers and be alert to the fact that the different papers may not always present compatible views.

### List of papers:

|  | page |
|---|---|
| Paper 1 – People and perspectives in social psychology | 43 |
| Paper 2 – Making sense of theories in social psychology | 60 |
| Paper 3 – Levels of analysis | 74 |
| Paper 4 – Behaviour and action | 81 |
| Paper 5 – The significance of meaning | 85 |
| Paper 6 – Research methods | 92 |
| Paper 7 – The construction of reality | 100 |
| Paper 8 – Nomothetic, idiographic and hermeneutic social psychology | 109 |
| Paper 9 – A note on assumptions of autonomy and determinism in social psychology | 122 |
| Paper 10 – A note on the nature of social psychology | 126 |

## Paper 1: People and perspectives in social psychology

*by Jeannette Murphy*

This paper provides a schematic overview of the intellectual traditions which have influenced the way in which social psychology has evolved during the past eighty or so years. Instead of presenting you with a narrative account of the historical development of the discipline, I have tried to organize the material as a set of charts, each of which traces a particular tradition, orientation or perspective which has made a significant contribution to social psychology. In addition, there is a preliminary chart which indicates where in the course you will encounter these traditions.

What I would suggest is that you glance at all the charts now, but without expecting them to make a great deal of sense at this point in your studies. The first chart is likely to be the most useful at this point. After completion of each course block, it would be well worth the effort to look at the charts again, noting which traditions you have encountered. (You might also check to see whether your own personal 'scheme' would differ significantly from that sketched in this paper.) Finally, you should return to the charts when you have completed the course and are revising for your exams. It is only then that all the names and theories will be familiar to you.

## 1: General comments that will help you to use the charts

*Chart 1 – Linkage of theoretical traditions and course themes*

This first chart gives you a sneak preview of the many perspectives and traditions that are woven into the course. When you look at the first chart, you should note the following.

(a) The ordering of the various traditions that feed into a research topic is arbitrary (i.e. it is *not* meant to imply time or relative importance or order of appearance in the course).

(b) Social psychology draws on many different traditions and orientations (the chart highlights the multiperspective nature of the course and the discipline).

(c) Any given theme or research area (e.g. groups or the family) has many different intellectual antecedents. Another way of expressing this is to say that there is a many-to-many relationship between theories and research traditions – each theory gives rise to a variety of research topics and methods of inquiry and each research topic (or block in the course) draws upon a range of different traditions. Thus, S–R reinforcement theorists have initiated work on interpersonal attraction, and socialization. At the same time, a topic such as interpersonal attraction or socialization attracts researchers from more than just one theoretical tradition. The reason for stressing this point is to counterbalance an impression you might get (from the other charts) of the cohesion or unity of the various intellectual traditions. Although there is undoubtedly a sense in which traditions are distinct, with a continuity of concepts and assumptions within the tradition, the important point to remember also is that theories do develop and change. Furthermore, when it comes to doing research there is an intermingling of traditions, thus it is inevitable that an exchange of ideas takes place across the boundaries. If you bear in mind that no perspective has a monopoly over a given field of research, this should help you to avoid thinking that the real world of theory and research is as cut and dried as these charts might seem to suggest.

*Charts 2–9 – The link between persons, perspectives and research themes*

Charts 2–9 provide you with a *chronological frame of reference* for the key theorists you will meet in the course. What each chart does is draw together material that is scattered throughout the course units. We do not expect you to absorb all the details of these charts at the beginning of the course (nor to memorize them for the examination), but we hope you will make *active* use of them. They should help to familiarize you with certain names, to alert you to which names are associated with which perspectives and to make you aware of the period when particular writers were professionally active. Some names and concepts you may have already met in the course, but there will also be many persons and perspectives that are new to you.

Although the charts are drawn in such a way as to emphasize the time when certain key figures lived, they are *not* intended to provide you with a comprehensive history of social psychology. By and large, the maps only include details of persons and perspectives *that are relevant to the course.* For this reason, certain key figures in the history of psychology and philosophy are omitted.

Most of the charts take as their starting point a theorist or a school that gained recognition in the late nineteenth century. However, you should realize that in the history of ideas it is impossible to specify a moment in time when an idea first gained currency. Thus, our starting points are in some ways rather arbitrary.

While each chart deals with a distinctive perspective, there are variations between diagrams. This will become clear when you read through them and study the notes that belong to each one.

> Each chart contains:
> – names of key writers;
> – names commonly used to label the traditions;

- an indication of the chronological sequence within and between traditions;
- information as to the country where the theorist worked (which is not always the same as his country of birth);
- identification of some of the main research topics which derive from the tradition;
- indication of key interactions that have occurred between traditions (this is shown by a double headed arrow).

If you have the chance to discuss these charts with your tutor or with fellow students, you may well discover that not everyone agrees with the way in which they have been constructed. While some of the links suggested are obvious and non-controversial, there are others that are more tenuous and indirect. No two social psychologists would tell the story of their discipline in the same way, nor would they necessarily draw their charts in precisely the way I have chosen to do. Thus, you may end up challenging my conception of 'what goes with what' as regards concepts, theories and historical influences.

## 2:   Detailed notes to accompany each chart:

*Chart 1 – Linkage of theoretical traditions and course themes*

What this diagram is intended to convey is the fact that each of the course blocks (represented by the 'labels' on the 'ropes') draws from many different intellectual traditions or perspectives. These latter are the 'strands' which intertwine to make up each rope. For example, you can see that we have identified eight different 'inputs' to the study of the family etc.:

> sociobiology/ethology
> anthropology
> history
> sociology
> feminist analyses
> psychoanalysis
> systems theory
> humanistic psychology

The relative importance of these inputs and the nature of their contribution will be made clear in the block. The ordering of these different inputs is arbitrary in so far as it is not meant to represent time or rank ordering.

In the charts that follow you will meet each of these traditions again. For instance, we will suggest that work on sociobiology/ethology is one strand in the much broader tradition of genetics and biology.

What you should also note after inspecting all the intertwining strands, is that some traditions figure in more than one of the course themes. If we take psycho-dynamic theory (psychoanalysis), for example, we see that it appears under the following course themes:

> the family
> children/childhood
> personal worlds
> attitudes/public opinion/mass media
> groups/leadership crowds
> social change/social movements/collectivities

What then you should extract from this chart is the fact that each block in the course draws on a range of perspectives or traditions *and* each tradition is likely to contribute to several blocks. You may find it helpful to treat this chart as a checklist to remind you of where you encounter certain perspectives. It would be a good idea to return to this chart after you have completed the course.

*Chart 2 – Biological/Genetic tradition*

1   This traces the tradition from Darwin, although the study of biology and genetics predated the nineteenth century. (The reason for selecting Darwin as the starting point is because this reflects the way the material is developed in the course.)

2   There are several interactions between traditions shown on this chart: ethology and the psychodynamic tradition have come into contact through work on attachment; biometrics has given rise to the mental testing movement and has in turn incorporated many of the techniques and research findings of this approach in the study of individual differences.

3   Comparative social psychology (the study of social behaviour and social structures in the animal world) is shown with many different arrows leading from it as a way of calling attention to the ongoing influence of such studies. Here it is not possible to specify a date or to link this type of research to a single individual.

4   On the extreme right-hand side of the chart you are presented with a list of the type of research topics which illustrate the concerns of people currently working within this tradition or influenced by it. This list is not meant to be exhaustive, but is intended to demonstrate how questions relating to genetics and biology continue to puzzle and fascinate social psychologists.

*Chart 3 – S–R reinforcement tradition*

1   Work on the conditioning of animals (by Pavlov and by Thorndike) laid the foundations for behaviourism as a psychological school.

2   It is important to note the way in which this tradition has split into a number of distinctive approaches: from behaviourism we branch out to neo-behaviourism/learning theory, social learning theory, Bandura's model of observational learning.

3   Unit 4 (Block 1) gives a systematic treatment of this perspective.

4   Two interactions are worth noting: exchange between the psychodynamic tradition and neo-behaviourism, which has given rise to one type of social learn-ing theory; and the bridge between learning theory and biology and genetics provided by Eysenck's work.

5   The current research topics listed on the right-hand side of the chart provide an indication of the measure of the extent to which social psychologists continue to find S–R reinforcement theory a valuable framework for their research.

*Chart 4 – Sociological social psychology (symbolic interactionism) tradition*

1   The writings of George Herbert Mead have been seen as providing an important bridge between the concerns of psychologists and sociologists.

2   Writers in this tradition are sometimes classed as sociologists and sometimes considered to be social psychologists.

3   What distinguishes this perspective from other traditions is the stress that it places on situational determinants of behaviour.

4   The main figures in this tradition are all American and many of them were connected with the University of Chicago.

5   A detailed account of this perspective is to be found in Unit 4.

6   Some explanation is required as to why the term 'sociological social psy-chology' is linked to this tradition. (This point is considered in your Course Reader, Chapters 1 and 5.) Social psychology has tended to use concepts and theories from general experimental psychology and to operate from the assump-tion that the basic starting point in any analysis of social life is the individual.

Consequently, some writers have used the phrase *psychological* social psychology, the implication being that it would be possible to construct a *sociological* social psychology. Mead's writings suggest one way of pursuing such a goal, and hence symbolic interactionism (or social behaviourism as it is sometimes called) carries this designation.

7   Although the term sociological social psychology has come to be equated with symbolic interactionism, this does not mean that other sociological theories are not of relevance to the discipline. In the course you will not be presented with a detailed or systematic account of the various sociological schools, but the ideas and concepts of the founding fathers of sociology do figure indirectly in the course. Rather than giving separate diagrams for these traditions, the table that follows summarizes areas of social psychological research which derive from sociology.

TABLE 1 – The impact of sociology

| *Founding father* | *Social psychological research* |
| --- | --- |
| Max Weber | studies on bureaucracy; social institutions; power and authority; achievement motivation; social change. |
| Emile Durkheim | social norms; conformity; morality; collective representations. |
| Karl Marx | study of ideology; radical critiques of social science; social structure and consciousness. |
| Karl Mannheim | study of public opinion/ideology; mass media/mass communication; voting studies. |

*Chart 5 – Psychodynamic tradition*

1   You will learn about this approach in both your set book *(Freud and Psychoanalysis)* and in Unit 4, although its ideas appear in many places in the course.

2   The psychodynamic tradition has served as a source of ideas for many other traditions. The main interactions highlighted in this course are with Marxist thought (Frankfurt School), with neo-behaviourism (social learning theory), with ethology (attachment, bonding) and with anthropology (culture and personality).

3   Many of Freud's followers went on to found their own rival approaches (e.g. Jung, Adler, Rank).

*Chart 6 – Study of language tradition*

1   This chart differs from the others in that it does not correspond to a homogeneous school of thought. What unites the persons named (and hence justifies grouping them together) is the fact that they have worked on a common area. So in this case the tradition we are examining is not a theoretical perspective, but a shared research interest. For this reason, the writers named (e.g. Chomsky and Skinner) often have diametrically opposed ways of explaining language.

2   As can be seen by reading down the list of disciplines to the left of the chart, many different specialisms converge on the study of language.

3   Language features primarily in Block 2.

*Chart 7 – Study of the person tradition*

1   Philosophical theories have set the agenda for this tradition. What the various theories have done is to pose as the central issue the question of what it means

to be human. By and large writers in this tradition are opposed to mechanistic conceptions of human nature. Starting from the assumption that people are not things or machines, this tradition also seeks to explore alternative ways of studying people, of doing psychology.

2   Block 4 *(Personal Worlds)* guides you through the ideas that form a common substratum for this approach to social psychology.

3   Since the main contribution of this perspective has not been empirical research, but a method of study, when you look at the right-hand side of the diagram, instead of finding a list of research themes, you will see the names of modern representatives of the approach whom you will meet in the course.

*Chart 8 – Study of persuasion and communication tradition*

1   This topic features in Blocks 5 and 6 of the course.

2   All of the notes for Chart 6 (The study of language) also apply here. What unites the divergent trends here into a recognizable tradition is the common interest in the study of communication processes.

3   From the outset, there has been a division between sociological and psychological approaches. At the methodological level, psychologists favoured the use of laboratory experiments and pioneered the development of attitude measurement techniques. Sociologists, by comparison, tended to conduct surveys and to carry out field studies.

4   Although the field of communication studies has tended to be subdivided, some interaction has taken place between the psychological and sociological approaches.

*Chart 9 – Cognitive social psychology tradition*

1   This arises from the philosophical traditions of phenomenology, rationalism and structuralism. In a sense, cognitive psychology represented a reaction to reductionist trends in science. What all cognitive theorists maintain is that the whole is greater than the sum of its parts. In addition, this approach emphasizes structure and perception.

2   From the point of view of contemporary social psychology, this is the richest, most varied tradition.

3   As with other perspectives, it is possible to distinguish a number of sub-varieties: there is the developmental strand associated with Jean Piaget; there are the descendents from Kurt Lewin, and finally there are European cognitive social psychologists.

4   A great number of contemporary American social psychologists either studied with Lewin or worked with him (e.g. Barker, Bavelas, Back, Cartwright, Festinger, Deutsch, French, Katz, Kelly, Lippit, Newcomb, Pepitone, Schachter, Thibaut, White, Wright, Zander). Hence, the continuity or chain of influence is very much the result of direct personal contact. (As was the case with Freud and also with Mead.)

5   The main treatment of this tradition is to be found in Block 6, and in Units 4 and 5.

### 3   Using the charts

Lest you feel a bit bewildered and overwhelmed after your first look at these charts, let us reassure you that you are not expected to make sense of them until after you have completed the relevant units. Nor will you be required to memorize them so as to be able to reproduce them in an examination. As explained at the outset, these charts are designed primarily as an aid to revision and as a way of helping you to perceive that, although each block has its own focus, there are common perspectives running throughout the whole course. Do make a point of returning to these charts periodically as you progress through the blocks and don't forget to use them when you are preparing for your examination.

# CHART 1 : LINKAGE OF THEORETICAL TRADITIONS AND COURSE THEMES
### TRADITIONS THAT CONTRIBUTE TO THEORY AND RESEARCH ON A THEME

**COURSE THEMES**

**THEORETICAL TRADITIONS**

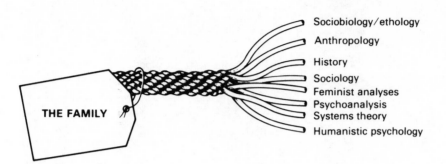

**THE FAMILY**

Sociobiology/ethology

Anthropology

History
Sociology
Feminist analyses
Psychoanalysis
Systems theory

Humanistic psychology

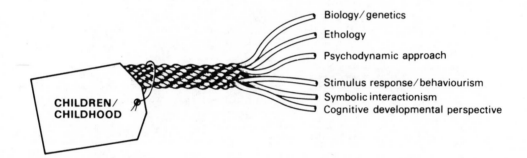

**CHILDREN/
CHILDHOOD**

Biology/genetics

Ethology

Psychodynamic approach

Stimulus response/behaviourism
Symbolic interactionism
Cognitive developmental perspective

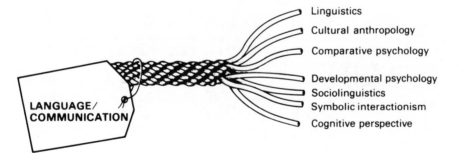

**LANGUAGE/
COMMUNICATION**

Linguistics

Cultural anthropology

Comparative psychology

Developmental psychology
Sociolinguistics
Symbolic interactionism
Cognitive perspective

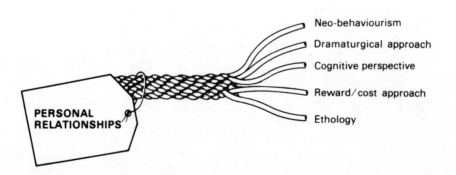

**PERSONAL
RELATIONSHIPS**

Neo-behaviourism

Dramaturgical approach

Cognitive perspective

Reward/cost approach

Ethology

**COURSE THEMES**                    **THEORETICAL TRADITIONS**

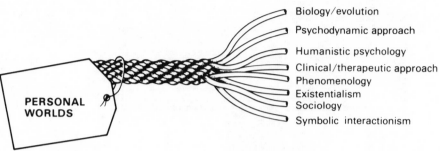

PERSONAL WORLDS

Biology/evolution
Psychodynamic approach
Humanistic psychology
Clinical/therapeutic approach
Phenomenology
Existentialism
Sociology
Symbolic interactionism

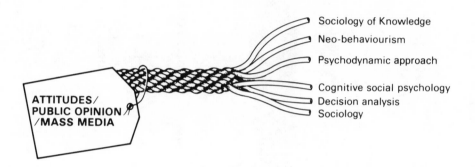

ATTITUDES/ PUBLIC OPINION /MASS MEDIA

Sociology of Knowledge
Neo-behaviourism
Psychodynamic approach
Cognitive social psychology
Decision analysis
Sociology

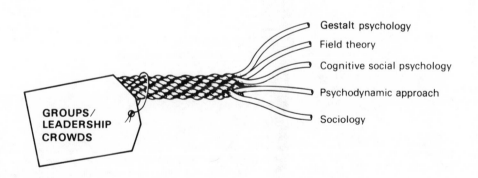

GROUPS/ LEADERSHIP CROWDS

Gestalt psychology
Field theory
Cognitive social psychology
Psychodynamic approach
Sociology

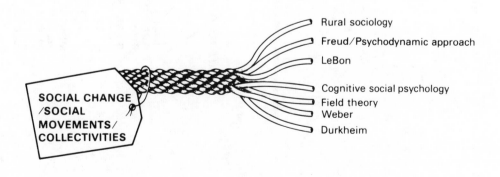

SOCIAL CHANGE /SOCIAL MOVEMENTS/ COLLECTIVITIES

Rural sociology
Freud/Psychodynamic approach
LeBon
Cognitive social psychology
Field theory
Weber
Durkheim

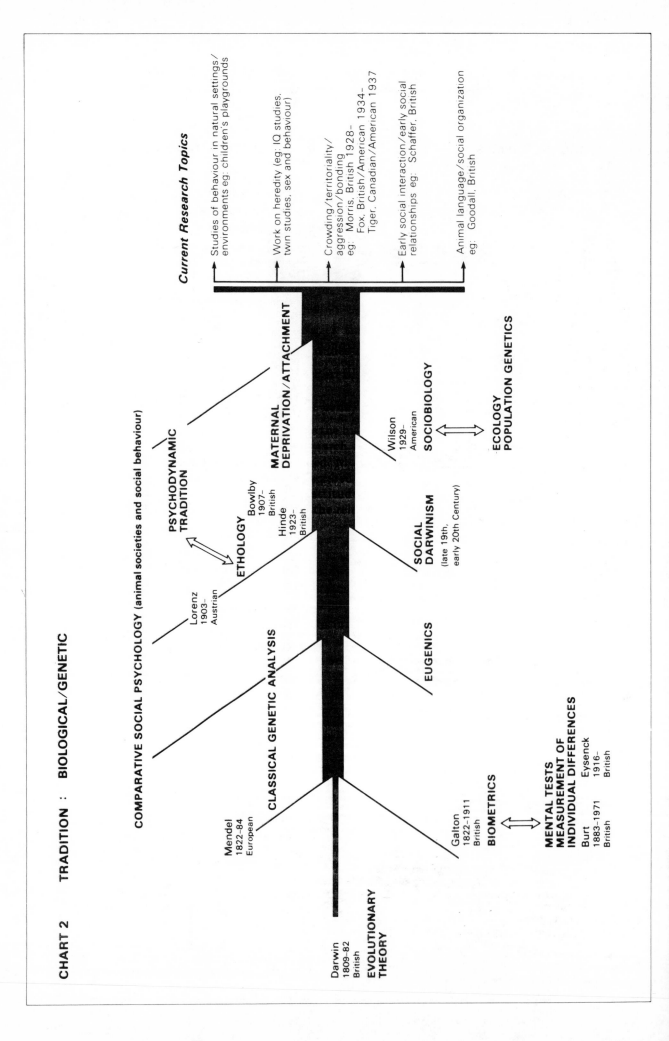

**CHART 2    TRADITION :   BIOLOGICAL/GENETIC**

**COMPARATIVE SOCIAL PSYCHOLOGY** (animal societies and social behaviour)

*Current Research Topics*

Studies of behaviour in natural settings / environments eg: children's playgrounds

Work on heredity (eg: IQ studies, twin studies, sex and behaviour)

Crowding/territoriality/ aggression/bonding eg:  Morris, British 1928– Fox, British/American 1934– Tiger, Canadian/American 1937

Early social interaction/early social relationships eg:   Schaffer, British

Animal language/social organization eg:  Goodall, British

**PSYCHODYNAMIC TRADITION**

**ETHOLOGY**

Lorenz 1903– Austrian

Bowlby 1907– British

Hinde 1923– British

**MATERNAL DEPRIVATION/ATTACHMENT**

Wilson 1929– American

**SOCIOBIOLOGY**

**SOCIAL DARWINISM** (late 19th, early 20th Century)

**ECOLOGY POPULATION GENETICS**

**CLASSICAL GENETIC ANALYSIS**

Mendel 1822–84 European

**EUGENICS**

Galton 1822–1911 British

**BIOMETRICS**

Burt 1883–1971 British

Eysenck 1916– British

**MENTAL TESTS MEASUREMENT OF INDIVIDUAL DIFFERENCES**

Darwin 1809–82 British

**EVOLUTIONARY THEORY**

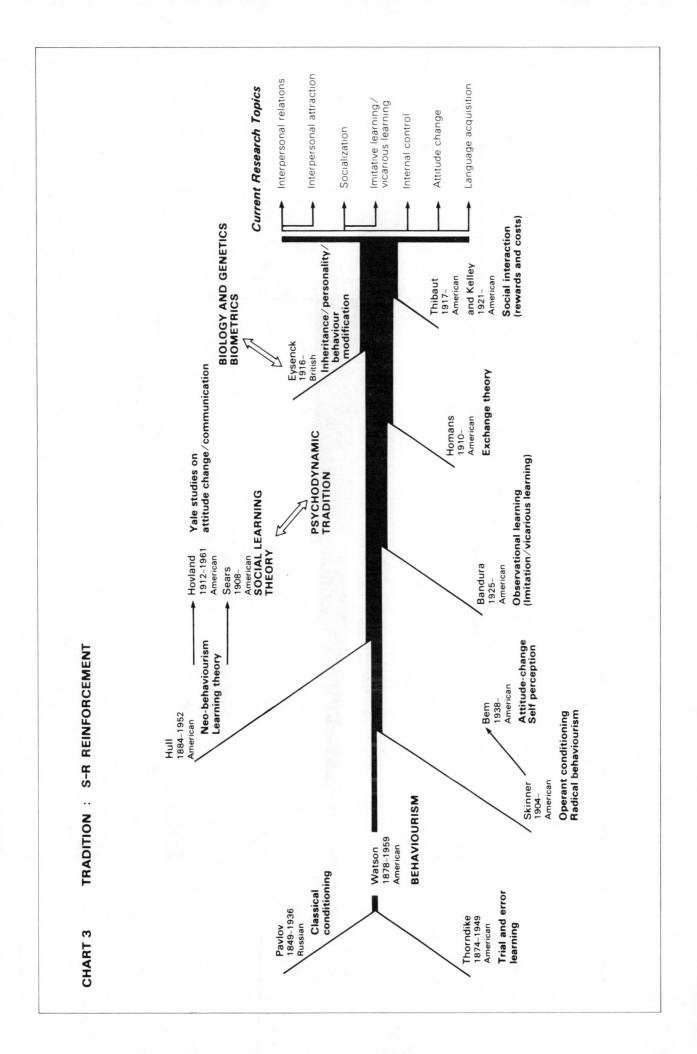

**CHART 3    TRADITION : S-R  REINFORCEMENT**

*Current Research Topics*

Interpersonal relations
Interpersonal attraction
Socialization
Imitative learning/ vicarious learning
Internal control
Attitude change
Language acquisition

**BIOLOGY AND GENETICS BIOMETRICS**

Eysenck
1916–
British

**Inheritance / personality / behaviour modification**

Thibaut
1917–
American
and Kelley
1921–
American

**Social interaction (rewards and costs)**

Homans
1910–
American

**Exchange theory**

**PSYCHODYNAMIC TRADITION**

Hovland
1912–1961
American

Sears
1908–
American

**Yale studies on attitude change/communication**

**SOCIAL LEARNING THEORY**

Bandura
1925–
American

**Observational learning (Imitation/vicarious learning)**

Hull
1884–1952
American

**Neo-behaviourism Learning theory**

Bem
1938–
American

**Attitude-change Self perception**

Skinner
1904–
American

**Operant conditioning Radical behaviourism**

Watson
1878–1959
American

**BEHAVIOURISM**

Pavlov
1849–1936
Russian

**Classical conditioning**

Thorndike
1874–1949
American

**Trial and error learning**

CHART 4     TRADITION :     SOCIOLOGICAL SOCIAL PSYCHOLOGY

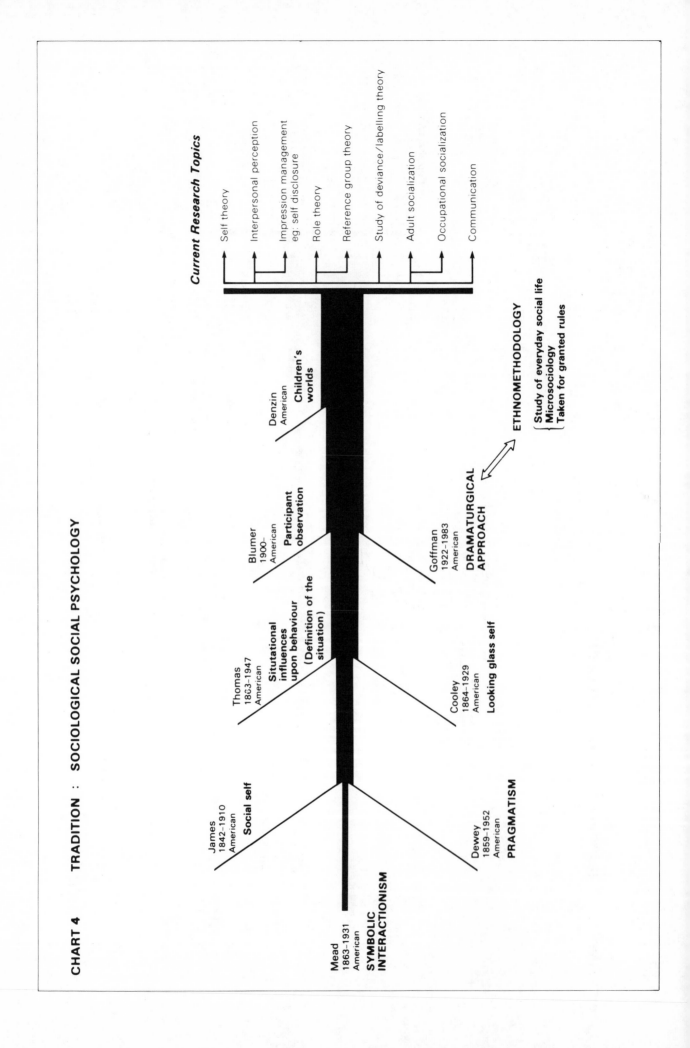

*Current Research Topics*

Self theory

Interpersonal perception

Impression management
eg: self disclosure

Role theory

Reference group theory

Study of deviance/labelling theory

Adult socialization

Occupational socialization

Communication

James
1842–1910
American
**Social self**

Thomas
1863–1947
American
**Situational
influences
upon behaviour
(Definition of the
situation)**

Blumer
1900–
American
**Participant
observation**

Denzin
American
**Children's
worlds**

Mead
1863–1931
American
**SYMBOLIC
INTERACTIONISM**

Dewey
1859–1952
American
**PRAGMATISM**

Cooley
1864–1929
American
**Looking glass self**

Goffman
1922–1983
American
**DRAMATURGICAL
APPROACH**

**ETHNOMETHODOLOGY**

Study of everyday social life
Microsociology
Taken for granted rules

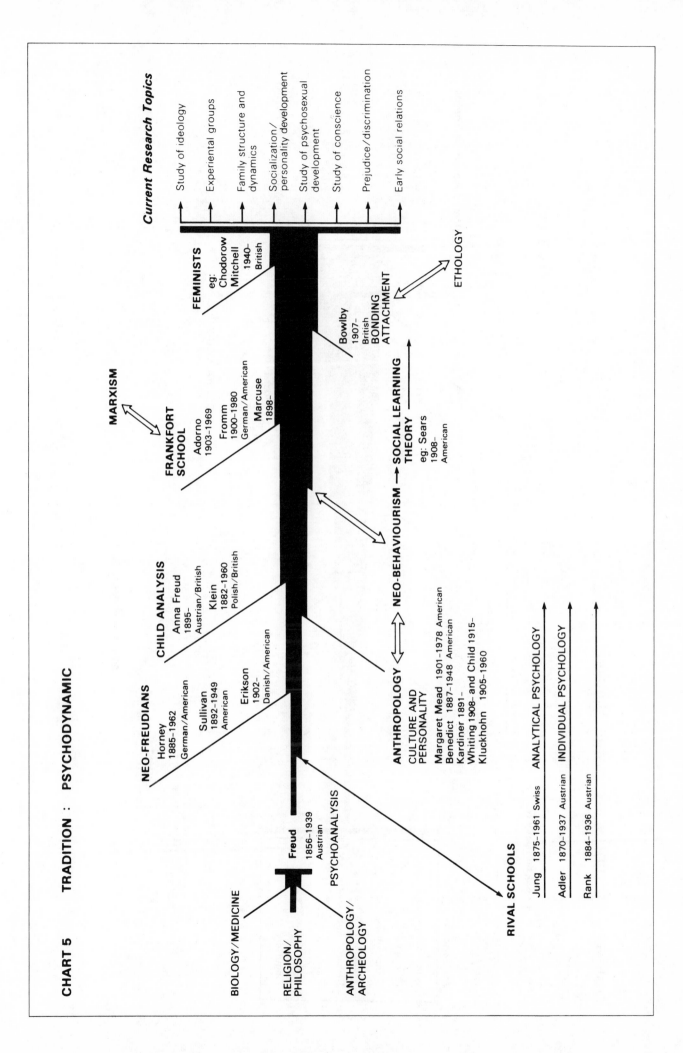

CHART 5    TRADITION :    PSYCHODYNAMIC

*Current Research Topics*

→ Study of ideology

→ Experiential groups

→ Family structure and dynamics

→ Socialization/personality development

→ Study of psychosexual development

→ Study of conscience

→ Prejudice/discrimination

→ Early social relations

FEMINISTS
eg: Chodorow
Mitchell 1940–
British

MARXISM

FRANKFORT SCHOOL
Adorno 1903–1969
Fromm 1900–1980 German/American
Marcuse 1898–

Bowlby 1907–
British
BONDING ATTACHMENT

ETHOLOGY

NEO-FREUDIANS
Horney 1885–1962 German/American
Sullivan 1892–1949 American
Erikson 1902– Danish/American

CHILD ANALYSIS
Anna Freud 1895– Austrian/British
Klein 1882–1960 Polish/British

→ NEO-BEHAVIOURISM → SOCIAL LEARNING THEORY
eg: Sears 1908– American

ANTHROPOLOGY
CULTURE AND PERSONALITY
Margaret Mead 1901–1978 American
Benedict 1887–1948 American
Kardiner 1891–
Whiting 1908– and Child 1915–
Kluckhohn 1905–1960

BIOLOGY/MEDICINE

RELIGION/PHILOSOPHY

Freud
1856–1939
Austrian

PSYCHOANALYSIS

ANTHROPOLOGY/ARCHEOLOGY

RIVAL SCHOOLS

Jung 1875–1961 Swiss    ANALYTICAL PSYCHOLOGY

Adler 1870–1937 Austrian    INDIVIDUAL PSYCHOLOGY

Rank 1884–1936 Austrian

55

CHART 6        TRADITION :        STUDY OF LANGUAGE

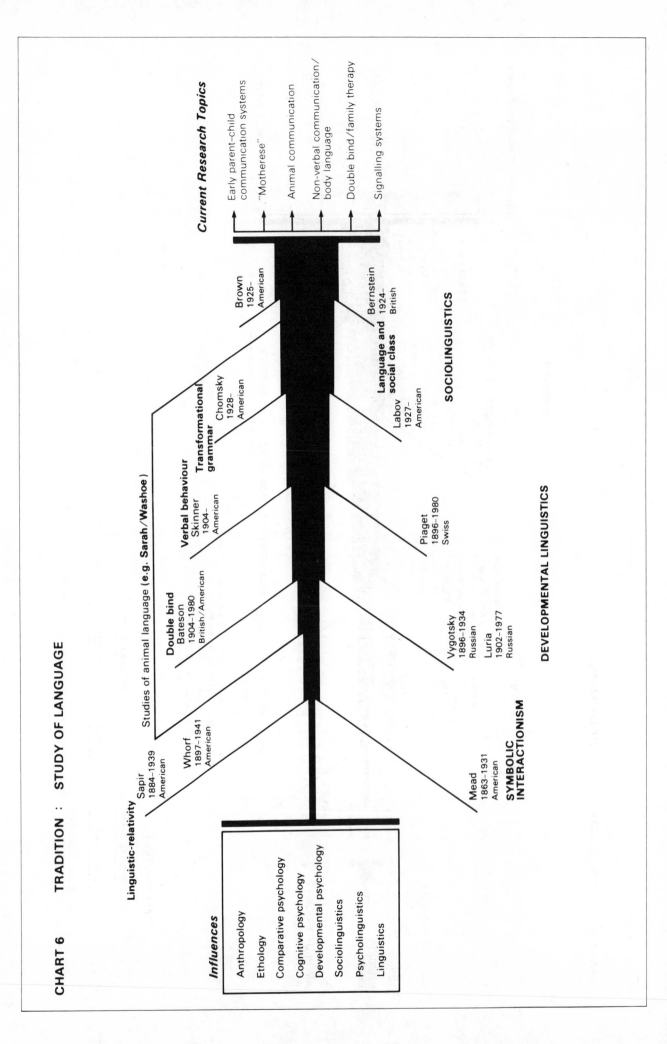

**Influences**

Anthropology
Ethology
Comparative psychology
Cognitive psychology
Developmental psychology
Sociolinguistics
Psycholinguistics
Linguistics

**Current Research Topics**

Early parent-child communication systems

"Motherese"

Animal communication

Non-verbal communication/body language

Double bind/family therapy

Signalling systems

**Linguistic-relativity**

Sapir
1884–1939
American

Whorf
1897–1941
American

Studies of animal language (**e.g. Sarah/Washoe**)

**Double bind**
Bateson
1904–1980
British/American

**Verbal behaviour**
Skinner
1904–
American

**Transformational grammar**
Chomsky
1928–
American

Brown
1925–
American

Mead
1863–1931
American

**SYMBOLIC INTERACTIONISM**

Vygotsky
1896–1934
Russian

Luria
1902–1977
Russian

Piaget
1896–1980
Swiss

Labov
1927–
American

**Language and social class**

Bernstein
1924–
British

**SOCIOLINGUISTICS**

**DEVELOPMENTAL LINGUISTICS**

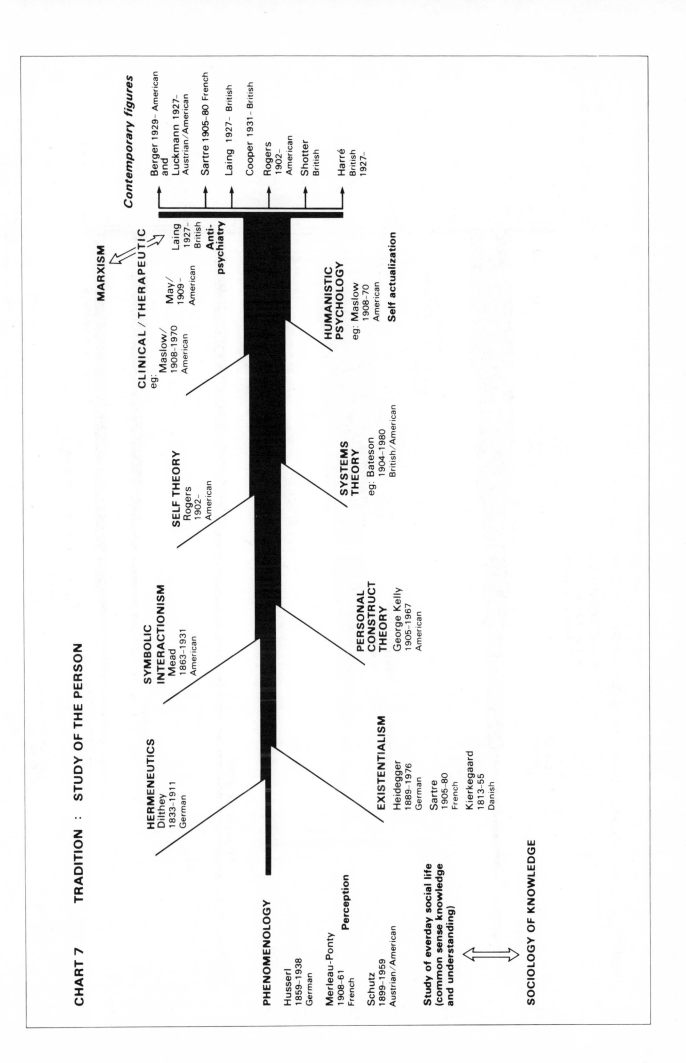

CHART 7     TRADITION :   STUDY OF THE PERSON

*Contemporary figures*

Berger 1929– American
and
Luckmann 1927–
Austrian/American

Sartre 1905–80 French

Laing 1927– British

Cooper 1931– British

Rogers 1902– American

Shotter British

Harré British 1927–

MARXISM

CLINICAL / THERAPEUTIC

Laing 1927– British **Anti-psychiatry**

May/ 1909– American

eg: Maslow 1908–1970 American

HUMANISTIC PSYCHOLOGY

eg: Maslow 1908–70 American    **Self actualization**

SYMBOLIC INTERACTIONISM

Mead 1863–1931 American

SELF THEORY

Rogers 1902– American

SYSTEMS THEORY

eg: Bateson 1904–1980 British/American

HERMENEUTICS

Dilthey 1833–1911 German

PERSONAL CONSTRUCT THEORY

George Kelly 1905–1967 American

EXISTENTIALISM

Heidegger 1889–1976 German

Sartre 1905–80 French

Kierkegaard 1813–55 Danish

PHENOMENOLOGY

Husserl 1859–1938 German

Merleau-Ponty 1908–61 French    **Perception**

Schutz 1899–1959 Austrian/American

**Study of everday social life (common sense knowledge and understanding)**

SOCIOLOGY OF KNOWLEDGE

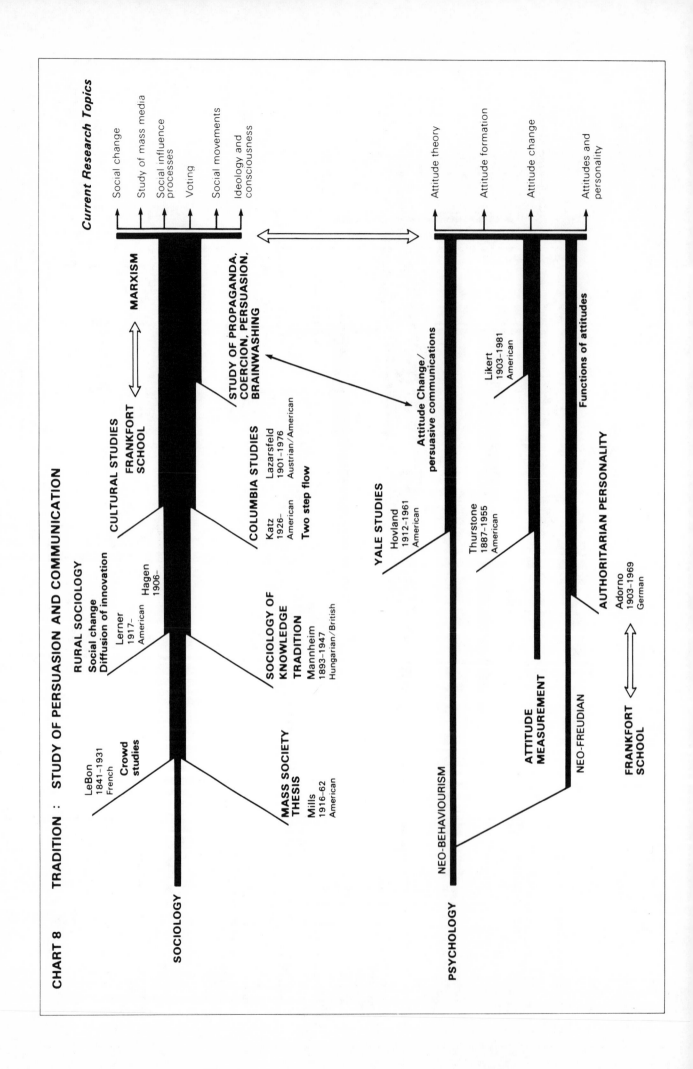

CHART 8    TRADITION :   STUDY OF PERSUASION AND COMMUNICATION

*Current Research Topics*

**SOCIOLOGY**

LeBon
1841–1931
French
**Crowd
studies**

**MASS SOCIETY
THESIS**
Mills
1916–62
American

**RURAL SOCIOLOGY**
**Social change**
**Diffusion of innovation**
Lerner
1917–
American    Hagen
1906–

**SOCIOLOGY OF
KNOWLEDGE
TRADITION**
Mannheim
1893–1947
Hungarian/British

**CULTURAL STUDIES**
**FRANKFORT
SCHOOL**

**COLUMBIA STUDIES**
Katz        Lazarsfeld
1926–       1901–1976
American    Austrian/American
**Two step flow**

**STUDY OF PROPAGANDA,
COERCION, PERSUASION,
BRAINWASHING**

**MARXISM**

Social change
Study of mass media
Social influence
processes
Voting
Social movements
Ideology and
consciousness

**PSYCHOLOGY**

NEO-BEHAVIOURISM

**ATTITUDE
MEASUREMENT**

NEO-FREUDIAN

**FRANKFORT
SCHOOL**

**YALE STUDIES**
Hovland
1912–1961
American

Thurstone
1887–1955
American

**AUTHORITARIAN PERSONALITY**
Adorno
1903–1969
German

**Attitude Change/
persuasive communications**

Likert
1903–1981
American

**Functions of attitudes**

Attitude theory
Attitude formation
Attitude change
Attitudes and
personality

58

# CHART 9 TRADITION : COGNITIVE SOCIAL PSYCHOLOGY

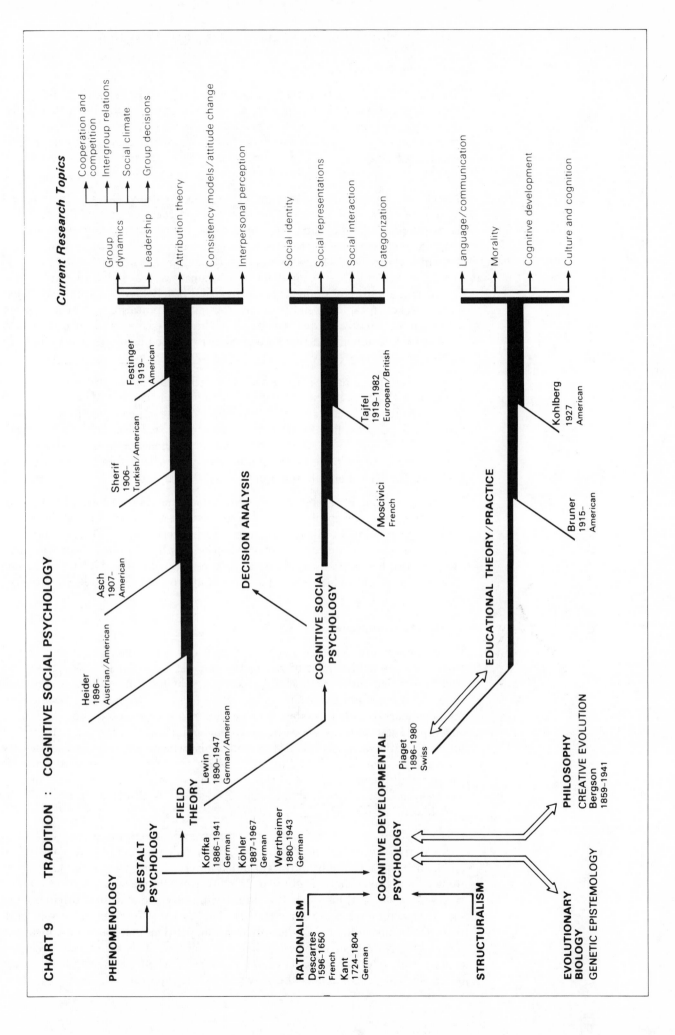

*Current Research Topics*

**PHENOMENOLOGY**

**GESTALT PSYCHOLOGY**

**FIELD THEORY**

Koffka
1886–1941
German

Köhler
1887–1967
German

Wertheimer
1880–1943
German

Lewin
1890–1947
German/American

Heider
1896–
Austrian/American

Asch
1907–
American

Sherif
1906–
Turkish/American

Festinger
1919–
American

Group dynamics

Leadership

Attribution theory

Consistency models/attitude change

Interpersonal perception

Cooperation and competition

Intergroup relations

Social climate

Group decisions

**DECISION ANALYSIS**

**RATIONALISM**

Descartes
1596–1650
French

Kant
1724–1804
German

**COGNITIVE SOCIAL PSYCHOLOGY**

Moscivici
French

Tajfel
1919–1982
European/British

Social identity

Social representations

Social interaction

Categorization

**COGNITIVE DEVELOPMENTAL PSYCHOLOGY**

Piaget
1896–1980
Swiss

**STRUCTURALISM**

**EVOLUTIONARY BIOLOGY**

GENETIC EPISTEMOLOGY

**PHILOSOPHY**

CREATIVE EVOLUTION
Bergson
1859–1941

**EDUCATIONAL THEORY/PRACTICE**

Bruner
1915–
American

Kohlberg
1927
American

Language/communication

Morality

Cognitive development

Culture and cognition

# Paper 2: Making sense of theories in social psychology

*by Richard Stevens*

*The aim of this paper is to clarify the kinds of difference you will find between theories in social psychology. It sets out ten dimensions along which they differ. You may find these useful as a conceptual tool for distinguishing between the theories which you encounter as you work through the course. The paper also serves to introduce several important issues which are dealt with in more detail in later papers.*

One of the problems facing anyone attempting to study social behaviour and experience is the multiplicity of approaches and theories that can be found in social psychology. The impact of this can be overwhelming and confusing. In designing a course in this area, one way to get round this problem is to adopt one particular theoretical perspective and to ignore, or discard by negative evaluation, all others. We have not done this because we feel it would totally misrepresent the nature of understanding in social psychology. To appreciate what social psychology is, the insights it can offer and its limitations, there is no other way than to study a varied selection of the approaches and theories which constitute it. You will find this variety right from the beginning of the course in the discussion of the family.

The purpose of this paper is to provide you with a *conceptual framework* to help you cope with the plethora of perspectives you will encounter. You can use this framework to set in context, and to contrast and compare theories at various points in the course and also when you come to revise. It consists of a list of ten ways or dimensions in which theories in social psychology may differ. By assessing theories in terms of these ten dimensions you will be able to compare, in a fairly explicit way, their different qualities and usefulness.

Do remember that any system of this kind is itself inevitably a conceptualization. So do not regard it as absolute: it is, to some extent, an arbitrary list and it would certainly be possible to think up a somewhat different system. Furthermore, it is not always easy to determine precisely the position of any theory in each category. But I hope that, as the course progresses, you will find it a useful means of integrating and contrasting the various approaches presented in different blocks.

## 1 Basic assumptions

Underpinning any theory is a set of assumptions, i.e. ways of approaching and looking at the subject-matter which the theorist takes for granted. These are usually implied rather than clearly asserted. They will have been assimilated from the intellectual traditions in which he has been trained (i.e. books read, methods learned, other 'models' to which he has been exposed and which have encouraged him to think about issues in particular ways). They may also reflect (or be a reaction against) the background of his own culture, because each society generates its own ways of thinking and looking at things. Another source may be the personal background of the theorist – his own needs and values. (The way theories constitute personal and social creations is discussed specifically in Metablock Part III, Paper 7, 'The construction of reality'.)

It is not always easy to uncover the assumptions underlying a theory. This is particularly true for the theorist himself and people working in that perspective, for the assumptions are usually very much a part of their way of thinking about things. I remember that one of the exciting features for me of coming to the Open University was working with the interdisciplinary group which produced the social science foundation course (D101). This was my first opportunity to work with academics from other disciplines (like political science, economics and sociology) rather than just with other psychologists. I found myself having to explain and reflect on all sorts of assumptions of which previously I, like most other psychologists, had never been aware, let alone questioned.

Underpinning each of the theories which feature in this course there are different *kinds* of assumptions. One, for example, is about what is the best (or only) *method* to use. As an illustration, take behaviourism (see Unit 4): this assumes that the only way to make progress in psychology is to use the methods of natural science. As precise observation and measurement are essential to scientific method, behaviourists (at least the traditional ones) consider that the study of subjective experience lies outside the scope of a scientific psychology. In direct contrast, other schools of thought in psychology (examples from Block 1 include psychoanalysts and symbolic interactionists) would argue that this is to put the cart before the horse. Subjective experience and the meanings which people attribute to themselves and their world are psychology's core subject-matter. We have to find ways which allow us to study this effectively, whether or not they fit with the traditional requirements of the methods of the natural sciences. Not surprisingly, these contrasting assumptions generate very different kinds of research concerned with very different questions.

Another assumption adopted from physical science and which underlies behaviourism and most experimental approaches in psychology (for examples of the latter see particularly Unit 9 and Units 10/11) is that the best way to study behaviour is to break it down into manageable parts for investigation. In contrast to this are approaches such as the interactional analysis of family processes as discussed in Unit 2, which assume that you can only understand an individual's behaviour by seeing it in the context of his or her relationships with other people. In other words, you need to study the *whole system* rather than the separated parts. The first approach in psychology to assert this 'holistic' approach (treating the wholes not the separated parts) was *Gestalt* psychology which was originally formulated by three German psychologists (Wertheimer, Koffka and Köhler) in the 1920s. (*Gestalt* is the German word for form, shape or configuration). The basic premise of *Gestalt* psychology is that *the whole is different from the sum of its parts*. To demonstrate this principle, Wolfgang Köhler used to play a melody backwards on the piano to his students. As he pointed out, even though all the components were the same, the *Gestalt* (or form) was very different. From this it follows that you should not assume, that because you understand the components, then you understand the whole. The operation of a part will depend on its context. (See Box 1.)

*[handwritten margin note: Gestalt ↓ whole different to sum of the parts]*

*[handwritten margin note: e.g. traits as integrated whole - trait is a function in relation to others]*

---

**Box 1**

An illustration from studies of the way we form impressions of others (a topic discussed in Block 3) may help you to understand the *Gestalt* principle. Solomon Asch (1946) found that if subjects were given a list of seven traits, e.g. intelligent, skilful, industrious, warm, determined, practical, cautious, they could happily provide a description of a person who might possess these traits. Asch discovered that, if one of the words in the list – 'warm' – was included with another set of traits, then it tended to convey a very different meaning. In the list above, 'warm' generally conveyed an impression of humanity and positivity. Set, however, in the list, 'obedient, weak, shallow, warm, unambitious, vain', the word 'warm' tended to convey passivity or a kind of 'dog-like affection'. Yet again, if confronted with the list, 'vain, shrewd, unscrupulous, warm, shallow, envious', subjects tended to describe a person who appeared to be warm but was not really so under the surface. Asch concluded that subjects perceive a list of traits as an integrated whole. The meaning of one trait is a function of its relation to the others. The whole is not merely the straightforward sum of its parts.

---

While *Gestalt* psychology itself does not feature specifically in this course, it has been very influential on approaches which do. Thus the 'phenomenological' or 'personal' type of perspective adopted by Block 4 assumes not only that studying the way a person perceives himself and his world is of central importance for social psychology but also that it is necessary to study this pattern as a whole. It maintains that you cannot understand subjective experience by breaking it down into component processes and studying these alone.

Another point of difference between theories is which *factors* are assumed to be *most significant in determining behaviour*. Learning theory (and the behaviourist approach in general) places the emphasis firmly on environmental factors. Watson, the father of the behaviourist movement assumed (as far as can be gauged from his writings anyway) that the environment is the *only* significant influence on behaviour. Later behaviourists, like B. F. Skinner, have modified this position and may acknowledge that biological processes may also be relevant. But they nevertheless assume that as the task of the behavioural scientist is to study observable behaviour; to investigate what happens inside the organism is not his concern – that should be left to other specialists such as the biologist and geneticist. Other very different theories, like those with a sociological emphasis, make similar assumptions about the importance of environment but conceptualize this differently – as social institutions and people rather than as specific stimuli and the reinforcements they provide. These all contrast, however, with the assumption which the sociobiologist makes – that to understand human social behaviour it is necessary to consider it first in the context of evolutionary development and biological processes.

Both Piaget's theory and psychoanalysis adopt an intermediate position here and see the determinants of human behaviour as arising from the interplay of biological and environmental factors. These theories assume the need to take into account the biological nature of human beings and also how this changes over time as a result of influence from the environments and social context of a person as he or she develops. One contribution which their theories make is to develop concepts (e.g. Piaget's accommodation and assimilation, Freud's defence mechanisms) which help us to unravel the complexities of this interaction process.

One way of looking at the set of assumptions held by a theorist is as a reflection of a particular *model of the person.* In the theory in question are people thought of as *self-governing machines* defined in terms of inputs and outputs, as *biological organisms* in a complex two-way relationship with their surroundings, or as complex *information processors* like a computer, or as experiencing beings influenced by unconscious feelings and capable of choice and will? Interwoven with implicit assumptions are also *values*. As Unit 1 pointed out, for example, most (though not all) of the theories applied there to understanding the family, take for granted that the preservation of society and social integration are to be encouraged.

It would be a major task to attempt here a list of the major theories and their key assumptions. I hope the comparisons I have given indicate the kinds of differences which can exist. As the assumptions underlying the theory are usually not made explicit and are often not apparent even to proponents of the theory concerned, they are not always easy to determine. They play a major role, nevertheless, in determining the kind of problem explored, strategy of research, interpretation of results obtained and the content of the theory. The aim of this discussion is to alert you to look out for such assumptions in the accounts of theories given in the units and elsewhere.

## 2 Concepts

Look through the following lists of concepts. If you can, identify the theory or general perspective from which they are taken.

*List*

A    animism, accommodation, equilibration, egocentricity, assimilation, conservation, concrete operations, sensorimotor stage.

62

*Interactional family therapy*
*ψ analysis*
*Learning Theory*
*construct*

B    circularities, rigid boundary, symmetrical interaction, disengagement, enmeshment, reframing, conflict detouring, paradoxical intervention.

C    rationalization, introjection, cathexis, displacement, identification, infantile amnesia, thanatos, libido.

D    vicarious reinforcement, contingencies, unconditional stimulus, operants, secondary drive, imitation, unconditional reflex, secondary reinforcement.

E    permeability, constructive alternativism, element, modulation corollary, core construct, range of convenience, grid, tight construing.

If you have already read the first block of the course you may have been able to identify most of the perspectives from which each list was drawn (although *E* may have proved a little more difficult). By the time you have finished Block 3 you should be able to identify them all.

Juxtaposing them in this way, may serve to draw your attention to the fact that, although psychological theories are usually expressed in a form of English prose, in effect they utilize very different concept languages. The concepts on each list are used by that particular perspective but rarely, if ever, by any other.

One important difference between theories, then, is the nature and range of concepts they use. Sometimes theorists employ neologisms or coin symbols especially to denote the significant concepts of their theories (e.g. libido, UCS to signify unconditioned stimulus). More often, they use words selected as approximations from everyday language and given a meaning of their own in the context of the theory (e.g. egocentricity, reinforcement, permeability).

The use of different sets of concepts in different theories means there are formidable problems in contrasting the propositions of one against those of another. It is often not easy to tell whether they are in direct opposition, are saying the same thing in different words, are complementary or bear no relationship to each other. Problems arise also in that the same word may be given a rather different meaning in the context of different theories. As an example, 'instinct' in ethological theory refers to an inherited behaviour pattern. In standard translations of psychoanalytic theory, it designates a more general instinctual drive which may manifest itself in a variety of ways. (One result of theorists annexing words from general language to designate their concepts is that the concepts may be given rather different connotations when the word is translated into another language. In the second example cited above, Freud's original German word, usually translated as 'instinct' was *Trieb* which in fact is probably more accurately rendered as 'drive'. For the problems which arise from reading Freud in translation see the set book *Freud and Psychoanalysis*, pp. 46–7.)

The concepts employed in different theories vary in explicitness (as do the theoretical statements themselves) from those given highly precise definitions (e.g. 'conditioned stimulus') to those which are used variably and whose precise meaning can only really be determined by the context in which they appear (e.g. 'internalization').

(In case you had any doubts, the lists above were drawn from the following theories: *A* Piaget, *B* Interactional family therapy, *C* Psychoanalysis, *D* Learning theory, *E* Personal construct theory.)

## 3   Kinds of explanation

A third way in which theories differ is in the *kinds* of explanation they propose. When we explain something, we demonstrate how it has come about. Explanations depend on the assumption that events, including behaviours and experiences, are interrelated and ordered in a consistent way. To explain why this behaviour rather than any other has occurred is to reveal the antecedent conditions without which that event would not have taken place in quite that particular way.

Almost all psychological theories assume some kind of determinism (i.e. that there will be antecedent or related events or experiences without which the behaviour in question would not have occurred). But they differ substantially in the *kinds* of answer they give to the question of *why* a particular behaviour or phenomenon has occurred.

## Hypothetical constructs

One point of difference between theories is the degree to which they rely on hypothetical constructs. A hypothetical construct is something which is essentially *inferred* but which is nevertheless assumed to be the source of the behaviour or characteristics in question. It is not then something you can actively observe or locate in itself. (A hypothetical construct is, in a sense, the opposite of an operational concept which *is* essentially specifiable in terms of observable operations or events.) Important examples of hypothetical constructs in psychology include personality, instinct, attitude and intelligence. None of these can be actually seen or observed, they are merely inferred from actions. As concepts, they can be of value nevertheless. They may enable us to tie together and to make sense of otherwise unrelated actions and statements. They may help us to predict what a person may do or say in the future. A danger here, however, is tautology. This is exemplified by the use of the hypothetical construct *instinct* in some theories in early social psychology. Thus aggressiveness was explained as due to the instinct of *pugnacity*, mothering behaviour as due to the *maternal instinct*. These are of course no explanations at all if, as was the case, the existence of the instincts were entirely inferred from the behaviours they purport to explain.

## Use of models

Many explanations depend on the use of *models*. A 'model' is the use of analogy to help make sense of the pattern of phenomena observed. So, for example, the way people interact together has been analysed by the use of the model or analogy of improvization or performing a play. Models are often devised on the basis of other processes whose operation is known. Models of thinking and skill performance, for example, have been developed on the basis of the design of computer operations.

## Kinds of determinant

Another point of variation between different theoretical explanations is in the *kinds of determinant* which they emphasize. This is not just a question of prior assumptions about which general aspects of behaviour should be focused on (see Section 1) but is a matter of the specific explanations which theories come up with. Such differences are best illustrated by contrasting the sorts of statement that different theories might typically produce to explain a hypothetical event – the actions of a child who repeatedly misbehaves in class. (It should be remembered that the following accounts are hypothetical. Within the framework of any one theory, different explanations are possible. In an actual, adequately researched and documented case more specific and possibly rather different analyses would be made. But they do serve to distinguish the kinds of explanation which selected theoretical perspectives would be likely to produce and the general investigative strategy they would employ.)

The *learning theorist* would seek for factors such as approval and admiration from peers which might make the misbehaviour rewarding for the child. Alternatively, he might assume that in the child's past history, good behaviour has not been sufficiently reinforced (i.e. rewarded) and therefore is not likely to be elicited in the classroom.

The *psychoanalyst* might search for the meaning that this behaviour has for the child. Is it, for example, a manifestation of a need for attention? If so, what factors in the past history of the child created such a need? Perhaps it represents an attempt to compensate for affection he had craved as an infant and been denied? Alternatively, perhaps the child's conflict with a male teacher represents the re-playing of an unresolved, residual hostility earlier experienced in relation to his father and now 'displaced' onto the teacher.

The *phenomenologist* would search for reasons in the experience of the child.

How does he perceive the classroom situation? Is he bored? Is it irrelevant to his needs? Does he see himself, each time he challenges the authority of the teacher and the school, as the hero defying the mighty? David against Goliath? Robin Hood against the Sheriff of Nottingham?

A *biologically based theorist* might look for an inherited need for a high level of stimulation. If, in the classroom situation, stillness, quietness and activities of a non-exciting nature are expected, this need for stimulation can express itself only in talking, fidgeting and playing pranks; activities construed by the teacher as misbehaviour.

A *sociologically orientated theorist* might see the situation in terms of the nature of the institution of schooling – its power dimensions and cultural expectations. In school, children are required to conform to the demands and prevailing social norms of society (or of a particular section of society). They are expected to behave 'properly', to achieve etc. It is not surprising that some children may express resistance to this in the form of 'naughty' behaviour.

The danger of any brief account of a hypothetical situation is that it can tend to sound a bit like a parody, nevertheless I hope these illustrations give some idea of the range of explanations which just a few theories might produce. Because they invoke different terms, such explanations may appear quite distinct. However, it is worth noting that on closer examination they do not *necessarily* turn out to be that much different. As with concepts, some differences between explanations prove on inspection to be more apparent than real. The use of different terms may serve to mask intrinsic similarities. For example, in spite of the very different concepts they employ, both learning theorist and psychoanalyst are likely to look for the source of the misbehaviour in the gratification it provides for the child (whether it be peer approval or attention experienced as symbolic affection). Both also consider past learning experiences (whether it be 'reinforcement history' or 'early family relationships') as likely to play an important role. The existence of such underlying similarities means that there is often potential for overlap and integration even between theories whose surface characteristics might suggest that they were irresolvable antitheses. Variations in the way analogous explanatory constructs are labelled by different theorists can also produce an appearance of greater fragmentation and conflict in social psychological theory than is necessarily really there.

One not uncommon failing of some proponents of particular theories in psychology (and in the social sciences generally) is to exaggerate the explanatory power of the theory they endorse. Behaviour and experience are inevitably the outcome of many factors. While a theory may provide an accurate account of one or two influencing factors, narrow over-emphasis on these may preclude taking into account other factors which are equally influential. This is particularly a problem if the factors concerned are interactive. Suppose, for example, we accept our biologically based theorist's assertion that the child's restlessness is a function of his temperament. This is still not sufficient to account for his misbehaviour. The latter arises out of the interaction between a child who gets bored easily and a situation which demands he sit still and not behave in the way that he wants to. In a different context, a different class even, which provided sufficient stimulation so that the child would not get bored, this temperamental predisposition would not result in misbehaviour or conflict at all. The point here is that behaviour is a function of the interaction between the biology and the environment of the person. Neither can be meaningfully construed as a factor influencing behaviour and experience without reference to the other. In order to understand fully a particular sequence of behaviour, it will almost surely be necessary to look at it from more than one perspective or level of analysis (for a further discussion of this issue see Section 9 of this paper and Paper 3).

The integration of different theoretical perspectives is not usually possible by merely 'adding' them together. The concepts provided within a theory interrelate and link together. Mere juxtaposition of theories results in two sets of concepts, unrelated to each other. Any real integration will almost surely require the development of new and higher-order concepts and principles which can link the phenomena denoted by both sets of concepts and explore their interaction. This is a critical problem for social psychology. Those theoretical positions which emphasize a holistic and integrative approach such as Piagetian theory and psychoanalysis (discussed in Unit 4 and in the set book *Freud and Psychoanalysis*) have tended to develop concepts of their own. The concepts and data of less holistic approaches – for example, those which utilize either biological or sociological concepts alone – are not easily subsumed within them.

(See Metablock Paper 3 *Levels of analysis*, Paper 5 *The significance of meaning* and Paper 8 *Nomothetic, idiographic and hermeneutic social psychology* for further discussion of kinds of explanation in social psychology.)

## 4   Emphasis on description or explanation

Theories are not only concerned with explaining. By originating concepts and ways of looking at the phenomena in question, they also serve as a means of *describing it* too. It is not always easy to separate out the two functions. The concepts used for a description may in themselves imply explanatory propositions. For example, if I say a piece of toast is *burnt* I am describing what it looks like (i.e. black and crumbly). I am also explaining how it came to be that way (i.e. by over-application of heat). To attribute to a person an 'anal personality' is not just a description of their personality (obsessive, scrupulous, miserly, creative etc.) it also implies a theoretical explanation (psychoanalytic) of how they came to be like that (over-emphasis on toilet training in early life).

Although descriptions and explanations are often intrinsically inter-woven, it is worth distinguishing between them for our fourth dimension along which theories differ. The emphasis on description and explanation varies from theory to theory. While almost every theory provides both, its descriptive and explanatory powers may not necessarily be equivalent. Thus a theory may be concerned with demonstrating *why* a particular behaviour occurs, but not provide concepts which allow one to describe the behaviour in question any better than in everyday terms. In the area of research into relationships (see Unit 10/11), for example, you will find that much of the experimental work is directed at discovering why a particular behaviour occurs (i.e. explanation) rather than making any attempt to provide a way of describing the behaviour in question. Thus Byrne (see Box 8 in Unit 10/11) has been concerned to demonstrate the hypothesis that you will find another person attractive the more similar to yourself you perceive that other person to be. A contrasting approach is the work of the ethologist Robert Hinde (see Section 6.1 in Unit 10/11). He emphasizes the need to *describe* the different kinds of relationship which are possible and has prepared a set of dimensions for doing this (e.g. intimacy, commitment etc.). The work of Goffman (see Section 3 of Unit 10/11) serves both descriptive and explanatory functions. The concepts he has developed (e.g. role, impression management, maintaining face etc.) serve to describe social interactions but at the same time can be used to understand why they take the form that they do.

## 5   Differentiation vs. testability

For our fifth dimension I want to introduce the notions of *differentiation* and *testability*.

*Differentiation*   By power of differentiation I mean the capacity a theory may have to encompass the detail, subtleties and nuances of human behaviour and experience. Clearly descriptions can vary according to their degree of differentiation. Take the example of a man and woman quarrelling. An observer from another planet may only be able to report 'two living organisms in close proximity to each other'. For 'it' (the alien from another planet) may not have concepts available to it to pick up and communicate attributes such as sex or emotions such as anger. With a little more familiarity with the human species, our green being from Planet *X* may learn the concepts 'male' and 'female' and so be capable of greater differentiation of the events it observes.

Human beings observing our quarrelling pair will be capable of much more differentiated descriptions. Even if they do not know the language the couple use, they can tell that they are angry. If they do understand it, they can describe what the quarrel is about and probably whether it is in play or a theatrical performance. An observer with special sensitivity and experience (a perceptive novelist or psychoanalyst, say) may pick up more subtle cues which would elude the more prosaic and, with their help, construct an even more highly differentiated description of the scene. Dispersed among the angry words and gestures he might note the occasional fleeting look and reaching hand. He scans the choice of words, observes the softness that colours the end of an embittered phrase, the eagerness that just occasionally lights up the woman's face. She is jealous, yes, but her jealousy brings with it not pain but a curious joy and excitement. In spite of her bitter words, her feelings are still of love not hate. This observer notes also the care with which the man picks his words and fends off abuse; the cautious, flattened tone suggests perhaps guilt, perhaps anxiety that this time he has gone too far.

Such descriptions form a continuum from simple to more complex. To describe an object, behaviour or event means placing it in a 'network of inference concerning their other observable properties and effects' (Bruner 1957). This involves going beyond the information given. Looking back at our descriptions, it might seem that the more differentiated they are so the more they tend to involve inference and to go beyond the information given. Concepts like 'organism', 'proximity' are closely tied to observables. The concepts in the more differentiated descriptions – 'quarrel', 'lover', 'jealously', 'guilt' etc. require the selection of, or inference from, subtle and complex patterns of attributes.

*Validity* Other things being equal, we might assume that a theory with a greater power of differentiation is better in that it can give us more information about what is going on. But (and it is a sizable 'but') the question arises of accuracy. However differentiated the description, it is of little use to the seeker of understanding unless it is more or less *valid*, i.e. unless it corresponds in some way to a 'reality' which we assume to exist independently of the observer. The difficulty here is that we do not have access to an 'objective reality' against which to assess its validity. As is argued in Paper 7 ( *The construction of reality*) the only awareness we have of reality is that which we, with the help of our culture and our sensory and cognitive capacities, construct. So what does the accuracy or validity of a description refer to? And how can we assess it?

In everyday life one way is by *consensus*. We invite other people to try out our description and to see whether it makes sense for them. This does pose problems though. Their constructions of what they see may be subject to similar limitations and bias as our own. History is full of examples of consensus on theories which turned out to be false (as one example, that the earth is flat).

A more powerful method is *predictive consistency*. No description can be made without the use of concepts of some kind. The meaning and implications of such concepts can be analysed. Further observation of what is implied by the analysis may then be made. Such situations may be spontaneous or, as in the case of experiment, deliberately contrived. The consistency between the observations anticipated on the basis of the description and those actually observed can then be assessed.

In further illustration of this point, let us return to our earlier example of the quarrelling couple. Our two sophisticated observers, as you will remember, described the woman as 'jealous'. Such a concept implies not only behaviour of a certain kind but a state of mind. As such, it goes beyond the information given. It is a probabilistic inference based on observation of styles of behaving (tone of voice, facial expression, particular utterances etc.) which are usually indicative of jealousy. But suppose our lady lied. Suppose she was an accomplished actress playing the part of a jealous lover. The observers' description is then inaccurate. The state of mind it implies is not present. The description then would certainly lack predictive validity. Given further information – suppose, say, we watch her subsequent behaviour, ask her what she genuinely feels or find out more about the context in which the interaction is taking place – we shall find this inconsistent with the description given.

*Testability*   There are different ways in which we can test for consistency and they differ in terms of their precision and rigour. In everyday life, we check the consistency of a statement against other relevant knowledge and experience which we have acquired. It makes sense to us or it does not. Sometimes we may purposely look around for evidence which either confirms or negates what has been said. Most of us are satisfied if the description seems plausible and there are no obvious discrepancies with our informal observations. The methods of science and philosophy are concerned with finding more rigorous means of eliciting criterial information and ensuring its appropriateness. In the first place, the statement must be rendered as precisely as possible so its key implications can be seen. A philosopher will carefully analyse logical relations with other concepts. A scientist will seek to observe, find or set up situations which yield the appropriate information to enable us to test effectively these implications. The most rigorous test is when the description enables us to make precise predictions which are then borne out by our observations. This is the reason for science's heavy dependence on experimentation and operational concepts (i.e. those that are definable in terms of observable operations or events). In a good experiment, appropriate situations can be set up, the influence of variables extraneous to the hypothesis can be avoided or controlled and the outcome can be recorded precisely and matched against predictions made.

The *testability* of any description or theory is thus a matter of degree. We can test the validity of a proposition in different ways of varying rigour. Although we may not be able to submit a proposition expressed in concepts of a non-operational type to a *precise* experimental test, we can evaluate its consistency with other events it purports to relate to. We cannot *know* whether or not a man feels anger or is repressing his natural impulses, but we can evaluate to some extent the degree to which the implications of such concepts are supported by other observations.

*Testability vs. differentiation*   One of the major paradoxes of social psychology is the tendency for testability and differentiation to be inversely related. Richness seems in inverse relation to reliability – in other words more meaningfully differentiated descriptions about social behaviour tend to be less likely to be potentially testable in a rigorous way. We can choose to demand highly reliable measures and lose meaning and subtlety of description, or opt for meaning and subtlety and run the risk of a less valid account, or, of course, select some mixture of the two. It is possible to describe a simple behavioural movement in operational terms and a description or proposition expressed as a series of linked concepts of this type may be fairly readily tested for accuracy or validity. However, as we have seen, a description confined to behavioural movements precludes experience, ideas, concepts, language and hence verbal communication – most of that which is interesting, relevant and significant about people. To go beyond simple observation of behavioural movement involves the use of hypothetical constructs. Propositions of this kind are far more difficult to test. To conceptualize the most subtle and complex areas of action and experience may require constructs definable only in terms of other concepts and thus not even directly relatable to observable behaviour. For example, the psychoanalytic concept of *latent* characteristics (e.g. latent aggression, latent homosexuality) can be defined only by reference to other hypothetical concepts such as *repression*. (Repression denotes a situation where, because it arouses anxiety or conflict, a feeling or desire is not allowed into consciousness. Nevertheless, it may still remain operative at an unconscious level.) 'Latent aggression' is where aggressive feelings are hidden or masked as a result of repression. Although they may not be expressed in directly aggressive acts, such feelings may still affect behaviour and experience but in different ways. Thus, it is not always easy or even possible to infer *latent aggression* directly from behaviour. Yet in spite of such limitations, it has been found a useful category by psychoanalysts and many psychologists and distinguishes a particular psychological pattern from others. Without a concept of this kind differentiation would be reduced.

As you will find as you work through the course, one way in which approaches and theories used in social psychology vary is in the emphasis they place on testability as opposed to differentiation. So, for example, symbolic interactionism, psychoanalysis, personal construct theory, and the phenomenological approaches discussed in Block 4 use concepts which are capable of encompassing the complexity and subtlety of social behaviour and experience and thus facilitate highly differentiated descriptions. However, they are difficult to test in any rigorous way. In contrast, much of the experimental work described in Units 9 and 10/11 of Block 3 uses tighter concepts (and relations between concepts) which can be put to experimental test but often end up by being somewhat limited in their power to capture the subtleties of human relationships.

This is one reason why it is not really possible simply to compare one theory with another and say which is the *better*. They are likely to have virtues and utilities of different kinds. One may allow more efficient hypothesis testing, another scope for richer and more differentiated description. Whether or not a particular theory emphasizes testability or differentiation will depend on the context in which the theory has been developed and the methods on which it has been based: on the purpose, therefore, and the context of the theorist. (Paper 8, on the varieties of social psychology, discusses this issue further in relation to the problem of generalization.)

It should not be assumed that the more experimentally testable theories are necessarily more valuable though many psychologists do make this equation. Such an evaluation is not *'objective'* as is often implied but, like any other evaluation, rooted in assumptions adopted by the evaluator. As testability is the fundamental criterion of value for experimentalists, it is not surprising that they cast a jaundiced eye on a theory which falls short of this, regardless of its differentiating power. But evaluation depends on your goal. If your aim is to understand or even predict complex human social behaviour or to offer people help in changing their lives, a theory with high power of differentiation and less rigorous empirical support may often prove more useful than one with greater experimental support but with propositions of limited applicability. Many psychologists retain a naive optimism that psychology is a young science; that some time in an indefinite future, differentiation and rigorous testability will go hand in hand. What they seem to ignore is that the most significant attributes of man – without which no account of complex behaviour and certainly experience can be complete – are concepts, ideas, thoughts, values and feelings. All of these can only be expressed as symbols (e.g. language); symbols which, by their very nature, permit no *precise* definition or quantification of the phenomena they denote, still less of the complex interactions operative between them (see Paper 5).

## 6  Methodological base

One of the interesting features of social psychology is the very different sources and contexts from which theories and data emerge. Many kinds of people have an interest in exploring social behaviour and experience. In addition to academic investigators concerned with understanding for its own sake, there are clinicians concerned with helping patients or clients, psychologists concerned with the procedures and problems of education and those facilitating personal growth and awareness; also occupational psychologists whose task it is to increase the effectiveness and satisfaction of people in their working environments. Each of these specialist areas has generated tools and methods appropriate to the task.

The nature and role of methods used in the study of social behaviour and experience will be discussed in more detail in Paper 6. They are introduced briefly here because the methods used play a very substantial part in determining the nature of theory. This can be illustrated by a comparison between psychoanalysis and learning theory. Psychoanalytic theory evolved in clinical work (on the couch, you might say!). The psychoanalyst's primary interest is to understand his patient, not to evaluate his own ideas. The psychoanalytic methods instrumental in the development of psychoanalytic theory are *elicitation* techniques designed to give the psychoanalyst access to unconscious material not readily available to the normal observer or to the person concerned himself. Examples are free association and dream analysis. Little or no use is made of methods for the *rigorous* testing of hypotheses. In contrast, learning theories have been developed by academic psychologists working in university laboratories. The goal is knowledge, whether or not this is immediately applicable to the complexities of everyday life. The methods used in the development of the latter theories (in particular the experiment) were primarily directed at evaluating hypotheses. The effects of such differences in methodological base show in the nature of the content of a theory. Psychoanalysis offers concepts which allow richly differentiated descriptions of a complex and subtle kind but concepts which are hypothetical and involve propositions which are often untestable in any rigorous way. Learning theories offer far more limited scope for differentiated description but are usually expressed in an experimentally testable form.

As you progress through the course, look out for examples of the link between methods and theory and the dependence of both on the context in which the theorist works.

## 7   Focus and range of convenience

The expression 'range of convenience' was first used in George Kelly's theory of personal constructs to indicate the breadth and scope of the constructs a person uses to make sense of the world. (Kelly's theory is discussed in detail in Unit 8.) I have borrowed the phrase to denote here the vast differences between theories in the range of phenomena to which they are intended to apply and are capable of accounting for. Theories in social psychology range from mini-versions which are hardly more than single hypotheses applicable to one aspect of social behaviour, to grand theories capable of accounting for (or so their proponents claim) virtually the entire repertoire of human behaviour and/or experience. An example of a theory with a restricted range would be social penetration theory (see Block 3, Unit 10/11). This is about what happens when people disclose information about themselves to each other and therefore it has a very limited focus. Psychoanalysis and learning theory, on the other hand, are two examples of the 'grand' variety and offer principles applicable to human behaviour of almost any kind.

A problematic feature of social psychology is the lack of an agreed and coherent theory. Many theories with very different characteristics and ranges of convenience co-exist and do not necessarily fit easily with one another, giving social psychology a fragmentary feel.

## 8   'Inside' or 'outside' perspective

A significant difference between theories of social behaviour is whether explanations are couched from the standpoint of the behaving person (i.e. an 'inside' perspective) or from the standpoint of the outside observer (i.e. an 'outside' perspective).

I choose to use the rather cryptic dichotomy *inside/outside* to denote this difference because the immediate alternatives which come to mind – *subjective/objective* and *experience/behaviour* – both have connotations which I do not wish to imply. An 'outside' view is not more objective in the sense of being more valid or real than an 'inside' perspective. Neither are explanations of an outside kind confined to behavioural studies. Explanations in terms of physiological processes and some psychodynamic explanations are also of an outside kind in that they adopt the viewpoint of an outside observer.

The methodological difficulties of the 'inside' approach are discussed in Block 4 *Personal Worlds*. Personal experience is inaccessible. You can only infer what another person is experiencing from his or her words and behaviour and on the basis of knowledge of the context and awareness of one's own experience. It is not always easy to communicate the quality of personal experience, let alone ensure that someone else appreciates what you mean. Nevertheless, as everyday intercourse, poetry and literature testify, it can be achieved. It is because of the difficulties of finding rigorous ways of investigating and conceptualizing personal experience that academic psychology has tended to emphasize the 'outside' approach.

Traditionally, the two perspectives have developed independently of each other and those who adopt one approach usually regard the value of the other with some scepticism. It might be argued, however, that the two perspectives complement each other: that each adds understanding which is capable of enriching the contribution of the other. This is the position adopted by the multiple perspective approach of this course.

## 9 Level of analysis

It is possible to conceptualize and analyse humankind at different, though related, levels. Imagine for a moment the view glimpsed by an observer in a plane. At this level all that may be seen are the *artefacts* of humans – houses, streets, roads, railways, canals and the chequered pattern of fields. Or think of an archaeologist's view of a civilization from long ago, pieced together from the fragmented traces left behind. Or think of China, Russia, America or any society outside your own. The view of humanity from any of these perspectives is one in general. Man is not an individual but a component part of an inordinately larger fabric – *society*. From such a perspective, people are conceptualized as units of an organized whole: units controlled by and given meaning essentially by their place in the larger framework – environment, communication and power structures, status hierarchies, work areas, resources, etc. At a lower level of analysis, people can be conceptualized as members of various *groups* and subcultures – family, gang, work-group, play-group, school, factory and office – each with its structure, interactions, roles and associated behaviours. Humankind is more tangible now; groups, if they are small enough, can be perceived as entities. But still the meaning of 'person' is a part and function of a larger, organized whole. At yet a lower level, we can study people as specific experiencing and behaving *individuals*. The analysis of people can be pitched at levels more molecular still. We can attempt to reduce an individual's functioning to physiological operations and couch our description and explanation in terms of neural, muscular or even biochemical processes.

What has been described is a hierarchy, but it should not be assumed that the levels are interchangeable or 'reducible', i.e. that explanations at any one level can be translated without loss to another. Each has attributes and meaning of its own. As the *Gestalt* postulate has it, each whole is different from the mere sum of its parts. But we must add the rider that, for some purposes, each *part* can often be understood more effectively when analysed and separated from the whole. So to understand people fully, we need somehow, in some way, ideally at least, to pitch our understanding at each level in turn; and to interrelate each with the other. Traditionally, each level has been the province of one or other discipline, ranging in order down our hierarchy from anthropology and sociology, psychology, anatomy and physiology, to neuro-anatomy and biochemistry. Some disciplines attempt to bridge two levels, physiological psychology for example. Social psychology is one of these. In this course, you will find analyses pitched not only at the level of individual behaviour and experience (for example, Blocks 4 and 6) but in terms of group processes or society (for example, Blocks 6 and 7). Some reference is even made, albeit brief, to more molecular studies in genetics (see Unit 3).

So far, we have discussed levels of analysis in 'outside' terms (i.e. in terms of the outward manifestations of behaviour). Different levels of analysis are harder to apply to the area of meanings and subjective experience (i.e. an 'inside' perspective). So experience has not been treated to the same amount of academic analysis. Karl Popper (1972) however has distinguished between the objective world of material things which he terms *World One*, and the world of personal experience which he calls *World Two*: he also conceptualizes a *World Three* – the products of organisms and minds which exist independently of those who created them. By *World Three* Popper refers not only to objects and changes in the environment made intentionally or otherwise, but also to the abstract creations of minds – ideas, art, languages, institutions, mathematics – complexes of symbols and communicated meaning. Thus the 'inside' sphere might be regarded as analysable at, at least, two levels; at the higher more abstract level of World Three (ideas, language etc.) as well as at the level of personal experience. A rather different, but perhaps complementary, approach is constituted by the analysis of different levels of consciousness by phenomenologists. These levels range from deep sleep through light sleep and dreaming, through waking experience when the mind is focused on the external world, to a level four which is reflexive awareness of self and subsequent levels of so-called 'cosmic awareness' (see, for example, de Ropp 1969). (As the question of levels of analysis is an important issue for social psychology, it is discussed in more detail and with particular relevance to course material in Paper 3.)

## 10   Formality of exposition

This dimension of variation between theories has been implied, if not expressed, in the earlier discussion of *concepts* and *kinds of explanation*. Theories vary greatly in the explicitness or formality with which they set out their propositions. Some theories attempt to define concepts carefully and systematically and make their principles clear. Others develop them in a more haphazard fashion, often embedding them in a discussion of experimental findings, case studies or general issues. It is probably true to say that there is a tendency for more molecular and 'outside' theories, because they are more likely to be able to specify concepts operationally, to be expressed in more formal terms. But an experiential approach or analysis at higher levels does not preclude the possibility of formal propositions. Kelly's personal construct theory is a good example. The theory is set out in the form of a series of corollaries (i.e. derived propositions) which stem from, and elaborate on, a fundamental postulate which expresses the basic principle of the theory (see Unit 8). The great advantage of stating a theory in this formal way is that it increases the possibility of supporting it with an effective research programme.

## Summary

I have suggested that ten ways in which theories may be distinguished are in terms of their:

1  basic assumptions

2  concepts

3  kinds of explanation

4  emphasis on description or explanation

5  differentiation vs. testability

6  methodological base

7  focus and range of convenience

8  'inside' or 'outside' perspective

9  level of analysis

10  formality of exposition.

It will be apparent from the preceding discussion of these dimensions that they are interrelated. For example, a theory whose basic assumption is that the methods of natural science provide the only valid approach (dimension 1) is likely to try to use concepts which are operationally defined (dimension 2).

---

ACTIVITY 2

Is such a theory also likely to adopt an 'outside' or an 'inside' perspective? What method is likely to figure prominently in research associated with this kind of theory? Is the theory likely to emphasize differentiation or testability?

---

*A learning and revision strategy*

It is suggested that, as you work through the course, you may like to use this scheme of ten dimensions to classify the theories you encounter. The dimensions should become more meaningful as you try to apply them to different theories. But bear in mind that it would be unrealistic to expect a definitive list or categorization under each heading. For example, it is not possible to identify *all* the assumptions on which any particular theory is based. Many of these are unclear and, in any case, can be made sense of in different ways. You should aim at identifying and categorizing as well as you can under each heading.

As a demonstration, each of the dimensions in turn will be applied to psychoanalysis. This is not intended as a *definitive* or complete analysis, you may come up with somewhat different ideas when you try, but at least it should serve as a way of starting you off by illustrating the way the dimensions can be applied.

**Psychoanalysis**

1  *Some assumptions*

(i)  Clinical method (talking with clients, applying dream analysis etc. to elicit the meaning of the experience) is the best way of studying the subject-matter of psychology.

(ii)  Important *influences* on behaviour
– biology (drives, pleasure principle);
– socialization and the conflicts it may produce (repression, sublimation etc.);
– early childhood experience crucial.

(iii)  It is important to take into account unconscious motivation.

2  *Concepts* – libido, id, ego, superego, cathexis, repression etc., etc.

3  *Kinds of explanation*. Explanation is in terms of drives, biologically programmed development and the conflicts produced between these and the experience of people and events and the internalization of that experience, particularly in childhood. Explanations are sought in the *meanings* (particularly unconscious ones) which events and behaviour have for the person concerned. Much use is made of non-operationalizable hypothetical constructs.

4 The theory provides the means for *both describing and explaining behaviour*. Descriptive concepts (e.g. reaction formation) tend to be strongly tied to explanatory assumptions.

5 Has great *differentiating* power but is weaker on *testability*.

6 Its *methodological* base is clinical. Hypotheses are derived (and tested) by talking with clients and are analysing dreams, associations etc.

7 The *focus* is on emotional experience and behaviour but the range of the theory is very wide indeed. It can be applied to the behaviour and experience of individuals as well as groups and also to the phenomena of culture (e.g. mythology, art etc.) as well.

8 It takes *both an inside and an outside perspective*. It is concerned with the analysis of behaviour and experience from the external perspective of the analyst but, in that it is concerned with meanings, it also requires viewing the situation from the perspective of the subject as well.

9 *Level of analysis*. It usually operates very much at the level of the experience of the *individual* though it has been applied to analysis at a group level.

10 Not originally set out as a set of formal propositions but research concerned with testing the validity of psychoanalytic ideas (see set book *Freud and Psychoanalysis*, Chapter 10) demonstrates that much of it is relatively easily convertible to propositional form.

### References

DE ROPP, R. S. (1969) *The master game*, London, Allen and Unwin.

POPPER, K. (1972) *Objective knowledge: an evolutionary approach*, London, Oxford University Press.

## Paper 3: Levels of analysis

*by Roger Sapsford*

### 1 Introduction

At several places in the course the idea of *levels of analysis* has been explicitly introduced and discussed. For example, in Unit 1 a range of theories about the family shows how descriptions of the family and its functions, and explanations of its role in society and human life, can be tackled in very different ways. Some of these differences can be attributed to different levels of analysis. Thus it is possible to focus on the family as an institution in society, or as a biological necessity, or as a source of intrapsychic satisfaction for individuals. In Unit 2 the family is treated as a system: a functioning group of interdependent people at a more micro-level than society or subculture and, furthermore, encompassing phenomena which cannot be described or understood at the level of individuals. This particular unit introduced a 'group' level, and also the idea that *what people create between them* in their personal relationships provides yet another, *interpersonal* level of analysis. Block 6 also explicitly discusses levels of analysis. In fact the idea of different levels is implicit throughout the course in the concepts, theories, research and even the underlying models of the person which are presented.

Before trying to classify 'levels', we should note that the whole concept of levels tends to imply some kind of hierarchy, which might suggest that we believe some levels to be higher than others in the sense of being superior or preferable or more important or more fundamental. This is not the intention here. One may describe 'a table' as an art object in a particular culture, or as a socially defined object which is used in certain ways – to eat breakfast from or to write essays on – or as a physical object of a certain sort, made of wood or metal, or as a certain pattern of subatomic energies. These are different 'levels' of description, but none of them is higher or lower in terms of being better or worse; each has its part to play in answering particular types of questions. In a similar way we shall, in this paper, elaborate various levels of analysis relevant to social psychology which are different, but not necessarily better or more important ways of asking questions about people, how they live and function. It is important to keep this in mind because outside social science the issue is not so clear-cut. The 'hierarchy of sciences', where, for example, the physics of subatomic particles is accepted as the most fundamental, can endow the lower levels of analysis with special explanatory power. Thus an embryological phenomenon can sometimes (not always), be 'better' explained by recourse to the concepts and theories of biochemistry; and similarly, problems about the structure and functions of material objects can often be best 'explained' by the properties of atoms and electrons.

## 2   Reductionism in physical and social science

The process of using concepts and laws from a lower level of analysis to provide an explanation for phenomena at a higher level is called *reduction*. It implies a deterministic relation between the two levels (i.e. that entities and processes at the lower level cause the phenomena that are observed and described at the higher level). Even though modern science is based on the working assumption that there *is* nothing but that which is physical, and that these physical entities are related in a hierarchical system of cause and effect, nevertheless, many scientists believe that the procedure (or philosophy) of *reductionism* is misguided. Reductionism implies that ultimately all sciences will (or could) be subsumed under a form of physics and that any other way of 'doing science' is, at most, second best. But a great deal of science involves description and explanation *within one level* – within one discipline – and, not infrequently, understanding is extended by hypothesizing relations with *higher* levels of analysis. Thus many practicing scientists and philosophers of science do not believe that reductionism is necessarily the route to understanding.

In psychology there are those who wish to build a *science* of psychology just like any physical science, and who therefore see the chief problem as being what the 'right' basic units are with which to explain more complex phenomena. Many who hold this view, for example, may argue that complex phenomena such as behaviour and cognition must ultimately be explainable in terms of changes in the physical state of the brain. Other branches of psychology which would not attempt to reduce psychological phenomena to biological or physiological causes would still make the claim that social and societal phenomena must be explainable in terms of some simpler kinds of process – generally something happening within or between *individuals*; this form of individualism is another kind of reductionism. In contrast, other sorts of theory (some sociological theories, for example) would deny any validity to individualistic approaches, arguing that everything of any interest or significance about individuals can be explained in terms of social structures or economic processes. This can be seen as a form of reductionism in that it explains the complex phenomenon in terms of simpler 'underlying causes'.

This last approach (known technically as *sociological reductionism*) has exerted considerable influence on recent social psychology because of the *political* role which many sociologists see traditional psychology as playing – distracting attention from society's inequalities by focusing attention on individuals. For instance, critics of the way our current society is ordered have argued that one way that inequalities of power are maintained and legitimized is by diverting attention from structural problems to the condition of individuals. Inequalities of wealth and opportunity are *structural* questions, but the people who steal because they have been taught to value a life-style to which they have no legitimate means of access are *individuals*. 'Theft', then, becomes a condition of the individual – either a 'badness' or a 'sickness'. (See the editorial discussion associated with the Hayley paper in the Reader, Chapter 4.) Social psychologists have been influential in having theft defined as a sickness – a pathological condition, susceptible to treatment or else incurable, but in any case not a condition which should rightly incur heavy punishment – which is a humane reform but also in a way strongly supportive of the *status quo*. If thieving is a property of individuals, then it is individuals who need to be treated for their deviation from the current social norm; society remains unchanged, and the idea that it might need changing does not even come up in the discussion.

The notion that crime is to be explained by something 'in' the people who commit it might well have an appeal for a lot of thinkers – despite the fact that self-report studies indicate that most of us have committed crimes at one time or another in our lives. Working at the level of the individual begins to appear more pernicious, however, when it leads to widespread prescription of drugs to 'cure' women's depression rather than looking at the nature of their lives and what might be wrong with the structures within which they live. (One may also question why the doctor's 'knowledge' is thought relevant – how medical knowledge is socially legitimized.) Most people in the West find the ideas of 'individual deviance' pernicious when it is used, as at times in Soviet Russia, to justify the 'treatment' of those whose political ideas do not accord with the prevailing state orthodoxy. Social psychology has often been judged conservative and state-supportive because its traditional pre-occupation with individuals' biology or internal states or the way individuals interact has seemed to rule out as irrelevant all criticism of the way things are currently ordered and organized.

What is emerging from our argument here is that the basic 'model of the person' with which social psychologists work must, in some sense, include many levels of analysis. A person is an animal of the species *homo sapiens*, with all the biological properties and constraints that this implies. For certain purposes we may choose to 'abstract' aspects of experience or 'chains of causality' and, for those purposes treat them as if the mind could exist in isolation, apart from a culture or social structure. Similarly it is possible to look at cultural traditions, or at social structures, *as if* they could exist in isolation from people. Ultimately, however, theories of social psychology have to be related back to the *whole* person, who is a thinking and feeling (biological) individual, interacting with others in an essentially social world.

In a way, all this sounds like an attempt to build an empire: if social psychology works at all levels of analysis, what need is there for biology, or cognitive psychology, or sociology etc., as separate disciplines? The nature of social psychology as a distinctive discipline is discussed in more detail in Paper 10, but we clearly need to have some preliminary thoughts on the subject in the context of 'levels of analysis'. Nothing which is said here is intended to detract from the separate importance of disciplines, such as the biological sciences, which try to work out the structure and function of the human organism, or from sociology's attempts to explicate the working out of forms of socio-economic relations through social structures and ideologies. Even though most research in social psychology is concerned with the behaviour and experience of social beings as individuals and with their personal interactions, I argue that *theory* in social psychology may require a wider knowledge and appreciation of other levels at which discussion about people can relevantly take place.

### 3 Levels of analysis in social psychology

Traditionally, three broad levels of analysis have been identified in social psychology: societal, group and individual. In this paper, we shall adopt a somewhat different scheme, one which rests on the premise that no *clear* hierarchy of levels exists (perhaps perspectives would be a better term) and that any attempts to identify a fixed number of levels is highly artificial.

#### 3.1  Societal levels

The first broad grouping of levels – traditionally the home ground of sociologists, though modern social psychology finds itself taking increasing account of it – comprises analyses in terms of 'the wider society' – or 'the nexus of social relations', where 'social relations' is understood to mean not relationships between individuals, but the relationships of whole groups or classes of people to other groups or classes as mediated and defined by social structures and the economic system inherent in a particular society.

Unit 1 of Block 1, for example, discusses 'societal' and 'cultural' levels of analysis: the broad structures of economic and social relationships in a society (societal level) and the dominant meanings and values which are expressed (cultural level). At the *societal* level we saw that the nuclear family functions as an institution which may largely determine what behaviour is possible for women, in combination with the institutional forms which 'work' takes in our society. Women are constrained to 'run the home' and care for children, irrespective of any other work they may take on, and irrespective of whether family finances in fact constrain them to seek paying work. These 'family responsibilities' make it less easy for women than for men to 'follow a career' and largely determine the kind of work they are free to take. *Culturally*, we noted that this situation is maintained in large part by the fact that all parties substantially accept it. It is 'normal', 'accepted', 'taken for granted' in our society that men go out to work while women look after the home and children – even where this does not actually happen – and these cultural expectations form another level of constraint, on experience as well as on behaviour. (One should note that men as well as women are thus constrained: the man who might wish to stay home and care for the children meets opposition from inside himself as well as from other people.)

A third level within this broad grouping involves looking not at the nature and influence of social structures, but at the *social position of particular individuals* – whether, for example, they are rich or poor, in work or out of work, and so on, and the implications of these facts for their lives and experience. This level of analysis is not much discussed in the course texts themselves, but the Rutter and Madge paper in Chapter 4 of the Course Reader looks systematically at 'Cycles of Disadvantage' and their consequences for those who are trapped in them.

### 3.2    Group levels

Traditionally, again, this level is seen as the next 'below' societal levels of analysis. However, in certain respects groups of people – whether small informal groups, families or larger organizations – can be understood in the same terms as were applied to the societal levels. Block 6 describes how the physical structure, communication channels and power hierarchy in groups affect the kinds of processes that occur and the behaviour and experiences of the participants. So too do the pre-existing roles and general 'cultural' expectations. Is the group level of analysis – for a social psychologist – the same as the societal level but involving a smaller number of people? There is probably not much mileage in such headcounting. Organizations and large groups may be treated as sub-cultures: homogeneous groups within society, identifiable in terms of internal structures somewhat different from those of society at large. Subcultures have different cultural expectations and values and, often, have a hierarchy of resources and advantage similar to that which we have referred to above as 'social position'.

What is particular about *small* groups, however, is that members have face-to-face contact and develop relationships. In small groups the opportunity to interact directly confers special salience on other psychological processes such as the ability to reward and punish each other, communicate in an extremely elaborated form, present and 'manage' selves and understand others. These processes lead to interpersonal influence which is probably different in kind, certainly in emotional intensity, from the sort of social influence processes that are described at societal and organizational levels. Furthermore, social interactions between people in small, longstanding groups or in personal relationships lead to phenomena that belong to a rather different level of analysis – *the interpersonal level.*

### 3.3 The interpersonal level

This level is concerned with what people create between them. It is *not* concerned with the interacting individuals and is *not* primarily concerned with how each participating *individual* (sequentially) perceives and attributes meaning to the other(s), a process of intersubjectivity which is more akin to the personal level (3.4) below. At an interpersonal level the focus can be either on the *system* of which the individuals are a part, or on the *discourse* they create between them. Thus in Unit 2 the family is seen as a dynamic system with identifiable and predictable features which are not properties of the individuals and cannot be explained by reduction to analysis at the level of individuals. The system can be said to have *emergent properties* which do not exist and cannot be explained except at the interpersonal level. This is also true when attention is focused on the discourse (or conversation, in its broadest terms) between people. Although it is possible to concentrate on conversation at the individual level – what each participant understands – at the interpersonal level we focus on the conversation or discourse as a thing in itself.

Unit 7 uses this approach to the growth of understanding in children and points out its importance in child development research and theory in general. The increasing use of the interpersonal level of analysis in child development theories signals dissatisfaction with the way that a rigid distinction between the 'public' and 'private' mental lives of children has been *imposed* by researchers, rather than *derived* from the phenomena studied. Researchers are less prone, now, to assume that what is happening in a particular social event, represents some permanent feature of the 'inner' life or disposition of the participants.

There has been a long tradition in Western thought of assuming that a private inner life is present in the individual from the very beginning. This has, claims Shotter (1982), misled us into always beginning our research with the study of individuals and 'into thinking of society as only a group or collective of interrelated individuals'. (You will see in Chapter 1 of the Reader the position adopted by Allport about the central place of the individual even in the study of social issues.) In the Reader we trace a gradual disillusionment with this position which leads up to the examination of a proposed new model of 'dialectical psychology' (Llewellyn & Lock, 1980) at the end of Chapter 4. Individualism has been a strong influence in developmental psychology, and has led to a very 'adult' conception of childhood. Children's behaviour is studied and inferences made from it to their 'inner states' on the basis of our own *adult* subjectivity. This means we treat certain behaviours in children as signifying what they mean *to us*. In so doing we are imputing a degree of maturity and self-sufficiency to the child's inner life that it may not have.

The way out of implicit 'adultmorphism' has been to drop the process of inference altogether and to examine instead *what the child actually does*, the 'discourse' of the child in his social context. This means the study is not concerned with what is in the children's minds, i.e. their 'mental furniture', but with the emergent qualities of actions in the here and now. The child is now seen by developmental psychologists not so much as made up of inner self-sufficient mental dispositions, but as characterized in the outer 'discourse' where individual and context are one. He or she has been relocated from inside the 'head' to inside the ongoing action. (Examples of this type of approach are to be found in Margaret Donaldson's classic 'Children's Minds' (1980) and Valerie Walkerdine's (1981) 'From Context to Text: a Psychosemiotic Approach).'

### 3.4 The level of the person

The traditional third level of explanation is that of 'the individual' or 'the person'. In Block 4, for example, we look at the person as a conscious entity, someone with a conscious awareness of being someone and an ability to make a separation between self and others. In Block 3 we spoke of George Kelly's model of 'man the scientist' and how people form their theories of the world by testing them against the reactions of others to their behaviour. One aspect of families explored in Block 1, Unit 2 was the way that individuals form their pictures of the social world in interaction with other family members. In Block 1, Unit 4 we looked at a symbolic interactionist perspective on socialization – how we form our understanding of our selves from the reactions of others to us, within the cultural matrix. In Unit 1 of Block 1 we looked at how individuals, in communes or more 'traditional' nuclear families, may try to change their opportunities for action and experience by 'going against' the norms of their society.

All these approaches presuppose the idea of the *individual* or *person* as something analytically distinct from the social world. They are rarely individualistic in the sense of ignoring social interaction – most, indeed, make great play of the idea that we are shaped by our interactions with others. All, however, are centred in the concept of the integrated and to some extent free or self-determining person, analytically distinct from others – even if most worthy of study when in interaction with others. This picture comes close to how we normally talk about ourselves and others in the ordinary language of common sense, and may therefore sometimes seem a trivial level of analysis. On the other hand, for the same reason it can seem seductively 'right' – it reinforces our everyday reasoning. In the view of many social psychologists it is an important part of what social psychology is about, and one which has been very much neglected until recently except among practicing therapists. One needs to remember, nonetheless, that the experience or 'feeling' of personal freedom is not incompatible with the presence of causation, and also that our current conception of the autonomous person is itself a cultural product with a socioeconomic history behind it.

### 3.5  'Below' the level of the person

Finally, let us consider the many theories in social psychology whose primary focus is what goes on *inside* the individual – explanations of what the person does in terms of internal dynamics or structure. In Block 1, Unit 4, for example, you were first introduced to four theories of socialization all of which deal explicitly with what goes on *inside* the individual as he or she develops: the perspectives of Freud, the learning theorists, Piaget, and the symbolic interactionists. All of these 'explain' current behaviour and/or experience in terms of how dynamic processes or cognitive representations have been established within people during childhood. George Kelly's theories, which you met in Block 3, centre around a view of how the world is represented within the person and how representations influence each other. Block 5 is specifically concerned with internal representations and/or tendencies to behave – attitudes. These *intrapersonal* explanations form a large part of psychological theorizing and are the 'stock in trade' of much applied social psychology.

The *biological* level of explanation which locates the basic 'units of explanation' literally within the physical individual was also introduced briefly in Unit 1 with the sociobiological notion that 'the family' can be explained as a syndrome of inherited behaviours which promote survival. (This was repeated at the end of Section 4 in Tiger and Shepher's explanation of why the *kibbutzim* have failed to eradicate apparently 'social' sex differences; Section 4 also gave another explanation predicated partly in biology – Spiro's – which did not call on the concept of inheritance.) The major treatment of biological explanations in Block 1 was reserved for Unit 3. Here we saw that the distinction between 'innate' and 'learned' behaviours may not deserve the amount of effort which psychologists and others have put into exploring it. There seems to be little point in disputing that *tendencies* towards certain types of behaviour may be inheritable, along with *potentialities* for some aspects of character and ability; farmers and dog owners have been breeding selectivity for such traits for many years. (At the very simplest level it seems fairly obvious that gross aspects of biology affect the nature of human experience: it seems fairly obvious that six-foot men have to some extent a different view of the world from four-foot men and that the blind experience a different world from that of the sighted.) However, Unit 3 made clear that any inherited tendencies or potentialities are dependent on the environment for their development. (Even clearly hereditable physical character-

79

istics such as eye colour depend on the environment for their expression; if we add certain chemicals to the baby's diet, he or she will have not brown or blue eyes, but *pink* ones.)

## 4   Which level?

Some of the theories mentioned above are in a way anomolous: for example Kelly's approach, as we said earlier, is primarily to be seen as located at the *personal* or even *interpersonal* level of analysis, dealing with personal meanings interpersonally negotiated. However, the 'atom' of Kelly's system is the 'construct', the belief about the world, and these are to be found *within* a person. Symbolic interactionism is an *interpersonal* or even a *cultural* theory, concerned with shared norms and their implications, but again a norm which is held *by the individual* is held in some sense *within* the individual. Attitudes are often treated as part of the 'whole person' – see, for example Smith, Bruner and White's article in the Course Reader. But they are also treated as being below the level of the person (see above) whilst their correlates in the social world (societal and cultural influences on the attitudes that individuals come to hold) firmly link attitudes to other levels of analysis. Thus the artificiality of trying to assign theories to particular levels of analysis is again underlined: a social psychological analysis maybe at a particular level, but a theory of any scope or power usually spans several levels.

We have distinguished, above, four broad and arbitrary 'categories' or 'levels' of analysis which social scientists bring to bear on the phenomena which they seek to explain. We noted, first, a 'societal' level whose exponents talk in terms of the broad structures of social relations and the 'culture' or 'ideology' which enforces them or legitimates them. A 'group level' was next elaborated, which similarly analyses what goes on in social life in terms of structures and hierarchies on the one hand and norms or ideologies on the other, but which also covers the truly *interpersonal* analysis of what goes on *between* people – the discourse, or system, or social process, seen as a property of the group (or dyad) rather than as the sum of properties of individuals. A third 'level' was that of the *person* or *individual*: the thinking, feeling, experiencing and decision-making subject of our everyday experience; and *intrapersonal* explanations in terms of traits, attitudes, internal representations, internal processes or, at the extreme, biological 'facts' about the organism. Traditionally, social psychologists in Britain and America have tended to locate their explanations mostly at the group level or at the intrapersonal level, or to a lesser extent at the level of the person. At what level *should* we be working, however? Which level is likely to be the most productive of future social psychological insights?

The problem is that each level in turn is demonstrably inappropriate as a candidate for the title of 'natural home of social psychology'. If social psychology is about the behaviour and experience of individuals, then societal-level explanations are of obvious relevance to it, as has become increasingly clear to psychologists during the last two decades: much of what we are and how we think is determined by the institutions and the ideology of our society. To say that *everything* about us is so determined, however, fails to explain the *variety* of possible behaviours and experiences which can be seen in different people's lives. (It fails to explain even how we can conceive of a norm as oppressive and try to change it in our lives – see Block 1, Unit 1.) Group pressures and group structures, similarly, are part of what determines who we are and what is available to us as experience, but again there is more variety between people and more apparent scope for creative and individual action than a purely group-level explanation can enfold (and it is obvious nonsense to leave out of account the wider society in which the group is located). At the other extreme, intrapersonal explanations were long thought to be the most promising path for the building of social psychology as a science, and they explain quite plausibly the variety between individuals, but they cannot of themselves explain all that individuals have in common; for this, group or societal level analyses are needed. Finally, explana-

*[margin note]* 4 levels of analysis
Societal
group
person/individual
Intrapersonal

80

tions in terms of *the person* come closest to what social psychology is aiming to be about, and they avoid the various 'reductionisms' associated with the other styles, but on the whole they tend not to be explanations at all, but only descriptions: as soon as we want to ask why the individual thinks, feels or behaves as he or she does, what led up to it, then we are working at one of the other levels.

Our tentative answer, therefore, would be two-fold:

1  Research into the causes and constraints on behaviour and/or experience will always be in one or more of the 'societal', 'group' or 'intrapersonal' levels. If theorizing about such determinants is confined to a single level, it is likely to be vacuous: one needs generally to consider internal dynamics or structures *and* immediate social influences *and* the wider society and its history to produce a rounded and socially situated explanation.

2  We should not forget, however, that we are individual people writing for individual people. The aim of social psychology may be to lay bare what determines behaviour and experience, but implicit in the aim must be a belief that people can change determinants, sometimes, once they know about them. To this extent, therefore, social psychology is always and inevitably to be related back to the level of the person.

## Paper 4: Behaviour and action

*by Kerry Thomas and Roger Sapsford*

In the course title, *Social psychology: development, experience and behaviour in a social world*, the word *behaviour* is used in its ordinary, everyday language sense to mean what we see people *do*, including what they say. Sometimes in the course, however, you will find that the word is used in a more technical sense, contrasted perhaps with the word *action*. A preference for using *behaviour* rather than *action* – or *action* rather than *behaviour* – to describe the visible and/or audible part of what people do is sometimes an important clue as to the sort of social psychology which an author espouses and to what sort of 'model of the person' informs his or her theories. It seems useful, therefore, to try to impose some kind of order on the variety of ways in which the terms have been used in the course and in social psychology in general.

It is possible to use the two terms in direct opposition to each other. When used in this way, they reflect quite different statements about what is going on. *Behaviour* is taken to mean *strictly what is observable* about the person's conduct, shorn of all assumptions, inferences or intuitions about what the observable behaviours might mean for the people who do them and without any implications about hypothetical processes underlying them. As we shall see later, this extreme position tends to be adopted by those psychologists who believe either that the meanings or processes do not exist, or that they do not matter, in the sense of having no part to play in a scientific explanation of *behaviour*. (Notice, incidentally, that one usually speaks of 'the scientific explanation of *behaviour*', not 'the scientific explanation of *actions*'.) At the opposite extreme, the word *action* is used for what people do deliberately and meaningfully. Psychologists who use the word *action* in preference to the word *behaviour* tend to assert that social psychology is about *making sense* of what people do rather than *explaining* what people do in a scientific way through the formulation of general laws of behaviour. They would tend to assert that such scientific explanation is not a relevant goal for social psychology because it usually implies a search for the *causes* of behaviour; they would probably also claim that we have at least some degree of *autonomy* in our actions, which renders the notion of causal explanation at least partly irrelevant.

An example of the first of these extreme positions is behaviourism. However, possibly the majority of behaviourists would *not* now take the *most* extreme position being instead what may be termed 'methodological behaviourists'. That is, they espouse behaviourism as a *methodology* – a set of premises upon which to build a psychological science. Among the main tenets of this position are:

(a) Psychology should be a science like any other physical science and, therefore, must be built upon objectivity and must aim towards general laws and universal statements (see also Paper 8).

(b) Inner states, including meaning and intention, are not accessible for direct observation and, therefore, cannot be objectively described and/or measured. In practice, only overt behaviour is amenable to objective observation. For this reason, only overt behaviour stripped of concomitant interpretation and mean-ingfulness is legitimate as data.

(c) Organisms do *experience* inner states, but the role of these in causation of behaviour is unclear. Because of the need for objectivity, these experiences are treated as irrelevant to the science of psychology. However, in theory, if some objectivity could be achieved (perhaps in the future of psychology-as-science) then knowledge of inner states could contribute to understanding the causes of behaviour.

The more radical position – typical, for instance, of Watson (behaviourism's founder) and Skinner (one of its now most notable adherents) – would revise the third of these tenets, claiming instead that 'inner events' are unrelated to the causes of behaviour – they are merely parallel events which are experienced by the organism. Even if such 'symptoms' could be objectively described and measured they would not contribute anything to our knowledge of behaviour. This position is the extreme for which we are looking: 'behaviour' stripped even in theory of all implication of meaning.

Behaviourists of this variety would claim that no class of event is beyond the scope of description as a behaviour. The three examples we give below will, we hope, help to make this clear. Translating the everyday language of social relationship, Watson (1930) wrote of one situation: 'Shortly afterwards the two men became friends . . . that is, formed verbal and manual habits towards one another and towards the same or similar situations.' In other words, he regarded similarity of response towards similar situations as sufficient reinforcement for continued and more frequent association with the similar responder and translated 'friendship behaviour' as a set of responses towards another person (e.g. spending more rather than less time in the person's company) set up and maintained by this and other reinforcers. The meaning of words can similarly be expressed in terms of behavioural contingencies, according to Skinner (1957): 'In making a distinction . . . between *send me two* and *send me, too,* we are specify-ing either the normal conditions under which the responses are made or their normal effects upon a listener.'

Even the question of reflexivity – the inclusion of the act of theorizing itself within the scope of the theory – was tackled by Watson in his 1930 book (although we may suspect a touch of humour in the precise formulation). Watson saw theoretical writing as an activity akin to speech about theory – consisting only of manual behaviours (e.g. writing) associated with *sub*-vocal behaviours (move-ments of the larynx not resulting in audible sound) rather than overt vocaliza-tion. Of a crux in his own career as a theoretician, he wrote: 'Since the advent of the conditioned reflex hypothesis in psychology I have had my own laryngeal processes stimulated to work upon this problem from another angle'.

To illustrate the other extreme viewpoint let us first consider Shotter's model of social psychology. He sees on one hand *caused behaviour* and on the other *reasoned action*, and treats these two as belonging to quite different kinds of explanation:

> In explaining our actions to others we have, ideally, to give our *reasons*, tell of our *aims* or *intentions* . . . (although) our intentions are often as obscure

to ourselves as to others – and this is where empirical investigation can prove effective... Unlike actions, [behaviours] just happen; they are no one's responsibility... To explain them, we must seek their causal principles, the laws of nature which seem to govern the structure of their appearances – the traditional task of the natural sciences. So we must be clear when investigating psychological phenomena whether it is *reasons* (or something having the logical structure of a reason) or *causal principles* that we seek; the two belong ... to distinct spheres of thought and investigation.

(Shotter, 1974, p.58.)

Yet another facet of the distinction between behaviour and action is revealed by the above quotation. Behaviourists, because of their theoretical position take an *outside perspective* – they remain 'psychologists' observing from the sidelines, effectively divorced from membership in the class of organism that is being observed. In contrast, Shotter's social psychologist who wants to understand reasons must probe within the experience of those she is studying *and* take on board and exploit knowledge which comes directly from her/his own experience as a member of humanity. So we have to include *reflexity* in our notions of what psychology is. But even from this *inside perspective* it is possible to use the term behaviour – as does Shotter – for things that we (or others) do but *experience* as 'just happening'. So we also have to consider the issue of what we do consciously and deliberately as opposed to what we do unintentionally or apparently unintentionally (determined by factors which are – at least at that instant – outside our awareness and/or control).

Thus, in Shotter's sense an 'action' is something which we can, in principle, explain by saying why we did it – what our purpose was – and the term pre-supposes autonomous rather than determined action. But whether 'actions', in this extreme form of the term, ever do in fact occur is a subject of heated argument in social psychology.

For instance, Freud argues that most things which appear to be *behaviours* are in *some* sense *actions* – they express an unconscious meaning and a purpose. Slips of the tongue, clumsy pieces of *behaviour*, apparently random behavioural events, can generally be seen in the context of the person's life-history as following a deliberate and purposive pattern (see for example *The Psychopathology of Everyday Life*). However – taking almost the opposing view – Freud would not assume that most or even much of this purpose and deliberation is consciously available to the person; most is repressed into the unconscious, and most of the reasons we give for our actions are 'rationalizations' – rational but inaccurate ways of not having to face the real unconscious motives. (This is the force of Shotter's point that our reasons may not be accessible even to us.) We may wonder at this point whether it is useful to think of these as actions as opposed to determined behaviour. A similar case could be made that much of what we believe about the world is not the product of reason and discovery, but rather an unthinking expression of the dominant ideology, i.e. determined by outside events. If either of these arguments is admitted, then the extreme distinction between 'behaviour' and 'action' loses a lot of its force, because the premise of deliberate and voluntary action is undermined: and the argument is not so much about behaviour or action as about what is and is not determined, about what is and is not 'freely chosen' and deliberately meaningful.

The extremity of the distinction can be undermined in yet another way. There are classes of 'doing' which it is very difficult to explain as *behaviours*, if by *behaviour* we mean physical movements devoid of meaning or intention. To use an example from Unit 15 of DS262, there may be *no* observable differences between a deliberate but bad shot at snooker, an accidental miscue by a competent player and the more or less random behaviour of a novice player who is succeeding for once in concealing his or her incompetence. The difference lies partly in the event's meaning for observers, and even more in the thoughts and feelings of the player; it cannot necessarily be established from the movements of the balls or the movements of the player.

Our use of the terms *behaviour* and *action* may, therefore, tend towards expressing theoretical positions such as those outlined above, but in practice we generally use them in a more method-oriented way, to indicate the level of analysis which we are currently (and perhaps temporarily) adopting. This kind of use is well expressed in a paper by Reynolds:

> The matter of definition is always at the heart of discussion in the field of animal behaviour or human action. . . Weber distinguished clearly between the physical, potentially observable part, which he refers to as behaviour (*Verhalten*) and the ideational, unobservable part, which he refers to as meaning (*Sinn*). The combination of the two, that is what an animal or human being does in its totality, he refers to as actions (*Handeln*). Putting these together, we can say the following. *If we describe what people or animals do without enquiring into their subjective reasons and/or interpretations, we are talking about their behaviour.*
>
> If we study these subjective aspects of what they do, the reasons and ideas underlying and guiding it, then we are concerned with the world of meaning. If we concern ourselves both with what people are overtly and objectively seen to do or not to do and the reasons for their so doing or not doing which relate to the world of meaning and understanding, we then describe action.

(Reynolds, 1982, ibid, italics added)

Finally, as Reynolds goes on to point out, what we need to be able to say about what people do is not exhausted by the two terms *behaviour* and *action*.

> . . . I should like to mention one aspect of the interpretation of human action . . . which I feel is probably necessary for a full understanding of action. This is the inclusion of a new element which has been called by Harré and Secord . . . the act.
>
> Act is used by Harré and Secord to refer to action in its social context. We, therefore, need to think of actions in terms of firstly the behaviour which is the part we can see and describe, secondly the meaning which is the part we cannot see but about which we can obtain information by asking the subject why he did something, and thirdly the act, or that perspective or part of what a person does which is intimately connected with the social situation in which he performs and represents the place or effect of the action in that situation. For instance we can see *behaviour*, a hand movement say, as a meaningful gesture, that is intended *action*, and *interpret it as an act of protest*.

(Reynolds, 1982, ibid, italics added)

### References

FREUD, S. (1901) *The Psychopathology of Everyday Life*, Harmondsworth, Penguin, 1976.

REYNOLDS, V. (1982) 'Behaviour, action and act in relation to strategies and decision-making', in von Craanch, M. and Harré, R. (eds), *The Analysis of Action*, Cambridge, Cambridge University Press.

SHOTTER, J. (1974) 'What is it to be human?' in Armistead, N. (ed), *Reconstructing Social Psychology*, Harmondsworth, Penguin.

SKINNER, B. F. (1957) *Verbal Behaviour*, New York, Appleton-Century-Crofts.

WATSON, J. B. (1930) *Behaviourism* (second edition), Chicago, Chicago University Press.

THE OPEN UNIVERSITY (1981) *DS262 Introduction to Psychology*, Unit 15 'Understanding People', The Open University Press.

## Paper 5: The significance of meaning

*by Richard Stevens and Roger Sapsford*

*A factor which is crucial to our understanding of the nature of social psychology is the growing realization within the discipline of the importance of* meaning *in any analysis of social life. This issue is also discussed in Chapter 11 of the set book,* Freud and Psychoanalysis, *which should be read in conjunction with this paper.*

A central debate in psychology throughout this century has been between those whose goal it is to build a science of human life on a par with and adhering to the methods of the natural sciences (collectively they are known as *positivists*) and those who are unable to accept the limitations which this goal imposes.

The positivist approach comes in many forms. The most extreme example in psychology is perhaps classic behaviourism. This is probably the most avowedly 'scientific' of all the schools of psychology which have grown up in this century. Its aim is to build, literally, a 'science of behaviour' which will be the equal in rigour of physics and chemistry. In the service of this aim, strict behaviourists try to ensure that their subject-matter includes only that which is observable. Concepts such as 'consciousness', 'meaning', 'intention' and 'feeling' are seen as mere verbal abstractions rather than as entities to be measured. If they can be translated into behaviour terms ('I like Joan' = 'I seek Joan's company rather than avoiding her'), then the translation is to be preferred on the grounds of scientific simplicity. If they cannot, then they refer to something mystical or mysterious which is not openly observable and therefore has no place in a science. Watson, the founder of the movement set out the essential idea of his 'science' very clearly in the preface to the second edition of his book:

> Behaviourism . . . was an attempt . . . to apply to the experimental study of man the same kind of procedure and the same language that many research men have found useful in the study of animals lower than man. We believed . . . that man is an animal different from other animals only in the type of behaviour he displays. . . The raw fact [is] that you . . . if you are to remain scientific, must describe the behaviour of man in no other terms than those you would use in describing the behaviour of the ox you slaughter.

> (Watson, 1930.)

Along with the disregard of consciousness goes the exclusion of notions like intention and purpose when explaining human behaviour. B. F. Skinner (1971) for instance, writes in his book *Beyond freedom and dignity*.

> In what we may call the pre-scientific view . . . a person's behaviour is to some extent his own achievement. He is free to deliberate, decide, act. . . In the scientific view . . . a person's behaviour is determined by a genetic endowment . . . and by . . . environmental circumstances.

and elsewhere in the same book:

> As a science of behaviour adopts the strategy of physics and biology, the autonomous agent to which behaviour has traditionally been attributed is replaced by the environment. . . What is being abolished is autonomous man – the inner man . . . the abolition has been long overdue. Autonomous man is a device used to explain what we cannot explain in any other way . . . only by dispossessing him can we turn to the real causes of human behaviour.

> (Skinner, 1971.)

Some modern behaviourists and many other psychologists who adopt a positivist approach may take a less extreme view. But all insist that we work only with variables which can be observed and measured, that we use only hypotheses which are testable. The great advantage of this is that the investigations of psychologists, like those of the natural scientists, become open to scrutiny and are potentially replicable by those with the interest and expertise. In effect, because subjective experience and the meanings which we attribute to events are difficult to translate effectively into observable form, such data can easily get left out of account and become treated as inappropriate as the subject-matter for a science.

The problem with an approach such as this though is how far does it tend to throw the baby out with the bath water? Is to do away with the study of meaning and subjective experience to do away with the essential subject matter of psychology?

First, it is evident that what goes on in our minds is often far richer and (if it could be made accessible) more telling about a person than his or her observable behaviour. The behaviours of a group of people listening to a lecture may well show only superficial differences. One or two may fidget or cough a little more than the rest, but on the whole individual differences in behaviour in such a situation are likely to be relatively few. But if you could tap their *experience*. . . Inside those many heads are as many worlds; some follow the lecturer's address, responsive in their ways to the immediacy of his words and gestures, others do not hear. Perhaps they are reflecting on a point made several minutes earlier, debating with themselves as to whether to go for a drink afterwards, or thinking confusedly of what to do about that letter that arrived today. This person consciously focuses on the shadow pattern made by the lights along the wall, that one speculates about a stranger across the aisle. Some slip into sleep or wake in a moment of silence in terror that all have heard their snores.

Second it is by knowing what a person is experiencing, by understanding the way they make sense of a situation, that we can most effectively predict what they will do. It is in subjective experience that we can most often detect the seeds of action yet to come. If we know that this still, intent woman is quietly worrying about the child she left behind at home, we might predict that she will leave before the questions begin.

Third, it is open to question how far we can, in fact, effectively describe behaviour without reference to meaning and to intentions. Scott and Fuller (1965) found this to be the case even in their classic study of genetic influence on the behaviour of dogs. Although they started out by trying to describe the behaviour of the dogs in terms of specific and observable behaviours of a relatively operational kind (e.g. 'scratched', 'walked down field'), they gradually realized that the dogs' actions could only really be described in terms of meaningful *behaviour patterns* (e.g. 'digging a bed in the dirt') even though, these involved ascribing 'intention' to the dogs and required the use of interpretation. It is certainly difficult to describe human actions economically and meaningfully using only concepts of an operational kind and without the use of terms that involve some inference and interpretation. If you doubt this, you might like to observe a simple social interaction sequence and try your hand at this kind of description. You would have to avoid any reference to the feelings and intentions of the participants as these can only be inferred and not specified in terms of observable operations. (See Project I on family observation for an exercise of this kind and where a similar point is made.) Words like 'try', 'pleased', 'happy', 'sad', 'angry' could not be used in their normal sense. Nor could a strictly operational description cope very well with conversation. Although the words might be recorded, the meanings they convey can only be inferred and thus strictly fall outside the notion of observable data.

Well you might manage such a description, though we are inclined to doubt it! And if you did, how much would a description in these terms (e.g. 'Hand raised, takes one pace forward', etc.) convey of what was going on? In the case of almost all social action, behaviour is not nearly as critical an aspect as meaning or intent. The same behaviour pattern may conceal very different social meanings. The vigorous shove that lands you under a passing bus may be an identical piece of behaviour whether it emanates from a careless person in a hurry or from evil Uncle Harry with hopes of your estate!

To effectively investigate human behaviour and experience, then, we must study meanings. We just have to wrestle with their intangibility and the difficulty of studying them as best we can.

In contrast to the positivist approach, there have been a number of influential psychologists who have placed a concern with *meaning* firmly at the centre of their theories. The significance of meaning in Freudian theory is made clear in the set book *Freud and Psychoanalysis* (see especially Chapters 9 and 11). It is true that Freud, no less than Watson, was seeking to build a *science* of human life, as would indeed be expected of someone whose early research was in neuro-physiology. And in his way he is just as deterministic as the behaviourists, just as prone to consider that the only valid explanations of behaviour are those couched in terms of antecedent causes. However, the data upon which he theorizes are bound up with the *meaning* of situations and actions and with the experience of the individual.

George Herbert Mead, who taught at the University of Chicago in the 1920s, was another psychologist who was concerned with the centrality of meanings and intentions. Although Mead writes about 'behaviour' and, like the behaviourists, emphasizes the importance of environmental influence, it is our interpretations of these which he sees as the subject-matter of psychology. Individuals are con-ceived of as acting within a world of meanings which have been generated by the wider context of society and which will determine the way things will be perceived by them. (For a more detailed discussion of Mead, see Unit 4.)

Kelly is another theorist whose work features in this course (see Unit 8) who has seen meaning as central to psychology but who has tried to devise systematic methods of discovering and conceptualizing the ways in which people make sense of themselves and their worlds. Unit 7 also makes clear how a lot of the new research in developmental psychology is essentially directed at exploring how our experience comes to be meaningful and our actions intentional. There, it is pointed out how development is not just a question of acquiring 'behavioural skills', but the gradual creation of a meaningful world of experience in which people are assumed to be capable of initiating their actions and of intending what they do.

It might be worth pausing here and reflecting on what we mean by the concept 'meaning'. It is one of those fuzzy terms which admits of many different defini-tions and uses according to the purpose of the writer. Here are some of the ways in which it may be used.

1   The connotations of an object or action – what other objects or actions it con-jures up or seems to the actor to be naturally associated with. This way of con-ceptualizing meanings is central to Freud's account of symbolization: how dream images symbolize wishes repressed from consciousness, or how objects or situa-tions may come to stand symbolically for early traumatic situations and therefore to elicit apparently inappropriate reactions. It is central also to Mead's account of the world as made up of symbols rather than objects, and to the theory of George Kelly.

2   The function of a set of actions – the linking 'story' which will make sense of them to an outsider or to the actors themselves.

3   The functions and the antecedents of a set of social circumstances – how and why the structures and institutions of society came to be as they are. This is in a sense akin to.2 above, but different in important respects. We are talking not about the 'script' of a person's actions but about the 'stage' and 'set' within which they take place.

4   The expressed intentions or reasons of the actors – what they wish to be seen

as intending to achieve. (This concept is central to Goffman's notion of 'impression management', which you will meet in Unit 10/11.)

5   The conscious experience of intention – what the actor thinks he or she intended to achieve.

6   The overall intentions or reasons of the actors – what they intend to achieve. (This is not necessarily the same as 5 if we accept that there may be meanings which are not accessible to the actor: Freud would say that people often *rationalize* their actions, making *post hoc* and sometimes mistaken sense of them in retrospect.)

7   The world-picture of the individual – what sort of a world he or she thinks this is, and where he or she locates the self within it.

8   The value or fulfilment offered by an experience or situation or life in general, i.e. the meaningfulness which it has for a person. (This is the sense in which meaning is discussed in Part II of Unit 12.)

9   The set of role-expectations implicit in a situation, as when we say that a situation would *mean* something different to a parent than to a teacher, because the actions which would most naturally follow from it are different.

As you can see then the concept of meaning constitutes a somewhat varied and fuzzy set of ideas. At their core lies the human capacity for 'symbolizing' or representing our experience of ourselves and the world (of which language is a prime example): also our capacity to do things with intention (even though we may not necessarily be aware of such intention). How this capacity develops is the theme of Unit 7 and there it is stressed how 'meanings' are not just personal affairs but arise over time through our *interactions* with other people. The meanings they ascribe to our actions and those which we create together by 'implicit negotiation' play an important role. Meaning is very much an interpersonal and cultural (i.e. a product of our society) matter.

If we accept that meaning is at the heart of the subject-matter of social psychology, what implications does this have?

Positivist approaches in psychology have tended to adopt a *nomothetic* position. That is, their aim is to establish, by experiment or other scientific methods, a set of 'laws' which explains why we behave as we do. If meaning is accepted as central, the appropriateness of this aim may be questioned. An action or experience does not exist as a simply observable, objective event. It is constituted by meanings of different kinds. These meanings will vary depending on the perspective of the person making sense of the situation (whether this be the actor him or herself or an observer). It will depend also on the kind of analysis which is made. Each of us is usually able to see several different meanings for the same actions depending on 'which way we look at it'. In the light of these considerations, the search for unequivocal and fundamental explanations in terms of 'causes' might be regarded as misconceived. A different kind of explanation becomes appropriate – one couched in terms of 'reasons' rather than 'causes'. (These issues are discussed further in Paper 8.)

Let us continue, for a moment, our consideration of the nature of explanations found in social psychology, which was begun in Section 3 of Paper 2. The positivist type of explanation is in terms of general laws usually of a *cause-effect* type, i.e. other things being equal, where $X$ occurs, $Y$ will follow. For example, most, if not all, of the principles or laws postulated by behaviourists are of this type. Behaviour is conceptualized as a *response (R)* to a *stimulus (S)*. The task of psychology for the behaviourist is to find out which kind of $S$ (or under what conditions an $S$) produces a particular $R$. Such principles are established by experimentation involving the isolation and manipulation of one stimulus while holding other factors constant, in order to observe its effect.

The difficulty with this cause-effect approach is that any piece of behaviour is (like any other event) the product of a whole complex of factors and the way these interact (influences which, in the case of behaviour, have their source both within the organism and outside it). The effect of a factor may be very different in one context than in another. An alternative approach which goes some way to overcoming this limitation of the cause-effect approach is to explain in terms of key structures or processes; in particular the way these develop and their functions and origins. Piaget's theory, which is discussed in depth in Unit 4, is of this *structural/functional* type and so, to a certain extent, is psychoanalysis.

There is a third approach which takes into account the key point of this paper – that meaning is central to social behaviour and experience. This presents a rather different kind of understanding in terms of beliefs, feelings, intentions and reasons. It is what John Shotter (1974) has called a *personal* approach to human affairs. He distinguishes between the three kinds of explanations as follows:

> ... At the moment psychological theory is deeply divided between at least three major schools of thought.
>
> One school believes that man's behaviour can be accounted for within a mechanistic conception or its equivalent (e.g. Sutherland, 1970; Broadbent, 1971; Skinner, 1953, 1972). For them, man consists of a number of objective parts, which, because they are thought to retain their character unchanged irrespective of their context of existence, can be investigated in isolation from the totality in which they play their part. The task of these workers is to discover the natural laws thought to be governing the behaviour of the parts, and from this knowledge plus a knowledge of the relations between the parts, infer man's total functioning. The second school, however, believes a more holistic, organismic (v. Bertalanffy, 1952, 1968) or a more biological approach (Piaget, 1971, 1972) is required. They feel that as man is an entity which grows itself, so to speak, it cannot consist of distinct parts like a machine at all. At any one moment in time, man's parts owe not just their character but their very existence, not only to one another, but to his parts at some earlier point in time – they have grown from them, and a temporal as well as a spatial, a historical as well as a logical aspect characterizes their interdependence. It is the task of this school, given the logical structure of the ends towards which organisms develop, to account for the developmental processes involved in attaining them.
>
> This is a far richer approach than the first. Piaget's constructive structural approach does what Sutherland's and Broadbent's simple mechanistic approach cannot: it makes the *construction* of 'mechanisms' within the organism a possibility, for mechanisms as such cannot be made to construct themselves. Organisms may be thought of as constructing 'mechanisms' within themselves during the course of growth – *viz.*, Piaget's 'formal operations' stage, where contingent relations finally make way for necessary ones. However, while these approaches may make the construction of mechanisms intelligible, neither can give an adequate account of *meaning*, an account of when, where, how and why a particular 'mechanism' is *used* in the co-ordination of one organism's behaviour with another's. Neither this school nor the mechanistic one treats the *social sphere* realistically: They make no mention of how the *source* of an action is ascertained and how the attribution of responsibility for it influences subsequent action; they make no distinction between what a person *does* and what merely happens to or within him. Yet, I shall argue, this is of fundamental importance in human affairs: it is just because a mother can (or not, as she so chooses) treat her child's actions as if 'he' were responsible for them that she can influence his development in the way that she does (see Ryan, 1974) ...
>
> Because of the above and other deficiencies in the social sphere an even richer approach than the structuralist one seems called for. A third school, to which I assign myself, feels that nothing less than a *personal* approach to human affairs is adequate. However, in taking this approach, psychology is

removed from the realm of the natural sciences and is placed among the moral sciences. This alters its character entirely. Most importantly it becomes concerned with *negotiations,* with negotiations between people rather than with interactions between things. Values, opinions, beliefs, feelings, intentions, etc., once again assume a crucial role in human affairs. While classical science demands that everything be studied ultimately as if it were matter in motion according to an absent God's pre-established laws, *persons* seem able on occasions to act from a belief, a mere *conception* of a law, thus, apparently, exempting themselves from this demand. And in attempting to live thus, according to the conception of a law, people may fail; they may act inappropriately, rightly or wrongly, legitimately or illegitimately, etc., for conceptions decree only what *should* or *might be* the case, not what is. Attempting to live according to laws inevitably involves the judgement of other people.

This, then, I shall take as a basic fact of life: that *people* living in relation to one another co-ordinate their affairs in terms of concepts. And what it is for people to conduct their affairs in a rational and responsible manner is for them to direct their behaviour towards the attainment of socially constructed and established goals, sensing and correcting deviations from this task in the course of their behaviour – constructing its own goals in this way is something no other species of animals can do. Man's social life is essentially a moral affair. And it's no use hoping, as many psychologists do, to replace the essentially moral practices regulating human affairs with 'natural' principles. . .

(Shotter, 1974, pp. 216–18).

If we accept the significance of meaning for social psychology as argued in this paper, Shotter's emphasis on the need for a *personal* approach would seem justified. As Shotter puts it, '*people* living in relation to one another co-ordinate their affairs in terms of concepts'. The ways in which we conceptualize situations and ourselves are a major influence on what we do. In the process of growing up we evolve a concept of self, of what we are and of what we should and should not do. We learn ways of behaving in specific social situations. We expect and are expected to behave differently in church, while shopping, at a party or at a business meeting. The institutions and role relationships of our society each carry with them their own prescriptions. Whether we go to the library to borrow a book, buy a drink from a pub, play a game of soccer, get married or buy a car, there are conventions governing the ways we should act. Such conventions may be often unvoiced and implicit but they affect us nevertheless. The meaning of actions can often be determined only in relation to them. What does 'offside' mean, or 'jilt' unless we know the conventions of soccer or courtship? It is important to note that such rules are social, they vary from culture to culture. They are matters of convention not laws of nature. So Shotter argues that psychology is essentially a 'moral' rather than a 'natural' science. It is concerned with 'negotiations between people rather than with interactions between things'. If one accepts that meaning is at the heart of much of human behaviour and experience, the problem of explanation in social psychology takes on a different character than it has in the physical and biological sciences. There is a certain immutability about physical processes. The nature of biological processes changes very slowly as a function of evolution. In contrast, awareness and concepts are a product of cultural evolution and individual development. They vary as a function of historical, cultural and personal contact. In this sense, human beings collectively and individually 'make themselves' and they can do so in an infinite variety of ways. It is by no means possible, therefore, to assume that an explanation which applies in the case of one person can be generalized in the same way as one instance of a biological or physical process can be generalized to another.

ACTIVITY

You might like to apply the three-fold classification of kinds of explanation discussed above to the five explanations of the child's misbehaviour which were given as examples in Section 3 of Metablock Paper 2 (pp. 63–6). For suggested answers see the end of the paper (top of p. 92).

Understanding meanings requires not so much a nomothetic approach (i.e. concern with establishing laws) but a *hermeneutic* one. This is outlined in Chapter 11 of the set book *Freud and Psychoanalysis* (see especially pp. 119–21). Essentially it involves *interpretation* of the meanings, uncovering the significance and implications of actions and social situations for the people involved both at a conscious and unconscious level and within the shared conventions of their culture. A hermeneutic approach would also involve exploring the *source* of such meanings as to how they are developed and maintained through our interactions with others.

The points made about meaning and the hermeneutic approach in Chapter 11 'The significance of meaning' in *Freud and Psychoanalysis* apply not just to psychoanalysis itself but to any approach which regards meaning as its central subject matter. There are formidable methodological problems. Meaning is not easy to measure or to subject to formal analysis. Nor is it straightforward to validate interpretations. Although ingenious methods have been devised for investigating meanings (see Kelly's repertory grid method for example) the emphasis of hermeneutic approaches tends to be on differentiated description rather than the testing of precise hypotheses. (See Paper 2, Section 5 and Paper 8.)

You will find then something of a split in psychology. On the one hand, there are those who are attracted by the rigorous testability of the methods of the natural sciences, assuming (and perhaps without justification) that they are the most appropriate to use with the subject-matter of psychology also. On the other hand there are those who, regardless of the methodological problems involved, prefer to attempt to investigate meanings. Yet other theorists fall somewhere between the two. As the setbook *(Freud and Psychoanalysis)* argues, a fundamental tension in Freudian theory is that it sets out to formulate fundamental laws of human behaviour while at the same time adopting an essentially hermeneutic approach in its practice.

It might be argued that if meaning is central, no approach which ignores or cannot accommodate it could have relevance to social psychology. In fact, many (if not most) systematic investigations of human behaviour have taken a positivist stance and most social psychologists would argue that such studies have many useful insights to offer. As this course is an introduction to social psychology, you will find both positions represented. Later, you can decide for yourself which approach seems likely to be most fruitful in the task of understanding social behaviour: or alternatively whether the two approaches are best regarded not as mutually exclusive but as complementing each other. (See Paper 8 for further discussion of related issues from a somewhat different perspective.)

### References

SCOTT, J. P. and FULLER, J. L. (1968) *Genetics and the social behaviour of the dog*, Chicago, University of Chicago Press.

SHOTTER, J. (1974) 'The development of personal powers' in Richards (ed) (1974) *The integration of a child into a social world*, London, Cambridge University Press, pp. 215–24.

SKINNER, B. F. (1973) *Beyond freedom and dignity*, Harmondsworth, Penguin.

*Suggested answer for activity on p. 91*
I would suggest that the explanations given are best classified as follows:

Learning theory — cause–effect.

Psychoanalytic — mixed but largely structural–functional (e.g. 'unresolved conflicts') and hermeneutic (focus on unconscious meaning of behaviour).

Phenomenological — hermeneutic (it investigates the meaning of the situation for the child).

Biologically based — cause–effect.

Sociological — hermeneutic (it is concerned with the cultural significance of the behaviour and the origins of this). (N.B. – This refers to this particular example of sociological-type explanation. In sociology it is possible also to find approaches of a positivist kind).

## Paper 6: Research methods

*by Roger Sapsford*

This is a paper about 'facts' and how we find them out. I put the word 'facts' in inverted commas because facts are not simple things like cabbages, to be harvested in due season; although facts are the test of theories, they are also the product of theories, because what we see as researchers is crucially determined by the theories we hold and the 'models of the person' which they express. (This statement is as true in everyday life as it is in research – Kelly's 'man the scientist' sees the world and acts in it only by virtue of a pre-existing construct system.) You have been faced with very many examples of research in D307, and this paper aims to give you criteria by which to judge whether they offer good, indifferent or poor evidence for the theories which they are said to support. More important, it aims to give you a framework within which to judge your own research work in the D307 projects and to help you diagnose and eliminate faults in your own procedures.

**survey** Let us begin with one style of research with which we are all familiar, the survey. The survey aims to *describe* a population in terms of pretheorized variables – things we already know we want to know. If we want, for example, to know the views of workers in a particular factory about an aspect of their work, one simple way of finding out would be to devise questions about it and go out and ask them of every single person in the factory. Alternatively, we might want to observe all the employees at their work and see how they actually react to it, counting categories of behaviour which we have decided tell us something about their views – systematic observation projects are surveys. This kind of research design **census** – looking at every member of the population under study – is called a 'census'; the best-known example is the population census which is undertaken every ten years in Britain and is aimed at reaching every member of the population of the United Kingdom.

Few studies use the census method, however, because it is incredibly costly to reach every member of a large population. In studies of child development, for example, no attempt whatsoever is made to observe every child in the country. **sample survey** Instead, we take a *sample* and hope to be able to generalize, from the results of that survey, facts about the whole population – we look at a sample of perhaps a hundred or two hundred or a thousand children. One major technology of surveys is associated with sampling – trying to achieve samples which are truly representative of the population (to use a technical term, trying to achieve **population validity** *population validity*). A good sample would be reasonably large and selected **random sampling** randomly from the population, with every member of the population having an equal, non-zero probability of being selected for the sample. Where we know something about the population under study we can do even better, constructing **stratified random sampling** what is called a *stratified random* sample; we specify groups of the population ('strata') according to variables which we suspect may be important, and sample

92

randomly within each group. For example, we might specify sex and race as criteria for stratification and draw random samples of white men, white women, black men, black women, Asian men, Asian women, and so on. This way we can make sure that we have enough of each group to draw reasonable conclusions even where the groups are very rare in the general population. Given random selection (within strata, if relevant and possible) statistical calculations can be made to specify the range of error within which the results for the sample can be generalized to the population. (We have not troubled you with such calculations in D307, as you are not required to carry out a survey yourself; however you may encounter them in several other Open University courses.)

The second great technology of the survey is aimed at validity and reliability of measurement. If we are to describe the distribution of variable $X$ in the population, then it is crucially important that we have a valid and reliable measure of $X$. (As we shall see, *all* researchers who measure have to put a good deal of effort into establishing validity and reliability; these problems are not confined to survey research.) To the extent that what we set out to measure is a stable and **reliability** consistent characteristic of the population, we need a *reliable* method to measure it stably and consistently, so that the tests we apply or the questions we ask could be applied to the same population at a different time and by a different researcher and give the same results; a yardstick is not much use if it measures a given distance as 2 feet for me and 2 feet 3 inches for you, or if it gives me three different readings if I use it to measure the length of the same object three times. (Note, however, George Kelly's tongue-in-check definition of reliability as 'that characteristic of a test which measures its insensitivity to change'.)

**validity of measurement** Given that a yardstick is reliable, we can then ask whether it produces *valid* measurements. Are we indeed measuring intelligence as a whole, if that is what we want to measure, or does our test actually measure verbal ability, or even **operationalization** ability at doing paper-and-pencil tests? Have we, in other words, *operationalized* our concept correctly? And this in turn, of course, depends on having a clearly defined concept which can be operationalized.

The point is that we can only measure directly what is immediately and openly observable, but that we wish to use these measurements as evidence for the presence or absence of traits, qualities or factors whose presence or absence can only be inferred. Let us say that we are doing research into 'intelligence', which is a researcher's hypothetical concept, an *un*observable fact about a person. We set out to observe it nonetheless by 'diagnosing' (inferring) intelligence from whether or not the person appears to behave intelligently or to make intelligent remarks or to have the ability to do certain tasks which we would theorize as needing intelligence for their completion. Our measure would be validated if it correctly predicted performance, or if it correlated with other measures which are already accepted as good indicators of intelligence, or in a whole range of ways which it is beyond the scope of this paper to list in detail. Much of the argument about what is measured in a survey (and other) kinds of research centre around whether or not the researcher has managed to establish, to the satisfaction of his or her critics, that the things which were measured actually do bear a logical relationship to the things (generally unobservable) which the researcher's theories say they do. (The technical term for using correct logic in the design of a **internal validity** study, so that the conclusions do indeed follow as they are supposed to, is *internal validity*. As we shall see, validity of measurement is only one aspect of it.)

The strengths of the survey at its best are high population validity and high validity and reliability of measurement. Its main weakness is the risk of low internal validity for any 'causal' conclusions that may be drawn from it. The pure survey, quite simply, constitutes a weak form of argument. Typically, one notes in surveys that certain variables are consistently correlated or associated (e.g. smoking and the incidence of lung cancer), but it is an old and obvious maxim of survey researchers that *correlation does not necessarily imply causation*. Height and intelligence, for example, are slightly but significantly correlated in the population, but that does not mean that either causes the other. A more plausible alternative explanation is that the occupations of one's parents is correlated with both, and is in turn correlated with income and dietary habits which allow an environment more conducive to development of potential. There is said to be an area of Germany where the number of storks observable is correlated with the number of babies born, but one doubts that either causes the other; a more plausible alternative explanation is climatic conditions – which can be shown to affect the mating behaviour of stork and man alike. Showing that two variables are associated in a population is only one step on the way to showing that either is causally related to the other. To establish a causal relationship you then have to demonstrate that there is no other, equally plausible, explanation for the correlation.

No full-blown surveys are provided among the course projects for you to do – you do not have the time to carry out extensive interviewing or observation. However, at least one of the projects does have elements of the survey about it: the Diary Project (which comes from a series of research studies which used fairly large numbers of subjects) involves the systematic collection of data in questionnaire format.

---

For an extended example of survey research in this course, see the study of political socialization by Himmelweit *et al.* described in Block 5 and the associated Set Book *How Voters Decide*. Block 5 also describes some of the ways in which survey researchers have tried to get around the problem of inferring causes from correlations (e.g. by path analysis) and some of the problems which have to be tackled in measuring attitudes.

---

**experiment**

The core of research into causal relationships is, of course, the *experiment*. Although you are not required actually to *do* any true experimentation in this course, you meet the results of experiments throughout the course (and particularly in Blocks 3 and 6), and the mother/child interaction project is treated like the early stages of a natural experiment. Although precise and valid measurement is quite as important in the experiment as in survey research, the great strength of the good experimental design is its internal validity – the rigour with which effects can be deduced from causes. Correlation does not necessarily imply causation because it is always possible to propose alternative explanations for what is observed; the whole point of experimental design is to control and eliminate these alternatives, until only the researcher's explanation remains as a possibility.

*correlation does not necessarily mean causation / experimental conditions to remove any possible alternatives*

Let us take a mythical new toothpaste as a trite but simple example:

1  If we just get people to use the toothpaste and see what their teeth are like afterwards, there is nothing we can logically conclude from our measurements.

2  So the minimum information we need is a measurement of the condition of their teeth before using the toothpaste and after using it, so that we can at least establish if there has been a change. (Comparison between two conditions that differ in one specified and essential element is fundamental to experimental method).

3  But any observed improvements might just as easily have happened because the people taking part in the experiment changed spontaneously over time, irrespective of what toothpaste was used (perhaps there is 'spontaneous remis-

**control group**
**maturation effects**

sion of tooth decay'), so we need a 'control group', a second and similar (ideally, identical!) sample who do not use the toothpaste, as a control for *maturation effects*. (If we want to be able to claim that the new toothpaste is better than the old ones, we shall need further groups that use other kinds of toothpaste.)

4   We cannot leave the choice of people for these groups to the experimenter; he or she might unconsciously (or consciously, even) pick the people most likely to improve for the 'experimental' group who try the new toothpaste. We also want to make sure that our two (or many) groups are not so dissimilar from each other that their dissimilarity could provide an alternative explanation; we do not want, for example, all women in one group and all men in another. Normally, allocation to experimental and control groups proceeds in two stages: (a) we split up the total sample into groups by the variables we know or believe to be important – the condition of their teeth and perhaps sex, age and social class; (b) we take each of these groups (e.g. 'middle class males aged thirty plus with bad teeth') and allocate its members randomly to either the experimental or control group. The matching by characteristics takes care of variables about which we know, and the random allocation makes it likely that any other variable which might turn out to be important is randomly distributed between the groups.

**history effects**   5   One of these 'other variables' which is particularly important is the possibility of *history effects* – the possibility that any observed changes are due to idiosyncratic events in the lives of the subjects. This is why we matched by age, sex and class in the example above – it seems intuitively likely that people of the same age, sex and class are most likely to have the same kind of experiences. Randomization should, with luck, distribute the rest of the unpredictable events equally between the groups. (In the true or laboratory experiment the environment would be controlled, so that both groups had the same history during the experiment. The toothpaste example, however, would almost certainly be a 'field experiment', occurring in the subject's 'real world', where such control is not feasible.)

6   Finally, we would control every other aspect of the situation which might affect the result. Perhaps the most important among these is the possibility that the experimenter may affect the results of the experiment, so we would probably isolate the experimenter from the subjects, or use the same experimenter for both groups. A really elaborate design would probably include a 'double-blind- component – neither experimenter nor subjects would know which was the experimental group and which the control group – so that the situation would be the same for both groups in that respect.

The strengths of experiments are apparent; their weaknesses, in ascending order of importance, are:

(a)   *Generally, low population validity*. This is not a *necessary* characteristic of experiments – it would be possible, in theory, to use the sampling technology of surveys to select representative subjects – but in practice most experiments are conducted on small, potentially unrepresentative groups of people. Very many experiments are carried out on small groups of students for example – because they are easily available – and no one has ever claimed that students are typical of the rest of the population.

(b)   *Inapplicability to certain kinds of research problem*. It is not possible to allocate people at random, for instance, to one sex or the other or to a social class, and therefore experiments for which these are key independent variables can never be used as a control for history effects – inevitably the subjects carry with them every aspect of sex or class, and these are confounded in the design.

(c)   The experiment – and, for that matter, the survey – tends to trivialize the area of study in the interest of reliable and precise measurement. We might want to investigate anxiety but we may finish up measuring responses to questions like 'Do you sweat a lot?'. We might want to investigate learning, but we may finish up with the causes of button-pushing in a laboratory. We might want to investigate conformity, but we may finish up looking at whether people agree on the length of lines. The art of experimentation is simplification without trivialization.

**ecological validity**   (d)   Low *ecological validity* – that is, poor generalizability from the immediate research situation. The laboratory is an entirely artificial setting and even field experiments (set outside the laboratory) are a particular type of social situation which may have different rules from those of ordinary life. Our ability to generalize from experiments to what people ordinarily do from day to day is therefore severely limited.

---

For examples of laboratory experiments, see the Latané studies in Box 16 of Block 6, and for examples of experiments 'in the field' see Newcombe (1952) and Siegel and Siegel (1957), in Boxes 2 and 3 of Block 6.

---

**quasi-experiment**
One way which has been advocated for retaining some of the strengths of the 'true' experiment while overcoming some of its weaknesses is the use of the 'natural' experiment or *quasi-experiment*. It is often possible to find events or situations in the real world which have some of the properties of an experiment – and, particularly, situations which embody a 'natural' experimental group and a control group. Social researchers have, for example, studied the effects of changes in motoring laws or police practice by comparing accident-rates in countries where the law or practice has been changed with countries where it has remained the same. Social researchers studied the effects of television on the viewer, in the early days of television in this country, by comparing areas where television *could* be received with areas where it *could not*. At their best, such studies display a considerable degree of the logic of experimentation: an experimental and a control group, an 'experimental manipulation' – the change in law or practice, or the introduction of television – and measurement before and after the change (or lack of change) for both groups. However, the logic is always imperfect because subjects are not randomly allocated to the groups. One cannot say that any observed difference between experimental and control group is unambiguously due to the experimental manipulation; it could be due to some other event which happened during the same time. (Note the relevance of this discussion for the mother/child interaction project.)

It is worth noting that most uses of surveys are based on the same logic of experiments or quasi-experiments: they are used to contrast differing groups (e.g. smokers and non-smokers) on some 'naturally occurring' variable. Conversely, some studies which purport to be experiments and occur in laboratories are actually nearer to quasi-experiments. Laboratory studies which explore sex-differences in performance, for example, are unable to allocate subjects randomly to one sex or the other, and their results may often, therefore, be explainable by some variable other than just the sex of the subject – differential behaviour of the experimenter, for example.

**Validity and reactivity**

Pausing to summarize, we have come across two broad criteria by which quantitative or scientific social research may be judged:

**internal validity**
1 Internal validity – the extent to which the researcher's findings and conclusions are consistent with the claims s/he makes on the basis of her/his theory, and cannot be explained away as the outcome of some other factor(s). Within this broad class we have distinguished the logic of experimental (or survey) *design* – to exclude alternative explanations by making sure the research is designed to exclude them – and validity of *measurement*, the extent to which we can demonstrate that the thing we set out to measure actually was measured in the research, rather than something else.

**external validity**
2 External validity – the general name for the extent to which the results of a piece of research can be generalized. We have mentioned two kinds of external validity – *population validity* the extent to which we can generalize from the research subjects to people in general; and *ecological validity*, the extent to which we can generalize from the research situation to the situations of everyday life.

**reactivity**
Two further technical terms may usefully be introduced at this stage – *personal reactivity* and *procedural reactivity*. These come from a quite different research tradition from the ones we have met so far. The concepts of reliability and

validity come originally from the tradition of positivism; although there are few positivists left in social psychology, the terms still suggest at root that 'facts' are somehow 'out there' waiting to be measured and that the main problem is to get at them in an effective and logical manner, free from personal bias and accidental confusion. More 'qualitative' or 'ethnographic' or 'hermeneutic' traditions, however, would take a different line. (The word 'ethnographic' simply means 'describing people' and 'hermeneutic' means 'interpreting something' – a text, for example.) These traditions have a model of the person as an interpreter of meanings in interaction with others, and they would say that all 'facts' are potentially specific to the way they are gathered. In ordinary life people shape what they say to us, and indeed what they think in certain circumstances, to fit what they think we are – George Kelly's point again, that we see the world through our constructs. Similarly, however, they can interpret *themselves* largely by how others seem to behave towards them, so no interaction can possibly be one-sided. Moreover, what the researcher understands from his or her research is not something *seen* but something constructed – we *construct* the world, as researchers as much as in our everyday lives. The questions an ethnographer would ask of a piece of research, therefore, are:

How did the person who carried out the research affect what was learned, by action or by interpretation (personal reactivity), and how did the constraints of the situation determine what was learned (procedural reactivity)? Ethnographers would put little faith in the results of experiments or standardized surveys, not because they doubt their logic but because they doubt whether these artificial situations have any bearing on what happens in 'real life'.

**qualitative research**

**ethnographic research**

'Qualitative' or 'ethnographic' research techniques have almost the exact opposite aims from those of experiments or surveys – they are aimed at overcoming what are perceived as the weaknesses of the 'scientific' approach. Ethnographers attack experiments and surveys for their artificiality and oversimplification, their tendency to trivialize and to force researchers' abstractions onto situations at the expense of explanations which might make better sense of them. In general, they see quantitative research as missing the point in the process of building scientific theories.

The ethnographer's aim, is to make research *naturalistic* – to disturb the situation as little as possible – and to examine the *whole* situation, concentrating on the full complexity of the many ways in which the actors interpret and describe their own world and the nature of what they unknowingly take for granted. They would acknowledge that both of these ideal goals are not achievable even in theory. The former requires the researcher to have no effect on the environment, but he or she must also be a part of it and therefore *must* change the situation – what is experienced is inevitably a product of negotiation between the researcher and the people he or she is describing. Similarly, the latter goal requires the researcher simultaneously to be immersed in the setting (to be able to understand it from the actor's perspective) and to be external to it, so that the 'taken for granted' elements are not taken for granted by the researcher as well. Nonetheless, it is these goals which shape this kind of research.

**participant observation**

The classic method of ethnographic research is covert participant observation, where the researcher becomes or passes as a participator in the setting, without other actors knowing that he or she *is* a researcher. Thus the student of factories becomes a factory worker, the student of gangs becomes a gang member and the student of homosexuals finds a role in homosexual society. (One very famous study of this type carried out by psychologists is *When Prophecy Fails,* in which several of Leon Festinger's research students joined an 'end of the world' movement to see what happened when the world, in fact, failed to come to an end – see Unit 16). The researcher makes copious notes on what he or she sees and hears, trying to 'move around' in the setting in order to gain different perspectives on it and thus become, in fact, better informed than any individual actor in the setting, but also examining his own experiences and what happens to him. Overt research may also be conducted, with the researcher identifying himself as a researcher and telling participants what the research is about. While this has the

*[handwritten margin notes: ethnographic – describing people; hermeneutic – interpreting something]*

disadvantage that the researcher makes a distinct impact on the setting it also has the advantage that the researcher can go to places and ask questions which would not be possible for the 'under cover' participant.

**unstructured interviewing**
Another more reactive, but more economical method is the informal or unstructured interview, in which the interviewer may slant the conversation in directions which he or she finds interesting, but is primarily concerned to obtain the participants' own accounts and to let them talk about what seems to be important to *them*. Ethnographic interviews range from full 'life histories' collected over months of interviewing to interviews of only an hour or two, centred around a particular topic. The former gives a deeper understanding of a particular informant and lets the interviewer 'enter' his or her life to some extent. The latter is inevitably more superficial but allows more participants to be included in the research.

Both the strengths and weaknesses of this kind of research must be apparent from the above account. The great strength of the research is its high ecological validity and the extent to which it is able to avoid procedural reactivity by its emphasis on naturalism. Its weaknesses are low population validity – as a method it is highly labour-intensive and not many people and settings can be reached in a given research programme – and its low internal validity. The ethnographic researcher can never say '*X* led to *Y*' but only, '*My interpretation of what I observed or elicited* is that *X* led to *Y*'.

However, within this limitation (which the ethnographers would say is true for *any* style of research), ethnography has its own ways of trying to provide rigour and therefore increase internal validity. The well designed ethnographic project does not consist just of a series of extended chats or a busman's holiday in an unfamiliar setting, but should fall into three phases with different aims (though in practice the phases will overlap and blur into each other):

**progressive focusing**
1  Initial exploration: the researcher goes into the setting, or finds a theoretically interesting group to interview, and 'feels his or her way' towards a picture or model of what is going on. Starting with broad interests and as open a mind as possible, he or she works gradually by *progressive focusing* to a 'story' or set of categories and relationships which appear to make consistent sense – always being open to negative instances and falsifying evidence which may force a change of model.

**theoretical sampling**
2  Model development: having come to a tentative model of what is going on, the researcher then goes on to develop it and make it more precise by a process of *theoretical sampling*. Two kinds of new setting or informant are explored: those which should resemble the original one according to the tentative theory, and those which should differ from it in known ways. This enables one to refine the tentative model and establish the boundary of the category for which it is appropriate.

**analytic induction**
3  Finally (sometimes – few projects proceed this far), comes the stage of testing, by a process known as *analytic induction* – a systematic search for falsifying information.

Two qualitative research projects are 'on offer' in this course. The first, the Interview Project, is a straightforward piece of ethnographic interviewing – insofar as ethnographic interviewing is ever quite straightforward! You will not have the time or scope in this to do much more than begin the process of progressive focusing towards a tentative model, but sufficient data should be generated to allow some small degree of testing at the boundaries of the model. The second is the Kelly Project. It may seem strange to label something as ethnographic which works by numerical analysis on a computer, but the Kelly Role Repertory Grid is as ethnographic in its original conception as one would expect from one of the founders of the interpretative side of modern social psychology. The Kelly Project provides an in-depth analysis of one person, or a comparison of two, with the aim of building an understanding of how this person(s) sees and acts in the world. Fewer data are generated than in interview – any given grid is at best a very small sample from the respondent's world – but in an interview the grid and the computer between them are able to 'ask questions' which with a live interviewer would be totally confounded by personal reactivity. The likelihood of procedural reactivity is high – filling in the grid is a very 'unnatural' activity. This, however, is the price which has to be paid for possible access to the judgements we made about the world but are seldom able or willing to put into words for others.

### History, geography and the 'armchair' researcher

Psychology is mostly an empirical discipline. That is, it builds its theories around how people think or experience or behave (with all the qualifications which are continually made in this course about how what we 'observe' is a construction of the observer, not a simple 'discovery'), and it continually checks and refines its theories against the behaviour and experience of people. However, some topics of central importance to social psychology are not amenable to empirical research in any simple way. If, for example, we are investigating the taken-for-granted ideology of our society and how it impinges on the life of individuals, we cannot readily find people who do not subscribe to the ideology, because *everyone* is affected by it in some way. Similarly, if we want to look at the effect of broad social structures – how families are organized, for example – we cannot find people who are not affected by them; even those who have 'opted out' and joined communes were themselves generally brought up in nuclear families, and they live in a society which treats the nuclear family as 'normal'. In these circumstances, you will often find that theory-building includes a fair amount of armchair speculation. Psychologists will ask themselves what it might be like if the world were different – what kind of a world would it be if men and women were treated equally, or if there were no genders at all? – and from their tentative answers try to tease out the essential taken-for-granted features of the current situation.

**thought experiment**  This (valuable) activity is sometimes dignified with the name of *thought experiment* – an attempt to 'do an experiment' in the head and without leaving the armchair – but it obviously lacks the experiment's status as evidence.

Even here it is sometimes possible to use quasi-experimental methods and found one's speculation on empirical data, by looking at what has happened in different places or at different times. In Block 1 we looked at how families are organized in non-Western cultures, for example, to explore the question of how necessary and inevitable the nuclear family actually is as an institution. In Block 2 we looked briefly at the history of how children have been viewed within our own culture, to discover that 'childhood' as currently understood is actually a rather recent social invention. This kind of comparison is becoming a more and more important tool of the social psychologist. However, one should note that questions of reliability and validity still apply – the data on which the comparison is based are still well or badly collected by someone and valid or less valid as measures of what we want to measure – and that the difficulties of understanding another culture or another period are at least as great as the difficulties of understanding our own.

### Index of concepts

| | |
|---|---|
| analytic induction | population validity |
| census | progressive focusing |
| control group | random sampling |
| ecological validity | reactivity |
| ethnographic research | reliability |
| external validity | sample survey |
| history effects | stratified random sampling |
| internal validity | theoretical sampling |
| maturation effects | 'thought experiment' |
| operationalization | unstructured interviewing |
| participant observation | validity of measurement |

## Paper 7: The construction of reality

*by Richard Stevens and Roger Sapsford*

A theme which is constantly reiterated throughout the course in different forms and guises is the idea that 'reality' does not exist 'out there' for us to discover but, rather, each of us is actively constructing or creating our awareness of it. Such constructions are the only reality we have access to. Our particular ways of constructing reality evolve over time through our lives and are a function of our particular patterns of experience and interactions with others. Because much of experience is common to all of us, there will be overlap between our reality constructions. (Indeed if there were not, much of social life would be impossible.) But there will also be considerable variation from individual to individual and culture to culture.

This idea that reality is constructed rather than given is found in three related forms in the course. Firstly, there are those theories (like personal construct theory) which focus on analysing and understanding the way an individual constructs his or her *personal reality*. Secondly, there is the question of *social reality*: people in the same society often share a similar consciousness and way of looking at the world ('collective representations'). The sources of such constructions can sometimes be traced in historical, economic and social conditions. Finally, there is the question of the construction of one particular form of awareness – *social psychological theories* themselves. Similarly, it is possible to some extent to relate these to the personal and social background of the theorists concerned.

### The personal construction of reality

The most obvious sense in which we ourselves construct our reality is that what we are able to perceive is a product of the nature and limits of our *senses*. There are many aspects of the world about us to which we have no direct access: information which, equipped only with your normal senses, you *cannot* perceive – for example, high-pitched tones which could be heard by a child or a dog but not by you, electro-magnetic radiation outside the visible spectrum, X-rays, heat patterns, signals emitted by innumerable radio stations.

The ways in which we make sense of our world depends by no means only on the characteristics of our senses. It is limited and shaped also by the *concepts* we have at our disposal. If I do not have a word or way for expressing something, that particular feature of my world may be far less salient to me. The way we construct our realities depends too on what aspects of experience we pick out as significant. In almost every situation there are a mass of 'cues' available – far more than we can assimilate at any one time. As I now look round the study where I am writing, I become aware of a hairlike, convoluted crack along a wall, a mark above a picture, a curtain ring slipped off the rail, a curious pattern in the carpet. I have used this room on innumerable occasions yet there are still things here I have not noticed before. We select, focusing on the functional, the familiar and the meaningful. (See Box 1.)

---

**Box 1  Language and the construction of reality**

The linguist Benjamin Whorf was most interested in the way the language we use both reflects and, he would claim, helps to construct the way we perceive reality. The eskimo, he points out, has several words to define different forms of snow whereas we have only one. Such a way of constructing reality is functionally relevant to the eskimo way of life and the concepts he has available make such distinctions more possible.

---

In everyday life, we are continually 'making sense' of events around us, of other people's behaviour and of our own feelings and experiences. Usually, our 'making sense' of these things consists merely of our implicit awareness that things are fitting together as they should. We have expectations; we assume that people will behave in particular kinds of ways; we have implicit theories about how and why people act in the ways that they do. It may take some effort to spell these theories out and it is difficult for us to describe explicitly what they are. We catch glimpses of them, for example, when some event occurs or when we have to explain something. Then, there may be partial articulation of the assumptions and theories we hold. It is also sometimes possible to infer them from the kinds of predictions we make and the expectations we have.

Each of us has a whole range of implicit theories which differ, not only in kind but in degree of *specificity*. Many are likely to be restricted in scope, applying only to specific situations or linking together specific attributes. A high-domed forehead, for example, may increase our expectation that the owner of the forehead will be intelligent. Other implicit theories may be of greater generality and related to a pattern or complex of characteristics. For example, we may assume that behaving in a friendly way towards people is likely to generate a friendly response. Or that children brought up without sufficient discipline are more likely to become delinquent.

Some of the implicit theories upon which we draw for our constructions of reality may be contradictory. Social situations are complex and many factors may influence their outcome so that what works in one situation may not in another. Proverbs reflect, in symbolic form, some of the implicit theories of a culture. Because of their generality, it is often possible to find seemingly contradictory statements made by different proverbs, for example 'Absence makes the heart grow fonder' and 'Out of sight, out of mind'. You will probably be able to think of many more. Each proverb has its own validity in certain circumstances, but not in all.

Through observation and action, we are continually testing our personal implicit theories and, as a result, they may be modified. We may observe, for example, that the last three people with high foreheads we met seemed to be more stupid than average, so we give up the theory or at least drop our expectation to a much lower level of probability. Or we may hedge a theory with qualifications, so that it applies only in certain prescribed conditions. For example, we begin to realize that friendly behaviour will not be reciprocated by all people; suspicious persons may remain on their guard. The expectations and opinions of others are also likely to play an influential role in the development of our implicit theories. Thus if a couple of close friends laugh at the idea that people with red hair are more predisposed to anger than those with blonde hair, then we may begin to lose faith in the theory. Neither the theory nor the testing of its validity is explicit or definitive, of course. Also, because our theories themselves filter and influence what we see, evidence which runs counter to them may often be ignored or reinterpreted. But over time, with experience and with education, we may gradually come to change the ways in which we construct our realities.

Several social psychologists have come independently to the concept of what we might call *the personal construction of reality* and developed it in a variety of directions. One aspect is dealt with in the course in some depth in Block 3. This concerns the way we perceive other people, form impressions of them and attribute characteristics and responsibility to them. As another approach to the personal construction of reality the humanistic therapist Carl Rogers has stressed the interpreting person as the centre and definer of his or her own reality, right or wrong:

> Every individual exists in a continually changing world of experience of which he is the centre. . . The world of experience is for each individual, in a very significant sense, a private world. The organism reacts to the field as it is experienced and perceived. This perceptual field is, for the individual, 'reality'. . . The world comes to be composed of a series of tested hypotheses

which provide much security. Yet mingled with these . . . are perceptions which remain completely unchecked. These untested perceptions are also a part of our personal reality, and may have as much authority as those which have been checked.

(Rogers, 1951, pp. 483–6)

The ideas of George Kelly are also directly concerned with the way we construe our personal realities. For all people, Kelly would say, the world in which they live is not simply *experienced*; rather, it is actively *constructed* by the perceiver. That is, we cannot make sense of what we see except in the light of our pre-existing *theories* about the world, and we cannot respond to the world unless we can make sense of it. We are, therefore, continually forming hypotheses about the world in the light of our theories, acting in the light of our hypotheses, and then (if necessary) reformulating our theories in the light of our actions' results. In its simplest terms this is what the scientist does in the laboratory, so the common 'shorthand phrase' for Kelly's view is 'man the scientist'. (For more details of Kelly's theories see Unit 8 and the Kelly Project, or Kelly, 1955, or the eminently readable account given by Bannister and Fransella, 1980.)

### The interpersonal basis of personal realities

Unit 7 showed how a person's concept of self and the way he sees the world intrinsically develops through interactions with others; and Unit 2 how people define us by their expectations and by the ways in which they act towards us. Seeing how others relate to and make sense of the world also helps to shape *our* construction of reality. The personal construction of reality is very much an *interpersonal* business.

The social psychologist who, in particular, has tried to alert us to this is George Mead. Because of the historical accident that Mead's lectures at Chicago were made compulsory for sociology students, his thought had much more immediate influence on sociology than on psychology and one may reasonably see him as an extremely strong formative influence on the *symbolic interactionist* movement in sociology. The symbolic interactionists took up one aspect of Mead's work – the stress on the social world as composed of meanings rather than objects and events, and on the need to explain individuals' behaviour as emanating from the whole social group, rather than the social group as built up from aggregates of individuals. The world is therefore seen as made up of *symbolized* 'realities' defined by the way that people and groups *interact*. The meaning of an event or a behaviour is therefore not given absolutely, nor imposed by individuals, but developed and negotiated between individuals in the context of existing 'social meanings' (see Unit 7).

Our experience of family life, to take the example used in Block 1, is crucially determined by the expectations with which we enter into it – the *norms* we accept for how families should function and the *values* we therefore assign to the actual behaviour of ourselves and others in the light of them. Such norms and values are partly constructed by how our parents and others whom we have observed run their families and partly negotiated as a compromise between the current family participants. The expectations of family life are also conditioned by the wider negotiation of symbolic reality which is conducted via television, the newspapers, novels, children's books and other channels through which the wider culture interacts with immediate interpersonal groupings. Our social reality is, therefore, interpersonally defined and culturally conditioned, a 'fact' which has had a considerable impact on recent social psychology (see, for instance, the discussions of shared constructs within families in Unit 2 of Block 1, or of the embedding of cultural expectations within language in Block 2).

One writer in particular who might be seen as belonging to this school and who has had a great influence on social psychology during the last fifteen years is Erving Goffman. One strand of his early work (e.g. *Asylums*, published in 1961) was to stress just how much people are concerned to take control of their world and how the behaviours even of mental patients may 'make sense' if taken in context, even if they make little sense to us as outsiders. The other major strand (started in *The presentation of self in everyday life*, published in 1957) is to explore (i) how we acquire (or give ourselves) social meaning by how we speak and act, (ii) how we constantly manipulate the information which we emit about what kind of a person we are, and (iii) how the way that others judge us is crucial to our own assessment of who and what we are.

### The social construction of reality

It could be argued that 'reality' (i.e. patterns of meaning which make sense of the world) exists not just at an individual level but at the level of a society or group. For example, proverbs, as has already been suggested, might be regarded as the implicit theories of a society. Within any society, there is a web of established conceptions of the way things are – particular ways of constructing reality which are the common currency of that culture. (Block 5 explores the nature and significance of such collective representations of the world.)

As personal constructions of reality can be traced to particular experiences, characteristics and backgrounds, so it can be argued that certain kinds of economic and social conditions may shape social consciousness or the typical forms in which reality tends to be constructed in that society. As one example, the analysis by Berger *et al.* of the way living in a technological society can influence the way we see things, is discussed in Block 4.

Social and personal constructions of reality are intrinsically interwoven. As we have seen, one important source of personal constructions of reality is in the assumptions and concepts of the culture and subcultures in which we live and grow up. For instance, depending on our background, we may come to see bizarre or deviant behaviour as arising because of possession by spirits or intentional malevolence or illness, disturbed family relationships in early childhood or prejudiced labelling by a powerful elite. We continually absorb assumptions and implicit theories from the social context in which we live. The language we learn to speak itself provides us with the concepts which underlie the theories we hold.

One reason why society may succeed in imposing its constructions of reality on individuals is the unequal distribution of power. Take the case of criminal behaviour, for example. A host of self-report studies have indicated that very nearly everyone has, at some time in his or her life, committed an act which would have rendered him or her liable to criminal prosecution if it had been detected or reported to the police and followed through into the criminal justice system. In one sense, therefore, criminal *behaviour* no more needs to be explained than breathing does. What does need to be explained is how some people and not others come to acquire a *criminal identity* in their own eyes and those of others – how they come to be *symbolized* as criminal. If we tackle the 'problem of crime' from this perspective, we find that there are structural social inequalities which lead poorer working class people to be more often apprehended (their transgressions tend to be more visible to the police), and that when the label of 'criminal' is once attached to a person by court proceedings it is very likely to be reinforced because of further inequalities which then come into operation – convicted persons are likely to have fewer job opportunities, for example, and again to be more 'visible' to the police than others. The process of labelling may therefore be seen as one main cause of the persistence of certain behaviours. There may also be changes in self-labelling as a result of persistent labelling by others, and consequent loss of equality of opportunity – the person concerned may come regretfully to accept 'society's' low estimation of his worth, or even rebelliously to 'join the out-group' and align himself with those who value such an identity.

Labelling theory, a development of symbolic interactionism, departs from the parent movement of symbolic interactionism by giving more weight to the fact that power is not equally distributed in negotiation; to a large extent how we perceive our reality is *determined* by what social institutions make of it. This point may be made from the labelling perspective in the case of mental handicap, for example. Severe intellectual disfunction has doubtless always been recognized, though not always distinguished from mental illness, but *mild* mental handicap (which might be thought of as *very* low average intelligence – i.e. in the range of 50–70 IQ points) is arguably a creation of industrialization and the introduction of compulsory universal schooling (Ryan and Thomas, 1980; Abbott, 1982; Tomlinson, 1981); unintelligent people could live normal lives working the land, but there is less scope for them in industry, and the state's commitment to educate all children to a certain level made *visible* a category of children who could not be brought up to this level and constituted them as a 'problem' for educational and social management. The social reality of mild mental handicap is therefore created not by the lack of intelligence but by the structure and goals of our education system. (Labelling theory is discussed in more detail in Unit 12.)

**Theories as constructions**

George Kelly's model of the person was 'the scientist'. The way we construct our realities is to hypothesize about the nature of the world, proceed to test these by our actions and modify the theory accordingly. But we could equally well reverse his postulate. For the process of constructing scientific theories could be regarded as merely a more specialized form of the way we construct our everyday models of reality. They may be more explicit and formalized but, like our personal constructions, they are not to be regarded as absolute descriptions of the 'way things are'. Even though they may draw on evidence and observations not normally open to us in everyday experience, they are still constructions and not reflections of reality. They too depend on selection and on whatever set of concepts and assumptions are brought to bear. (For a further discussion of this issue, see Paper 2, Sections 1 and 2.)

Although it is not an easy task, it is sometimes possible to trace the sources of a theory in the personal background of the theorist or the social and intellectual traditions of the time. Behaviourism emerged in the USA in the early part of this century. Its insistent empiricism, emphasis on environmental influence and rejection of introspection and the idea of hereditary influence, is very much in keeping with a non-reflective, pragmatic, practically-minded frontier society: a society whose dominant myth was that any person can achieve what he or she will and whose constitution enshrined the doctrine of equality for all. Psychoanalysis is, in contrast, so clearly a creature of late nineteenth century Europe. Its emphasis on instinctual drives and its preparedness to grapple with complexity and paradox are very much in tune with European philosophical thought of the nineteenth century. Its 'hydraulic' model of psychic energy as a constant which will find an outlet of some kind leans heavily on the concepts of nineteenth century science. Piaget, similarly, is in the European nativistic tradition. His theory revolves around the idea that the structure of the mind shapes our conceptions of reality as much as do the characteristics of the external world. Although he used observation and experiment, he was far more concerned with theory construction and ideas than with methodological rigour.

A growth movement in psychology in the past few years has been the use of computer analogies and development of the information processing approach: a shift in theoretical perspective clearly and explicitly influenced by developments in machine technology. Concepts like 'feedback', 'information bit', 'retrieval', have been taken over and applied in a new conceptualization of the way the human mind works. Would it be too fanciful also to suggest that contemporary movements in psychology which seek to bring in an experiential perspective, to explain in terms of 'reasons' rather than 'causes', are linked to the cultural realization of our time of the limitations of a single-minded dominance of scientific and technological modes of thought? Or that the contemporary shift from an absolutistic search for fundamental laws of behaviour to a more relative view of knowledge (for example, as propounded by this paper) has been influenced by the slow permeation of the basic concepts developed by Einstein (e.g. relativity) which revolutionized twentieth century physics? Such illustrations yield more than a strong suspicion that theories and approaches to the study of social behaviour are creatures of their time and cultural context. (See the Course Reader and Unit 13, Section 3.1 for more detailed elaboration of this theme.)

Similar analyses can be made of the influence of the personality of the theorist on individual theories, particularly where these have developed, as in the case of psychoanalytic theories, partly at least on the basis of self-examination. The Freudian idea of personality as conflict between drives, reality and assimilated sanctions imposed by culture and by parents fits well with the picture which emerges from biographies and Freud's more personal writings, of a man of rich inner thought and emotion whose outward life-style was conventional and sedate. Freud's focus on male development is consistent with the fact that a rich source of his own ideas was his own introspection and possibly also with the paternal and male-orientated pattern of a Jewish family. The shift towards pessimism characteristic of his later theory may well be linked to the impact of the First World War and to personal tribulations (the first traces of cancer appeared then and his beloved daughter Sophie died shortly after the war). Carl Jung split with Freud because of what he felt to be Freud's over-concern with sex. An interest in religion and mysticism permeates his own work. Interestingly, Jung was the son of a Lutheran pastor. Those of Freud's followers like Karen Horney, Erikson and Fromm who left Europe as the Nazis came to power and made a new life for themselves in the very different cultural context of America, characteristically placed far more emphasis on the importance of culture in shaping personality. Karen Horney notably takes specific issue with Freud's emphasis on the importance of anatomical differences in the psychic development of males and females. Erik Erikson is one of the few people without a university degree to hold a chair at Harvard University. His intellectual and cultural background is in history, languages and especially art. This background shows through in his sensitivity to patterns of feelings and observations, his capacity to convey vivid impressionistic accounts of people and cultures and his awareness of the importance of historical development. He would be the first to admit a weakness of logical clarity and precision of thought which he ascribes to lack of philosophical training. B. F. Skinner, the doyen of a very different approach, neo-behaviourism, also agrees that the scientist is the product of his own unique history. His own self-confessed stubbornness (he cites as descriptive of himself a statement from a character in his novel *Walden Two* (1962): 'I'm stubborn. I've had only one idea in my life – a true *idée fixe* . . . to put it as bluntly as possible, the idea of having my own way. "Control" expresses it, I think. The control of human behaviour . . .') fits well with his adherence, in the face of much opposition, to the dogma of behaviourist methodology and his intense concern with the controls of human behaviour. His avowed lack of retrospective self-concern ('the first thing I can remember happened when I was twenty-two years old' (1959, p.361)) is what one might expect of a man who believes that introspection can make no contribution to understanding why we behave as we do. Early academic work on animal behaviour and an enduring interest in gadgets are not surprising in the background of the man who invented the Skinner box (see Figure 1). In a lecture at Oxford (the Herbert Spencer lecture of 1974) Skinner argued for the need to resist the temptations of the 'primrose path' of alternative approaches to the study of psychology and to rigorously keep on the 'steep and thorny way' described by behaviourism. The tenor of his imagery as well as the assiduousness of his personal work programme is in keeping with the puritanical single-mindedness of his approach.

These are but speculations as to origin. Brief sketches hint at but do not conclusively demonstrate links between a theory and its personal and cultural context. But if theories are, as we have argued, constructions and equally a function of the theorists and the cultural context in which he works as of the phenomena theorized about, then to evaluate and appreciate a theory properly, we must try to tease out such links; to examine not merely its content but its

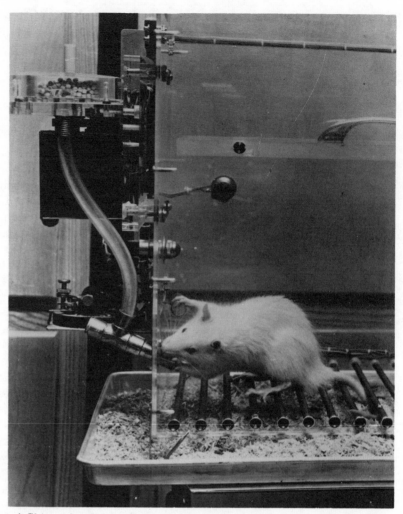

Figure 1: A Skinner box (photo: Public Affairs Division, Pfizer Inc., New York.)

personal and historical origins as well. This 'reflexive' procedure enables us to contrast and compare different theoretical perspectives more meaningfully. It may shed light also on our own evaluation of any theory. One criterion of evaluation is the personal relevance and meaning it has for the evaluator. It seems quite probable that theories appeal when theorist and evaluator hold key values or characteristics of cognitive style and personality in common; for instance a theory emphasizing testability and precision is likely to be both generated and appreciated by persons with a high need for certainty and low tolerance of ambiguity.

---

*Related reading*

Chapter 12 'A personal creation' in the set book *Freud and Psychoanalysis* suggests some of the possible social and personal influences on Freud's theory. It provides a detailed case study of the way a theory is a construction of the theorist and will reflect his background and characteristics.

Personal and social constructions of reality are intimately interwoven and the relation between them is two-way. Personal constructions of reality can come to influence prevailing social ones through the assimilation of scientific, philosophical and social theories into current ways of thinking. The following chapter of the set book (Chapter 13, 'Moral implications and social impact') briefly examines this issue in relation to psychoanalytic theory.

If you have not already done so, you might like to read these two chapters in conjunction with this paper.

This two-way relation between research and society is a major theme of the

Course Reader. It tries to demonstrate not only how political and social considerations influence and structure research but also how psychological ideas, in their turn, impinge on society.

## Implications for social psychology

Given this argument – that both our awareness of reality and scientific theories are constructions – what implications does this have for the study of social psychology?

The important implication is that we should realize that theories and research findings are not intrinsically 'objective'. For they will be rooted in and influenced by the personal and cultural background and development of the theorist or researcher. Absolute knowledge in social psychology (or in any other discipline) is not possible. All understanding is always open to revision and conceptualization in new ways.

Note, however, that to say that theories are constructions does *not* imply a position of (to use a distinction formulated by Erikson (1968)) *relativism*, i.e. that any theory is as good as any other. Although a theory is a construction and a function of the characteristics of the theorist, it is also a function of the characteristics of what is being theorized about. Rather, the constructivist position implies a position of *relativity*, i.e. that one theory can be judged only from the standpoint of another. There is no objective standpoint against which they can all be compared. We may have criteria we want to apply – how far is the theory testable, for example, is it consistent with other observations, how differentiated a description of the phenomena in question does it provide? (For discussion of these criteria, see Paper 2.) But the choice of any or all of these criteria is itself a construction. What we can hope to do though is to explicate a theory's content and approach, evaluate its degree of differentiation and consistency and the cultural and personal factors likely to have influenced the theorist; and then to contrast this complex against the respective patterns presented by other theories. And, although we cannot prove the propositions of a theory, we may be able to demonstrate that they are *not* valid as they stand; i.e., if the form in which they are expressed allows us to do this, we may be able to falsify them. (See Popper, 1968. For a discussion of falsifiability in relation to psychoanalysis, see set book *Freud and Psychoanalysis*, pp.114–6.)

The problem of understanding in social psychology is compounded by the fact that the subject matter itself – people's conceptions of reality and their actions and relationships – are themselves constructions. The understanding of social behaviour is subject to cultural and historical change. What washes in one context may not in another. Erikson has expressed this well:

> When it comes to central aspects of man's existence, we can only conceptualize at a given time what is relevant to us for personal, for conceptual, and for historical reasons. And even as we do so, the data and the conclusions change before our eyes. Especially at a time when our conceptualizations and interpretations become part of a historically self-conscious scene, and when insight and conduct influence each other with an immediacy that hardly leaves a pause for any new 'tradition' to form – in such a time all thinking about man becomes an experiment in living. The newness of man's self-awareness and his attention to his awareness has, at first, led to a scientific mythology of the mind or to a mythological use of scientific terms and methods, as if social science could and would repeat in a short time, and in view of immediate practical goals, the whole long progress of natural science from natural philosophy to pure and applied science. *But man, the subject of psycho-social science, will not hold still enough to be divided into categories both measurable and relevant.*

(Erikson 1968, p.43 (italics added))

All this suggests that an effective course in social psychology would be unwise to confine itself to a single theoretical perspective. Rather, we should adopt what we might term a 'multiple perspective' approach – looking at a range of theories and perspectives on our subject matter and contrasting them from each other's point of view. As constructions, theories are useful in different ways. They have their own particular ranges of convenience (see Paper 2). A theorist can do some tasks well, in others he may be less adequate. Skinner's strength, for example, is his capacity for rigorous application of operational principles; Erikson's lies in his penetrating insights and his subtle and delicate impressionistic comprehension of the complexity of human experience. The strengths and characteristics of a theorist will largely determine the questions he asks and the kinds of answer he seeks and finds. The way he is evaluated will also depend on how useful and relevant these are to achieving the goals and solving the problems which concern the evaluator – be these to design a more effective teaching system, get employees to work harder, bring up a child, give advice to a friend or make sense of personal experience.

Theories then do not stand merely in complementary or contradictory relation to each other. Sometimes, the propositions of one do contradict those of another. Sometimes they are complementary in that they construe reality in similar terms but deal separately with factors that interact and which need to be considered in relation to each other. But some theories and approaches represent *different faces of the same reality*. It is not simply the case that if the explanations they offer are different then one is right and the other wrong. In this case, understanding of phenomena is likely to be enhanced by the ability to look from each perspective in turn. One view may pose questions which are not generated by or meaningful in terms of the other.

Finally, bear in mind the point made earlier about relativity – that any evaluation is also a construction. In criticizing and viewing the theories and research presented in this course, try to be aware of the implicit assumptions underlying the assessments you make.

### References

ABBOTT, P. (1982) *Towards a social theory of mental handicap*, unpublished Ph.D. thesis, CNAA/Thames Polytechnic.

BANNISTER, D. and FRANSELLA, F. (1980) *Inquiring man*, Harmondsworth, Penguin.

BERGER, P. L., BERGER, B. and KELLNER, H. (1973) *The homeless mind*, Harmondsworth, Penguin.

ERIKSON, E. H. (1968) *Identity, use and crisis*, London, Faber.

GOFFMAN, E. (1957) *Presentation of self in everyday life*, Harmondsworth, Penguin.

GOFFMAN, E. (1961) *Asylums*, Harmondsworth, Penguin.

KELLY, G. (1955) *The psychology of personal constructs*, New York, W. W. Norton.

MURPHY, J., JOHN, M. and BROWN, H. (eds) (1984) *Dialogues and debates in social psychology*, London, Lawrence Erlbaum (Course Reader).

POPPER (1968) *The logic of scientific discovery* (2nd edition), London, Hutchinson.

ROGERS, C. (1951) *Client-centred therapy*, Boston, Houghton-Mufflin.

RYAN, J. and THOMAS, F. (1980) *The politics of mental handicap*, Harmondsworth, Penguin.

STEVENS, R. (1983) *Freud and psychoanalysis*, Milton Keynes, The Open University Press (Set Book).

TOMLINSON, S. (1981) *Educational subnormality*, London, Routledge and Kegan Paul.

WHORF, B. (1940) 'S :ience and linguistics', in E. E. Maccoby, N. Newcomb and E. L. Hartley (eds) (1966), *Readings in Social Psychology*, London, Methuen.

## Paper 8: Nomothetic, idiographic and hermeneutic social psychology

*by Kerry Thomas*

### 1 Introductory summary

This paper describes and evaluates three approaches to explanation and understanding in social psychology. It complements the methods paper (Paper 6) and extends some of the discussion of 'dimensions on which theories differ' (Paper 2); it also touches on the topic of autonomy and determinism (Paper 9).

The basic argument is that the kind of multiple perspective approach to social psychology that we have presented in this course, exemplifies, *in practice*, how nomothetic, idiographic and hermeneutic explanations are used in combination and rarely treated as mutually exclusive. But there are deeper issues at stake and the discussion needs to be placed in a wider context. The paper therefore touches on age-old arguments about how to do science, including modern notions of what physical science (like physics) is like, and debates about how to do social science. It also relates the three kinds of explanation to the history of social psychology and current ideas about its nature. Paper 10 ('A note on the nature of social psychology') tends to argue the case for hermeneutics and the idea that perhaps social psychology should be a 'moral' science. The present paper, whilst not decrying these arguments, is more sympathetic to the methods and aims of physical science, in its *modern* form. At the end of the day, however, it has to be remembered that the choice of how to explain people – be it nomothetic, idiographic, hermeneutic – rests on the theorists' models of the *nature* of people, and of the nature of the relationship between individuals and society, and their basic view of what social psychology is for.

### 2 An outline of the different approaches to explanation

The terms nomothetic and idiographic have been used in psychology and in social psychology for a long time. Hermeneutics has been adopted more recently as an appropriate way to study people and the social world. The idiographic approach has developed into something rather different from its beginnings. Therefore we need to look at the history of these terms at the same time as trying to set up definitions.

The terms *nomothetic, idiographic* and *hermeneutic* describe different ways of trying to understand and explain: all three have been used and discussed throughout the course. The nomothetic approach is basically that of any physical science: seeking general laws, often of cause and effect, using methods and concepts which are objective, clearly operationalized, replicable, usually empirical, and free from value judgements or any other bias that cannot be quantified (and thus discounted). This approach was adopted by psychology at a time when it was much closer to its biological roots than perhaps it is today. (It remains strong in areas of psychology that are biologically oriented.)

The beginnings of social psychology – as distinct from psychology and other social sciences – encompassed both the nomothetic tradition, which was particularly strong in psychology at that time, and a more qualitative, meaning-oriented approach. (Unit 16 'Attitudes and behaviour' charts some of this history.) The nomothetic approach stressed the 'common' aspects of human social behaviour, thus sacrificing the richness of individuality for general laws. For example, survey research (in all social sciences) relied on statistical principles and representative sampling, and social psychological experiments were conducted and described in a way that permitted replication, and specified the samples used. The extent to which findings could be generalized to other populations (e.g. from male students to men and women in general) was always problematic – but generalization, possibly to the extent of finding *universal* laws, was the overall intent.

In contrast, what was then termed the *idiographic* approach explored single cases in depth. This might be as case studies in sociology, anthropology and other social sciences and in social psychology it often implied seeking out individual people who were not representative but 'one off' special instances. But the idiographic approach also often implied that an in depth study of individuals could contribute to our understanding of people and social process *in general*. Thus, compared with the nomothetic approach, the idiographic approach was never so clear cut. Sometimes the study of individuals over time (as in psychoanalysis) can lead to clarification of general processes *for all people*; sometimes it can lead to generalizations which hold only for that *one individual* in terms of his/her personal meaning systems. This second kind of idiographic enquiry is closer to more recent views of psychology as the study of the *whole person*; and to hermeneutics. Before going any deeper into these definitions let's look for examples in the unit tests.

In Block 3, Unit 8 describes George Kelly's way of understanding others. This is an *idiographic* approach based on an in-depth exploration of each individual's unique way of construing other people and construing other people's constructions. In the text, Kelly's construct theory is contrasted with attribution theories which are examples of the *nomothetic* approach. In practice, the repertory grid does not help the research toward general statements which can be applied across the board to other situations, circumstances and people; instead, understanding is rooted in the rich complexity of each unique individual and her/his actions. (Although the theory is constructed in the light of general propositions about what social living entails.) In contrast, attribution theories set out to establish general laws which account for the more or less universal processes of attribution by which we understand other people. In so far as general laws of attribution have been discovered (see Unit 9) these serve as both *descriptions* of the processes and are, in themselves, the *explanation* of what is happening.

Another example of the two approaches applied to similar topic areas occurs in Unit 15 ('Individuals and their attitudes'). We can contrast the idiographic case study of Smith *et al* (1956), who explored how the attitudes of individuals relate to each person's way of coping with his life, with the authoritarian personality of Adorno *et al* (1950) which looked for the patterns of responses made by a large number of people to standard attitude questionnaires. Part of Adorno *et al's* study looked for evidence of a generalizable personality type – whose responses to further questionnaires about political and ethnic issues could, as a result of this 'typing', be *predicted*. They then went on to relate the authoritarian personality 'type' to a cause – a certain definable type of upbringing. (Part of this research was idiographic – in-depth and clinical interviews which provided the fundamental psychodynamic hypotheses on which the 'authoritarian personality' is based. But even the psychodynamic aspect of the work was essentially concerned with general, perhaps universal, processes (see Unit 15, Section 4.4).) A further example of the nomothetic approach in the unit texts, where the general law is more obviously one of straightforward *cause and effect* (rather than process), is the voting study (Unit 17/18). The aim of this survey, amongst other things, was to establish which beliefs on the part of the electorate led to their voting for a particular parliamentary party. The assumption is that a statistical model of the relationship between beliefs and actual voting behaviour would allow researchers, on another occasion, to use information about people's beliefs (or clusters of beliefs) to predict patterns of voting. But it would not necessarily imply that the voting behaviour of *every individual* could be accurately predicted.

The examples from attribution theory, the authoritarian personality and voting behaviour can be seen as the kind of systematic and generalizable enquiry that is, in many basic ways, the same as that which physical scientists might use to explain, say, processes of metal fatigue or the underlying causes of a mechanical failure. In contrast, Kelly's personal construct theory and Smith *et al's* in-depth research of the 'opinions of ten men' place the main focus on understanding individual cases *in their own terms* (within their own meaning systems). Often this is the starting point for nomothetic research. For example, Smith *et al* began to make hypotheses about the *general* functions of opinions based on their idiographic research. But, to the extent that this idiographic approach does not make inferences to people in general and tries to locate understanding of what is happening within individuals, it is different from the traditional way of doing science.

There was a tendency in the past to treat nomothetic and idiographic approaches as the basic alternatives open to psychologists; but more recently *hermeneutics* (the study of meanings – personal, social, conscious, unconscious) has gained ground as an appropriate way to do social psychology (and other kinds of social science). In this category we might include well established theories such as symbolic interactionism (and also the interpersonal development of meanings and discourse analysis introduced in Unit 7); the interpretive side of psychodynamic theories and psychoanalytic practice; and the phenomenology of personal worlds discussed in Block 4. (Kelly's approach might also be classified here by some – 'rich' theories tend to defy attempts at neat classification.)

### 3   Paradigms

The three approaches, nomothetic, idiographic and hermeneutic, are different kinds of epistemological endeavour – although, as we shall see, in practice they are not mutually exclusive. Adopting one or other of these approaches to social psychology entails a number of important implications about the subject matter and about the ways it should be studied. By epistemology I mean a consideration of what are the most appropriate means by which to understand and explain people. It encompasses what sort of questions to ask about the subject matter, what sorts of evidence to look for, the choice of criteria to apply to explanations, and the kinds of methods to use. Nomothetic, idiographic and hermeneutic social psychologies differ on all these dimensions. And these dimensions of epistemology are the outcome of the *model of the person* we choose to adopt. In essence, then, the three ways of explaining and understanding are basic to the *paradigm* that is adopted, i.e. the set of interlocking and compatible assumptions about *what* exists and *how* to gain knowledge of it.

The nomothetic approach is that of any science (like classical physics and chemistry, etc.) and it sets out to understand *via* the formulation and testing of a general law (e.g. if $x$ then $y$: meaning whenever $x$ then always $y$). Usually such a law is one of cause and effect. The general law is, in itself, the explanation. The idiographic approach can also be scientific in its thoroughness, its attempts at objectivity and sometimes its search for general statements about individuals' behaviour *over time*. There are, however, some fundamental problems in treating the in-depth study of individual (single) cases as science in the traditional sense. I shall return to these later. Hermeneutic enquiry is most clearly removed from traditional ideas of science in that exploration of meaning is not only frequently directed to single cases and the uniqueness of meaning but since its subject matter is subjective experience its practice is intrinsically bound up with the methodological problems of subjectivity – something that science has been at pains to minimize. Because the three approaches describe different scientific aims and different ways of *doing* science, the adoption of a nomothetic or idiographic or hermeneutic approach tells you at least two things about the paradigm the psychologist is working with. First, the choice of approach to explanation (epistemology) tells you how the psychologist thinks of psychology: a nomothetic perspective implies that social psychology is a science just like any other; an idiographic perspective implies that social psychology is a special kind of science –

perhaps not a science at all; and a hermeneutic perspective implies that science, in its traditional cause and effect seeking form, is inappropriate – that social psychology is a subject that requires a quite different approach if its true essence is to be studied. Second, the adoption of one or another stance also tells you something about the 'model of the person' that the psychologist is using.

A nomothetic, science-like-any-other approach implies that personkind can be understood 'mechanistically', in the same cause and effect terms that have been used to explain the physical universe. In other words, people are seen as determined by states, conditions and events in their biology and physical/social environments – all of which are potentially open to investigation and complete explanation. An idiographic approach, at least suggests that personkind is rather different – although just what this difference is, is not very clear. This approach tries to take account of the fact that people and their behaviour – compared with things and their happenings – seem more complicated; less certain; that they seem to be autonomous agents at least some of the time and thus not fully determined and not open to cause and effect explanations which lead to prediction; that they appear to be more than the sum of their parts and therefore are not open to complete understanding via segmentation nor through reduction to explanation at lower levels of analysis (see Paper 3). The idiographic approach aims for a holistic understanding of the complete person. Hermeneutics as applied to social psychology makes even more of the difference between people and other organisms, and between people and the physical world since the study of meanings is only applicable to people and their creations. Thus the essentially symbolic nature of much of human experience is at the centre of enquiry and in this sense the subject matter is in a quite different domain from any other. Faced with these very different approaches to social psychology how can we evaluate them? Ultimately any evaluation has to be in terms of what one believes social psychology is trying to achieve.


## 4   What is social psychology for?

Is the aim of social psychology knowledge for knowledge's sake like the study of old English or an exploration of Henry James' novels? Or is it more like physical science where usually (although not always) we want to *do* something with our knowledge of the physical structure of matter and of living organisms? In social science (and perhaps history) it is difficult to separate knowledge from its political implications – perhaps such knowledge stands in the same relation to policy as does knowledge of physics, chemistry, electronics etc., to technical innovation. Is social psychology for putting things right, be it clinical intervention through understanding people as individuals, or social intervention through understanding social processes? Or is it to extend our visions of what human experience might be – to confer a maximum of cognitive autonomy on each of us individually and on our social institutions so that we may live our lives to the full (a moral science)? You may well conclude that social psychology is for all these ends. And that theorists will choose paradigms which are appropriate to what they want to achieve in their practice of social psychology.

The particular paradigm in which theorists choose to work can be seen as part of their general orientation to the world, their attitudes and values, and the influence upon them of the place and time in which they live. (This 'sociology of knowledge' approach is basic to the Course Reader.) For example, early studies in the attitude area (see *The Polish Peasant*, Thomas and Znaniecki, 1918 – discussed in Section 1 of Unit 16) were idiographic. Thomas' idea of what constituted a social psychological investigation was influenced by European philosophical traditions and was essentially directed at helping individuals in society. For many people idiographic social psychology has remained part of 'a helping social science' but concerned with helping individuals rather than with intervention at a societal level. If you see social psychology as a 'moral science', as a means to extend our vision of what human experience might be then your chosen paradigm may be idiographic or hermeneutic or some combination of the two.

If you think that social psychology is for understanding the human condition in more general terms; for explaining the influence, for example of biology, social structure or culture; for understanding and perhaps intervening in wider social processes, then you might well be content to sacrifice detailed knowledge of individuals and meanings in order to describe the 'patterns' of social life or to make generalizations about what causes people to behave in a particular way. If you see social psychology in this way then your chosen paradigm is likely to be nomothetic.

Although the nomothetic approach has been dominant, especially in American social psychology, the radical social psychological movement of the 1960s and 70s argued very strongly that the methods and assumptions of physical science are *inappropriate* to the study of people and social life. This is the antipositivist standpoint that has been widespread in social science. (I shall return to some of the specific points in this argument, later.) I should make it clear that my own position is anti-antipositivism (not quite the same as pro-positivism.) It seems to me, given modern views of how to do physical science (and what the physical universe is), that these days antipositivism can only be espoused by those who are deeply committed to the idea that people are utterly different in kind from the physical universe – autonomous, i.e. in no way determined, and unpredictable – perhaps a return to vitalism. And I imagine that not many people would agree with this model of the person. Most social psychologists who are unhappy with positivism nevertheless acknowledge that some parts of behaviour and experience are determined and that social life exhibits patterns and regularities that can be described – even if, at the end of the day, people's awareness of what they do frees them from complete determinism. Therefore I would argue that science of some kind, premised on the search for regularities and general laws, must be relevant, indeed important, to social psychology.

Another tenet of antipositivism – perhaps more difficult to dismiss – is the question of ethical and political implications of being able to predict human affairs. Science (as in physics) aims for explanations which fit together into an ever-increasing (and increasingly precise) network of general laws, a network which in turn shows the way to further generalizations. This 'nomological network' provides understanding *and* as a by-product (perhaps intended or perhaps not) of its systematization it provides a means to predict, and to change, and thence to control. In the world of physical science this leads to innovation and technology. In *social* science, in so far as it succeeds in setting up such a network, then the same by-products are possible. But since we are now talking about prediction, change and control of people and society, then ethical and political issues have to be considered. (See, for example, the issues raised by Skinner's *Beyond Freedom and Dignity* (1971).)

The spectre of social engineering has always been associated, quite rightly, with the kind of knowledge that is gained from a nomothetic, as opposed to an idiographic approach. But it can be the outcome of any social psychological endeavour that generalizes beyond single individuals. The hermeneutic approach can be directed toward understanding structures of meaning in different societies, cultures or subcultures. Here any generalizations that emerge, however fuzzy, for instance about social representations of family roles, or social class differences in perceptions of technological risk, are also potentially open to misuse – perhaps in the design of welfare, or birth control policies or in the siting of nuclear power stations.

I'm not suggesting that hermeneutics can provide predictability of the same degree as the quantitative methods of physical science – but in a sense the fundamental intent of both kinds of procedure, even when hermeneutics is directed at understanding a single individual, is the same: it is to gain understanding by casting what is 'unknown' in terms of what is 'known'. And this is basically a process of generalization.

Generalization is at the centre of doing science, it is also at the centre of all understanding and explanation. Here I come to the nub of this paper: rather than disputing whether or not traditional, quantitive, deterministic science should be adopted wholesale in social psychology (or any social science), if we instead focus on generalization as the basis of understanding and the procedures it requires, then the differences between nomothetic, idiographic and hermeneutic social psychology – as practiced – can be placed on a continuum rather than on different sides of an ideological divide.

## 5  Doing social psychology

### 5.1  Generalization

My central argument is that nomothetic, idiographic and hermeneutic approaches to social psychology all have to face essentially the same kinds of difficulties in order to generalize, given that generalization is necessary for any kind of understanding and usefulness. I also see these difficulties as being broadly of the same kind as are faced in modern physical science.

You might doubt my insistence that generalization is necessary for understanding. If so, stop and think about what 'understanding something' might mean to you. I would say that it depends on relating ideas one to another, searching for structures and patterns, comparing instances, extrapolating, expecting, predicting. Even 'meaning' itself encompasses 'implications' and similarities (metaphor) and structure. Thus understanding is built on principles found in science – a search for a form of simplification which will then permit extension through generalization to other instances. You can find examples of this in poetry, where plumbing the depth of meaning of an object or experience involves the poet in a search for *partial* (i.e. simplified) similarities with other objects or experiences; and where such metaphors succeed the meaningfulness generalizes across the two objects (events).

Of course, the kind of generalization that is implicit, say in poetry or metaphor or in literary criticism, is far removed from the precision of general laws in science. But some of the essentials of the *process* are the same. At one extreme is abstraction (including segmentation, simplification and choices) of some known similar common feature from two or more (instances) images – perhaps in a poem or within one's personal experience – so that a comparison can be made and thence generalization set up, using what is known to extend understanding into what is unknown. These are the processes that are used in hermeneutics.

At the other extreme is the comparative method which is fundamental to science, of which the clearest example is in experimentation. Physical science seeks *universal* laws – that hold for *all* similarly defined instances. (But it is worth remembering that cosmology now questions whether the most universal physical laws would have been true for all time.) In social science and certainly in social psychology, general statements are usually of a relatively limited kind, other than in biological areas. For example, the postscript to this course questions the appropriateness of looking for universal explanations that hold across cultures. But this doesn't rule out the value of limited generalization – so long as the conditions under which it holds are acknowledged and can be described – and it doesn't rule out the contribution of nomothetic social psychology.

There are plenty of examples in the course material of findings that are of limited generality, but nevertheless important contributions to social psychological understanding. In a hermeneutic tradition, the exploration of meanings of *Health and Illness* (Herzlich, 1973, Unit 15) are limited to a small section (not even a sample) of the French, urban, middle-class. An important feature of this study is that it also, again in a limited way, extends understanding by setting up a *comparison* with rural people.

In Block 6 the studies on conformity in groups arrives at several *general* statements (e.g. that conformity is a function of the size of the majority, of the difficulty of the task etc.) and also suggests that these statements may be limited

114

by cultural factors or historical period. But does this rule out their interest and usefulness – or does it perhaps potentially increase our understanding? Now we can see other possible influences that might be at work and which can be explored.

Generalization plays a part in all three approaches, although its importance varies. And to the extent that it is primary, then the research aims for objectivity; and to the extent it is subordinate to rich description, then objectivity is replaced by subjectivity. Much of idiographic, and certainly hermeneutic social psychology, deals with subjective data; but can we claim with equal force, that nomothetic social psychology deals with objective data – with objectively defined situations, conditions and variables as would be demanded by a positivist view? It should be clear from several of the examples above that even when the aim of the research is nomothetic the practice is not really positivist; it is as much an art as a science, and *objectivity* is at the centre of the problem.

### 5.2   What is objectivity?

This course has tended to present a constructivist view of the world – which entails a fundamental subjectivism: we each create our own social world (although not necessarily in circumstances of our own choosing). In early science, in contrast, objectivity was the base line and was usually accepted as a reflection of the absolute properties of the physical world. Later, it became clear that properties of the physical world appear to be 'absolutes' (whether they are or not) because so many people, including the scientific community, have direct access to and frequent experience of these states and events and *agree* about what the definitions and measures stand for. But in social science (and modern physics and cosmology) the status of objectivity is more provisional. It is no longer appropriate or useful to think of objectivity as an approximation to the ideal where that ideal is an exact correspondence with a reality that exists out there. As we move into the realms of unobservables and the world of symbols, whether in physical science, psychology or social science, it becomes clearer that objectivity is no more than *consensus* about terms, definitions and operations and meanings. Once objectivity loses its absolute quality (or the criterion of 'real reality' against which it can be assessed), then any scientific endeavour can choose its place on the continuum objective – subjective. Furthermore, choosing and evaluating the *extent* of consensus and the *methods agreed* for *achieving* consensus themselves become an important part of the practice of doing science.

As we saw, it is nomothetic social psychology which aims for the most extensive and rigorous generalization, thus requiring strong criteria for testability, and, in turn, objectivity. But there are many problems in *doing* nomothetic social psychology which revolve around the extent to which objectivity (consensus) is (or isn't) achieved. Consensus about *observable* behaviour is the least problematic (hence the role of behaviourism as the best practiced variety of nomothetic psychology), though consensus about what is to be counted as a 'behaviour' to be observed may be more difficult to achieve. But once attention is turned to 'experience' or inner states or unobservable hypothetical constructs (like attitudes) then the difficulties of attaining objectivity (if that is possible) or of evaluating the degree of objectivity achieved, are considerable.

Maximum consensus (i.e. best efforts at objectivity) is more likely to be achieved when the subject matter is drastically simplified, a process which can lead to trivialization, a major criticism of positivism. Complex social phenomena have to be sliced up into manageable parts, which largely rules out a holistic treatment of people, another criticism of positivism. It is a moot point whether this problem is specific to the study of people, i.e. different in kind from the study of the physical world.

### 5.3   The art of simplification and segmentation

The art of simplification, in any science, applies across the board, from theory and concepts through the descriptions of controlled and uncontrolled aspects of environment (in so far as these are known or can be estimated) to the coding of variables and measurement, and procedures for collecting data. It is cogently illustrated in Box 1 below which describes interactions between mothers and infants – a method described in Unit 7.

---

**Box 1    Steps toward objective coding procedures in observation of mother–infant interaction**

Before we had videotape and computers, when coding, tabulating, and counting were costly and time-consuming, investigators were under more pressure to plan their analyses in advance and to limit themselves to testing prior hypotheses. Our work today is more exciting and more revealing ... We must begin to do something no one has yet done: to devise a set of procedures for using these tools without deceiving ourselves or our readers about the amount of fishing – casting, reeling in, casting again – that we have done ...

To a certain extent, the problem is a basic paradox in the nature of coding. Science is simplification; the reduction of chaos to order; recasting the unknown in terms of the known. The process of coding, our particular type of simplification, is not-seeing. The challenging part of learning to be a good coder is learning to not-see most of what is happening and to see only certain categories of things. One has to ignore the differences within categories, trusting one's intuition that the gross category is important. We do this first between the videotape and the coding sheets or the keyboard; then we do it again between the computer disk and the printout, and again between the printout and the published article.

In fact, by positioning the camera and zooming in on only a portion of the scene, we commit ourselves to not-seeing most of what is in the room. This process is merely continued as we define each coding category. 'Smiling' commits us to not-seeing a dozen variations in smiles that our eyes and minds are perfectly capable of seeing, indeed beg to see; but we learn to shut them out. We commit ourselves to a guess about a class of smiles we think might be equivalent, at one level, ignoring the ways in which every smile is different. (This, in fact, is exactly what the parent has to do in coding the infant's expressions and what the infant has to do in coding the world.)

The paradoxical aspect of all this selectivity is that its goal is to discover relationships we did not know about before. We want to see as much as possible: if we have to narrow our vision, we want to be able to open it up again, refocus, and try narrowing it in a different way.

(Kaye, 1982)

---

This extract vividly describes the early stages in doing science. Kaye states later in the article that he believes microanalytic studies of mother–infant interaction to be nomothetic; here he illustrates the 'art' of creating sufficient simplicity for consensus objectivity about coding, about equivalences and ultimately, for consensus about the data and hypothesis testing. Choosing what part of a problem to study and choosing what kind of simplification to impose illustrates the way that subjectivity underlies attempts to create objectivity; and perhaps illustrates that, in practical terms, there is less of a division between meaning-based hermeneutics and the generalizations of nomothetics.

Perhaps the idea of *creating* objectivity may seem strange – certainly it flies in the face of most people's stereotyped image of what happens in a physical science. But *is* objectivity unproblematic in the physical world? We tend to forget that much of the scientific progress that has been made rests on laws which relate to highly specified, unnatural conditions known as 'ideal states' (e.g. Boyle's law for expansion of gases – familiar to those who have studied 'O' level physics and chemistry). Laws based on ideal states, for the most part, give sufficient precision for prediction and use; and they fit alongside other similarly derived laws, into nomological nets which can be used to generate and test hypotheses and to extend knowledge. Thus they are an important contribution to the testability of theories – as discussed in Paper 2 of the Metablock – but at the same time they are based on simplifications on nature. They also represent one way of approaching the problem of carving up the 'whole' into manageable parts – parts which can be rendered sufficiently objective for definition and operation. But writing and solving equations for the non-ideal, interacting, chaotic, naturally occurring states – states of matter that are often observed, is a different kind of enterprise – perhaps one that is closer to understanding the complexity of what we have to deal with in social science.

## 6  Complexity, prediction and understanding

One of the arguments most often quoted against positivism, and therefore against nomothetic efforts in social psychology, is that *'Even if there is a causal order in the phenomena of human behaviour and experience it is so complex as to be permanently beyond description'*. But it is worth asking whether there is indeed a difference in *kind*, on the dimension of complexity, between the social and physical world. The extract reprinted in Box 2 from a BBC Radio 3 discussion on 'doing science' might serve to jolt some psychologists out of the assumption that people and their affairs are more complicated than the physical world and (by inference) that it is not appropriate to use a nomothetic approach.

No one can doubt the success in physical science of seeking to establish general laws, general laws with respect to ideal states; but increasingly, theoreticians are turning to a search for the laws which govern the occasional emergence of patterns and order from randomness. In Box 2 a theoretical physicist (Berry) and an embryologist (Wolpert) discuss how modern mathematical physics deals with non-ideal (i.e. not simplified) states, complexity and non-predictability.

---

**Box 2   The electron at the end of the universe**

WOLPERT: Physics is regarded as the hard edge of science. For most non-physicists the paradigm is still that of Newtonian physics, according to whose laws it is possible to predict the effect of forces on bodies so reliably that one can land a man at a precise spot on the moon. I was thus rather shocked when, at a recent meeting in Cambridge on 'the evolution and origin of the universe', Mike Berry told me about 'the electron at the end of the universe' which, he said, ruled out our comfortable ideas about predictability.

I had heard of the uncertainty inherent in quantum theory, but this was quite new. Chaos now appeared to be an integral part of the more familiar physical world and modern physics a very different kind of activity than I had imagined . . . Using a type of mathematics known as catastrophe theory he has found it possible to describe the complexity of such patterns as those of sunlight seen at the bottom of the swimming pool, in terms of a few universal structures or forms which appear again and again in many different settings . . .

BERRY: In the past, a person who studied waves, a theoretical physicist, would have been conceived of as a person who found the solution to certain types of equation, and the equations were well known, long known, very, very simple to write down . . . But, all of those solutions had the property that they were possible only because of some simplifying circumstances in the physical situation – the cylindrical symmetry of a lens for example. Now, it's been realized recently that in what's called the generic case (that is, the case that has nothing special about it, which previously was a case that people would have thought that they could say nothing about except it would be computers that solved the equations) actually is the case to which a wonderful new regime applies. There are universal forms which emerge in these generic cases . . . an example of a wave problem which is a generic case, is the refraction of sunlight by the wavy water of a swimming pool: you see the bright lines of refracted light focus on the bottom of the pool. Now, if you had asked an optical scientist ten years ago, 'How do I explain those lines?' then he could have said one of two things. Probably he would have

---

begun by saying, 'Oh, that's a rather trivial problem, it's just refraction of light and we all understand the law of refraction'. But if you'd pressed him and said, 'No, no. That's not enough. I want to know how the law of refraction gives rise to these morphologies that I see on the bottom there'. 'Ah', he would say, 'that's a very difficult one, you need a computer for that . . . just a big enough computer and you can work out what those patterns are'. Now, that would indeed provide you with a simulation and you would indeed find that with quite simple patterns of waves on the water surface you would get quite realistic looking patterns of focal lines on the bottom of the pool, but still you would be missing the understanding. You wouldn't be able to answer the question. 'Well, why is it I always see, for example, junctions of lines of this sort and not that sort?' He wouldn't have been able to answer that, but now one can answer it because precisely this kind of morphology is classified by catastrophe theory and it means that one has a sort of library . . . a very small library of universal forms out of which such short wave patterns and they are short wave patterns, because I'm thinking of the waves of light now which are very, very small compared with waves of water. These short waves of light patterns have built up and that's a very intensely developing subject – now one can really hit the heart of what actually one sees with one's eyes which one previously was unable to do.

WOLPERT: Is this a new kind of physics that you're dealing with or is it all within conventional physics?

BERRY: I would characterize it in the following way: The image of a physicist often is of somebody who's seeking to discover the laws of nature. Now, as it happens it does appear that those laws are mathematical and so one speaks of trying to discover the fundamental equations for elementary particles . . . But what's being realized now is that concealed in the old fashioned equations, long known, that describe matter on more familiar scales, there are new solutions, new phenomena which can only be brought out by using these modern kinds of mathematics. One of the most important problems in theoretical physics, apart from the elementary particles, is understanding the problem of fluid turbulence: Why is fluid motion so often unpredictable? And that's precisely a problem of understanding the solutions of the fluid equations which were worked out 150 years ago (so it's certainly old physics from a particle physicist point of view) and understanding how those equations contain in them chaos. Now, it's very easy to find solutions which aren't chaotic but they're not the ones you observe very often. You can't use catastrophe theory to solve that problem, it is the wrong sort of mathematics – they're more difficult problems and they've been very intensely worked on but they still fit into this category of simple equations having complicated solutions. In a way, that's a very satisfying answer to problems which people who aren't scientists often bring up: they say, 'Well, here you work with these few equations and you can write them down and cover one sheet of paper, and all the equations of theoretical physics can be written down there, but I see the world as a rich and complicated and beautiful place – aren't you brutally truncating it in that way?' And the answer is actually that simple equations have complicated solutions – it's a very, very compact encoding and now with the aid of mathematics, one's making very substantial steps in a whole new class of decodings.

WOLPERT: Chaos, that's not a concept that I would have thought of as associated with physics, because I have this image of physics that's a highly ordered image of the world or of the universe. I don't understand this concept of chaos – would that imply that there's no predictability?

BERRY: Sometimes, strangely enough, it implies just that. Now, we as theoretical physicists were brought up to believe that fundamental chaos only entered with quantum mechanics, you had the indeterminacy principle and so on. Before the advent of quantum mechanics, the universe was predictable in the sense that you had, for example, Newton's laws of motion, even as modified by Einstein. These will tell you that if you know the initial state of the universe, for example, for all these particles and positions and velocities, you can predict for ever more. And we believed that, swallowed that particular myth, although it flies flagrantly in the face of anybody who has ever used a pinball machine. What's realized now is that it's very common, not just some special case, for dynamic systems to exhibit extreme unpredictability in the sense that you can have perfectly definite equations, but the solutions can be unpredictable to a degree that makes it quite unreasonable to use the formal causality built into the equations, but the solutions can be unpredictable to a degree that makes it quite unreasonable to use the formal causality built into the equations as the base for any intelligent philosophy of prediction. I give an example – suppose you've got lots of colliding particles (you can think of them as molecules of oxygen let's say in a gas) and they're in a box and you believe that they obey Newtonian mechanics (they don't quite, but let's suppose they do). And you measure their initial position and velocity precisely (of course, one couldn't do that but suppose one can), then one could predict their motion for all time. But wait a minute, you can only do that if the system is completely isolated and so you say, 'Well isolate it as best you can according to the laws of physics as we now know them'. Well, there's one force that you can't screen out and that's gravity. So, unless you could know the position of every single external particle in the universe which would have a gravitating effect on your molecules, you couldn't predict the motion. So, let's estimate the uncertainty that arises from this source by considering the gravitational effect of an electron at the observable limit of the universe. You agree it's not possible to think of a smaller perturbation than that. A single electron just one; there it is, say ten thousand million light years away. Okay, there it is and it has gravitational effect, but you don't know *where* it is exactly so that's the uncertainty. 'Well', you ask, 'after how many collisions will the little uncertainty that's produced in a motion by that electron be amplified to the degree where you've lost all predictability in the sense that you make an error in predicting the angle which a particular molecule will emerge from a collision by say 90° – reasonably you could say you've lost predictability then.' And the amazing thing is – that number of collisions is only about fifty or so which is of course over in a tiny, tiny fraction of a microsecond. And that means that it's pretty unreasonable, in the large class of systems, to consider Newtonian mechanics as being predictable. The more realistic case actually is if you think of the particles as billiard balls on the actual billiard table and imagine a perfectly flat, perfectly smooth billiard table and so on and you're considering the uncertainties as being produced by the gravitational force of people, moving about near the billiard table – there always are such people milling about – and you want to know after how many collisions of the billiard balls will their motion be uncertain from this cause and the answer is six or seven. And that's why no billiard player, even the best in the world can ever plan a shot which would have even three or four consecutive collisions and have some reasonable expectation that he'll be able to successfully carry it out.

WOLPERT: Now one always had the image of physics as an exact science. Do you think this undermines physics as an exact science?

BERRY: No, I don't think it undermines physics as an exact science because generally when one can't predict something accurately as in these cases, one then finds that actually one didn't really want to, it's statistical properties that one really is more interested in. But it has implications for other sciences which would seek to use physics as its model . . . Knowing the laws doesn't enable them to predict the future and that's something which is just slowly filtering into other sciences which would seek to use mathematics. In other words, they have an outmoded paradigm of physics.

(Wolpert and Berry, 1983)

Perhaps this extract gives enough emphasis to the order of magnitude of complexity and interaction in the physical world to give new meaning to the 'uncertainty principle'. Perhaps we should think again about claiming that the social world, behaviour and experience are different because of their complexity and holism. Furthermore, does the extent of interaction between influences on matter in the physical world perhaps limit the idea that it is humans who are uniquely unique?

## 7 People are unique

As I said earlier, the question of cause and effect in human affairs is crucial to antipositivism. One of the most common points in the argument is: *Human behaviour and experience is not amenable to causal analysis because each individual is unique (i.e. nothing is replicable).*

I also argued earlier that most social psychologists, including antipositivists, would accept that cause and effect plays some part in human behaviour and experience, despite the observation that each of us is ultimately unique. Berry's billiard ball example, above, is an instance from the physical world where understanding of a particular case (i.e. particular movements of those billiard balls in that setting with the particular movements of that audience) rests both on knowing the general laws and principles – which give some predictability – *and* on knowing when and why predictability will break down. Perhaps this parallels the distinction in human affairs between the general principles of psychological *process* (to include biochemistry, biology, heredity, maturation and cognitive processes like memory and attention, and even personality dynamics) and the unique *content* of each person's consciousness. If we accept this, then it would appear that there is value in using a nomothetic approach to explain some parts of human behaviour, but that the content of individual experience is in a category of its own and only amenable to hermeneutic exploration. And this is problematic since it tends to isolate the content of consciousness from the study of the undeniable influences of society, biology and the physical environment – thus emphasizing individuality and autonomy.

There is, however, a further problem of doing science that arises from uniqueness: causal laws require that the same pattern of antecedent and resultant events *always* occur. It follows that there must be a population of identical antecedent conditions and identical outcomes which can be sampled so as to test the law. In so far as people's behaviour and experiences are unique, can we ever say, as traditional science demands, that $X$ always causes $Y$ and that $X$ is always $X$ and $Y$ is always $Y$?

Suppose that $X$ is an affect-laden belief about the government in office; and $Y$ is a vote in a local government election. We may be able to show that holding this belief is antecedent to voting against the party in power's candidate – but this 'cause and effect' statement is a statistical generalization. It need not hold for every individual. So far, this is no different from statistical prediction in the physical world. But in social psychology this kind of nomothetic statement glosses over the fact that the affect-laden belief is not going to be *identical* (in content or intensity) for every individual who holds it. So too, the act of voting against the candidate in question is going to *mean* something different (unique) for each individual. Thus although statistically $X$ leads to $Y$, what we really are observing is that $X_1$ leads to $Y_1$ for individual $I_1$ and $X_2$ leads to $Y_2$ for individual $I_2$. The general law only holds in so far as we are prepared to call $X_1$ and $X_2$ and $X$ and similarly $Y_1$ $Y_2$ and $Y$ equivalent. In other words, only if we forego the richness of the unique beliefs and behaviour. This is another instance of simplification losing information but permitting a useful nomothetic advance.

Another way around the uniqueness problem is to search for causal laws *within* individuals over time, using an idiographic approach. Thus it is possible to search for consistencies and repeating patterns within one person's life. Smith *et al* (1956) is an example of this; so, too, would be the interpretation that a psychoanalyst might arrive at after a long period of work with a patient. However, it is still unlikely that, over time, each instance is experienced by the person as identical – so there is still a degree of simplification needed to get round the problem of uniqueness.

But suppose that a person believes something on just one occasion – never to be repeated; but that following recognition of the belief and feeling that person forms an intention and then *acts*. Would we be justified in calling this an example of cause and effect? According to the traditional view in physical science this would be cause and effect although some psychologists and philosophers of science would treat it as a special form of causality known as 'singular causality'. This might seem an unneccessary complication but it is important because it does imply determination, whereas the alternative is to recast the same situation as an example of future-oriented, autonomous action. In this case, the person is seen as *not* determined and as free to choose not to act from that intention or to act in that way despite having the same affect-laden belief. This interpretation of uniqueness – as you can see – implies a very different model of the person and brings us back to the question of determinism.

## 8   Determinism

Some of the strongest arguments against positivism are about the fundamental nature of people: (1) *In the physical sciences a present fact is always determined by past facts, but in humans present behaviour and experience is oriented to future goals.* (2) *Since humans are aware of what they do (or can be made aware) then they can deliberately behave in a way which puts them beyond deterministic laws.* (3) *Since the social world is the creation of humans, and since social experience is actively construed, continuously (i.e. is essentially concerned with meaning), it is inappropriate to search for deterministic laws as explanation.* These are the kinds of arguments that most strongly support the practice of idiographic and hermeneutic social psychology, against nomothetic approach.

A determinist would respond to someone's reasons given after the event as *post hoc* rationalizations of a determined sequence that has been forgotten, repressed or was always below the level of awareness; and 'reasons' for doing something which are stated in advance (intentions) would be treated as *present* internal representations of the world, caused by past experience and, which, in turn cause the future behaviour. This sequence can be written formally as a practical syllogism, after Von Wright (1971):

(1)   *My goal* is to talk to a colleague about a book.

(2)   *I believe* that to have this conversation I must telephone him between 8 p.m. and 10 p.m. tonight.

(3)   *I intend* to telephone him between 8 p.m. and 10 p.m. tonight.

(4)   *I act* accordingly.

By specifying the reasoning in this way, it is possible to express both the detail of the content (the hermeneutic approach) *and* to maintain a formal structure representing an instance of singular causality which, in practice, would help a researcher to simplify and encode the content as a preliminary to looking for patterns of cause and effect (the nomothetic approach). This kind of procedure is similar to some of the research on beliefs, attitudes and behaviour described in Unit 16 and Unit 17/18.

The antipositivist standpoint would be that people's beliefs, feelings and intentions should be seen as uniquely construed and future oriented 'reasoning' and thus open to conscious choices which would seem to rule out deterministic relations. In other words, it is possible for people to become consciously aware of potential determinism in their lives and 'side-step' the cause and effect chain. This, of course, is the basis for programmes of consciousness-raising, counselling and, particularly, psychoanalysis – where the aim is to direct processes of unconscious determinism by bringing them into awareness. But the counter-argument to this reflexivity is simple: the conscious choices we might make – to avoid determinism – are themselves determined by other factors. It is possible that conscious awareness of choices can 'lift' any determinism that is operating into a different sphere. That is, into a determinism of our conscious and deliberated choices and decisions – which in turn can be consciously examined etc. (Harré (1971) has called autonomy the awareness of awareness.) But how is it that we are able to create new (new to us) 'possible worlds' to choose from? This seems to be the point where positivism is weakest since here the stress must be on generating, actively seeking and choosing.

Paper 9 on autonomy and determinism suggests that such creativity is like language – the raw materials and rules are given but new combinations can be evolved. But notice that even here one of the basic requirements is a grammar – or some similar structure of rules – whether for creative cognition or novel behaviour. The emergence of novel phenomena within a structure of natural laws is not uncommon in the physical world; so why should this be taken as unique to human nature? Further, in human affairs rules may be followed unthinkingly as templates. (Harré (1972) has called social rules 'formal *causes* of action'.) Consciously choosing to follow social rules could also be seen as determined by deeper lying convictions, values or even personality. It seems to me that the creation of novel *content* and *meaning* through the operation of rules or a grammar need not be seen as autonomy, i.e. as non-determined; whether this is called 'autonomy' or not does exclude the possibility of using a nomothetic approach – as, in the formal statements of the practical syllogism.

In this paper I have argued that social psychologists' rejection of positivism needs reassessment. Too often we reject it on ideological grounds without sufficient awareness of what we are doing. And too often we exclude with positivism, the possibility of using a nomothetic approach to those aspects of human affairs where it is valuable. It is possible to have a nomothetic social psychology which does not conflict with the essential 'humanness' and uniqueness of people and which does not invoke a totally mechanistic view of the person. But I also 'believe' that we should not reject the determinism that underlies positivism without due attention to modern developments in conceptualizing structures and causal relations, and methods, in the task of explaining the physical world; and without reconsidering that deterministic relations *can* be unique and unique outcomes *can* be determined. *And* until we can explain to ourselves why the idea of autonomy is so much more seductive than determinism.

### References

HARRÉ, and SECORD, P. F. (1972) *The explanation of social behaviour*, Oxford, Blackwell.

HERZLICH, C. (1973) 'Health and illness: a social psychological analysis', *European Monographs in Social Psychology, 5*. H. Tajfel (ed.), London, Academic Press.

KAYE, K. (1982) 'The moral philosophy of microanalysis', in T. Field and A. Fogel (eds), *Emotion and early interaction*, Hillsdale, New Jersey, Lawrence Erlbaum.

SKINNER, B. F. (1971) *Beyond freedom and dignity*, London, Jonathan Cape.

VON WRIGHT, M. G. (1971) *Explanation and understanding*, London, Routledge and Kegan Paul.

WOLPERT, L. and BERRY, M. (1983) 'The electron at the end of the universe', BBC Radio 3 Talk.

## Paper 9: A note on assumptions of autonomy and determinism in social psychology

*by Richard Stevens*

Many of the theories and research studies in this course are based on the assumption that each of us is the product of forces which are ultimately outside our own choosing. If we look back at the first two blocks which are concerned with the foundations of social behaviour, we might well come away with the impression that social life is generated by interactions between our biological make-up, social environment and the ways in which we are brought up.

Unit 3, which examined the possible relevance of genetic and biological factors to social life, indicated that our potential not only for intelligent behaviours but also for the powerful bond between a child and his or her mother may be 'built in' genetically. It also raised the question of a possible genetic basis for our potentials for certain complex social behaviours such as aggressiveness and the different behaviour patterns which may characterize the sexes.

While acknowledging that the existence and continuation of family life have been explained by reference to evolution, Unit 1 also emphasized the importance of social structure. This determines the form which families take in any particular society as well as related institutions like work which help to define the roles of family members. Society creates a framework which shapes and constrains the behaviours which are open to individuals within that society. It also creates a framework of expectations about what behaviours are to be regarded as normal and which as deviant, expectations which exert their own shaping influence and constraints. Unit 2 made us more aware that an individual's behaviour should not be viewed in isolation. In a family (or any close group) the behaviour of one member is radically influenced by that of the others.

Developmental theories in psychology tend to add weight to the notion that what we regard as freely chosen behaviour may well have been determined by factors in our past history or generated by the particular stage of biological maturity we have reached. Social learning theory conceptualizes this shaping process in terms of patterns of reinforcement and imitation; psychoanalysis in terms of oral, anal and phallic phases: but both presume that what has gone before makes us what we are today. Piaget's theory emphasizes the importance of maturational stages in determining the ways in which we will make sense of the world about us.

In short, much theory and research in psychology is premised on the assumption of *determinism*. This may be seen as a relatively straightforward mechanistic process of cause and effect, or it may be conceptualized as a system of some kind or it may even be viewed as shaping by the creation and manipulation of expectations and meanings. But all such theories presume that ultimately we are the products of factors which are outside our control; that whatever subjective experience of autonomy we may have (i.e. the sense that we can be the creators and arbiters of our own faith) is essentially illusory. The task of the psychologist is seen as uncovering the factors which determine what we are and the processes through which these factors work. The aim of the majority of such approaches in psychology is nomothetic: that is to formulate general laws to explain how behaviour and experience come about (see Paper 8).

But there are dissentient voices. In Units 2 and 7 we saw both in family interactions and in early development that the individual is not just passively shaped by the actions of others. Rather, each individual makes a contribution him or herself to the 'negotiated' process. Each helps to construct the interpersonal realities created by the process of social interaction. Unit 7 explicitly introduces the notion that human persons can be regarded as 'agents' – capable of initiating actions and carrying these through, and capable of making sense of situations in different ways: in other words, capable to a considerable extent of creating our own actions, experiences and lives. Block 4 'Personal Worlds' enlarges on this theme. One attribute which seems to help free us from simple determination by factors outside our control is our capacity for reflexive awareness. We can become aware that factor $X$ influences what we do. This very awareness may then undermine the effect it has. An important method for increasing our autonomy is 'consciousness-raising' – making us more aware of the factors which influence and shape what we are.

Several theories, either directly or indirectly, support this conception of a person as, within limits, an autonomous being. George Kelly's personal construct theory, for example, postulates 'constructive alternativism' – that individuals have the capacity to construe their experiences in different ways. Symbolic interactionism with its emphasis on negotiated meanings in social interaction also allows for a degree of autonomous input from individuals. We may even include Freudian theory here in that it supposes that it is possible to modify the effects of unconscious influences from the past by insight and the process of analysis. (As the set book *Freud and Psychoanalysis* argues (see especially pp.123–5) Freudian theory accords *both* with a model of the person as determined and also as possessing the capacity for creating oneself.)

Theories which allow for human autonomy do not seek to deny that we are shaped and influenced by factors outside our control. But, within this context, they will argue, individuals can play some part as active agents and creators of their own fate. Human beings have the capacity to initiate actions and to some extent create how they will be. Such capacity for autonomy would appear to be linked to the centrality of meaning in our personal and social lives. It is precisely because the meaning of actions and experiences are not fixed, have to be constructed and are open to reframing and change, that we are offered particular power in creating the personal and interpersonal realities we inhabit. Certainly in our daily lives, we generally assume that we ourselves and other people are capable of choosing what they do – we attribute each other with a *modicum* of autonomy at least. It is an essential key to our understanding of what it is to be human.

Different conceptions of persons then – as determined or as possessing a degree of autonomy – mark a fundamental controversy within social psychology.

Much of psychology is in the positivist mould. It assumes that the subject matter of psychology is potentially measurable and that, with application, psychologists can eventually discover the fundamental causal laws which 'make us tick'. The goal of psychologists becomes to understand why people are as they are – their fundamental psychological nature. However, as other psychologists have suggested, perhaps there is no such thing. Both as individuals and as joint creators of our cultures we are in part capable of creating our own nature.

> We begin our studies in psychology from the fact that our nature as human beings is a puzzle to us. But . . . is this a puzzle we face . . . because we have not yet done enough research and amassed enough information . . .? Or is it, perhaps, because we have no real nature, no natural nature, because we are self-determining, self-defining animals?

(Shotter, 1975, p.11)

If we take this view, we shift from a psychology of the way people are to a psychology of the ways they might be. Such a psychology is not concerned with formulating fundamental laws but rather with possibilities, of stimulating our capacity to create what we are – both as individuals and societies. Psychology becomes a moral rather than a natural science. Not only the aims but the forms of understanding and the methods used in these two different approaches to psychology will differ. Explanations in a moral science of psychology tend to be couched in terms of *reasons*: for a psychology as a natural science in terms of *causes* (for further discussion of the differences see Paper 5 and Paper 8). Methods in psychology as a moral science will emphasize the unravelling of meaning (hermeneutics) rather than the testing of hypotheses.

Confronted with such different assumptions about the nature of being, each with its implications for the aims, nature of understanding and methods of social psychology, how are you the student to choose between them? Or at least how are you to come to some kind of resolution of the controversy? The issue of autonomy and determinism (or 'free will' and determinism as it is sometimes called) has been with us down through the history of human thought and no doubt will remain so. Two points though may be of help to your thinking about these issues.

(1) The first is the question of conceptualization. In everyday life, we automatically assume a degree of autonomy. Few of us regard ourselves and others as mere automatons like a car or a washing machine. We tend to hold each other responsible for what we do and assume ourselves to be capable of initiating actions or of holding back. We presume that we have reasons for what we do. It would be hard to imagine what social life would be like if we presumed otherwise.

The perspective of the traditional psychologist in fact is very different. His task is to go beyond the everyday reasons we give. The psychoanalyst, for example, looks for unconscious motives; the sociobiologist for the influence of genetic potentials; the learning theorist for the effects of reinforcement histories. In these kinds of psychology behaviour and experience are looked at from a different perspective from that we adopt in everyday life and with a different end in view. It is not surprising that human beings are construed differently. The positivist and/or scientifically minded psychologist finds it hard to conceptualize (at least in his thinking *qua* psychologist) what could be meant by autonomy. What factors other than heredity and environment, both ultimately outside our control, could be responsible for making us what we are?

However, there is a model available which goes some way to providing a conceptualization to reconcile these separated positions. That is language. As we can see from Unit 5, the basis of language is determined. Our capacity to use it depends on both the possession of appropriate physical structures and exposure to a particular language system. Our capacity for language rests then on both biological potentials, social context and developmental learning. Yet an extraordinary feature of language is its openness – that we are capable of saying something that, to us at least, is totally original, something that we have never heard anyone say before. This is possible because language rests on our capacity for generating (and interpreting) elements which are patterned according to implicit rules. We do not learn sentences by rote but rather acquire the elements and rule systems which give us the means to create and understand them. Such capacity for openness – to create the novel and unique – could well be regarded as an example of autonomous process. We may well posit a similar process as being involved in generating both actions and the ways in which we make sense of the world. Thus we have a model for a process which is at once determined in that it rests on factors outside the individual's control and yet permits of autonomy in its capacity to create the original and unique.

(2)   The second point is to emphasize the complexity of the nature of being. We are clearly biological organisms, rooted in our bodies and subject to its vagaries and eventual decay. But the extraordinary feature of being human is our developed capacity for symbolic thought. We live in a world of meanings. There are two faces to humanness then – the biological and what we might term the 'experiential' (the reality of experience or awareness). It has been argued elsewhere in this course that the latter represents a fundamentally different kind of subject matter than the physical world. For not only are our theories of it constructed but it is constructed in itself. Such worlds of meaning (e.g. our experience and awareness) do not exist in definitive 'objective' form but are continually open themselves to reframing and reconstruction.

Both Paper 5 'The significance of meaning' and Chapter 10 in the set book *Freud and Psychoanalysis* present the argument for making such a division and explore some of the implications this has for social psychology (and the social sciences generally) as a field of study. The point to stress here however is that we are creatures of both worlds (and of course the two interrelate and influence each other). If the notion of the person as both determined and autonomous seems to be a paradox, it is perhaps because such a paradox is at the heart of being. As we are both biological and existential beings so we are both determined by factors outside our control and yet capable, to some degree, of transcending their influence. One important factor in developing our autonomy is increasing our capacity for reflexive awareness, i.e. increasing our understanding of the ways we are shaped and created. This, if anything, might be regarded as the ultimate aim of a course such as this.

---

Although the set book *Freud and Psychoanalysis* is primarily concerned with psychoanalytic theory, many of the points made there apply to the study of social psychology. The question of autonomy, determinism and the implications for psychology are discussed in Chapters 10 and 14. For further consideration of these issues you might like to turn there.

### References

SHOTTER, J. (1975) *Images of man in psychological research*, London, Methuen.

STEVENS, R. (1983) *Freud and psychoanalysis*, Milton Keynes, The Open University Press. (Set Book.)

## Paper 10: A note on the nature of social psychology

*by Richard Stevens with a contribution from Roger Sapsford*

*It would seem appropriate, towards the end of the course, to reflect on the question – what then is social psychology? What kind of knowledge and understanding does it offer? What sort of discipline is it? Several issues with direct bearing on this question have been dealt with in the preceding papers in this part of the Metablock, nevertheless I think it might be helpful here to make a few concluding remarks. (Bear in mind, however, that, as the term 'note' suggests these do represent the views of the authors. There is some disagreement among social psychologists about the nature of social psychology and what social psychology should be doing.*

It must be obvious from the variety of theories and approaches which you have encountered in the course that social psychology is not a unified and monolithic discipline. It embraces a range of traditions, each with its own particular assumptions about the nature of people, their relationship with society and the best methods for studying them. The course has deliberately adopted a multiple perspective strategy as a way of offering a fuller appreciation of what social psychology may have to offer.

Within this heterogeneity, however, we can detect broad groupings or themes. One key difference here which deserves comment is related to both the way the subject matter of psychology is conceived (i.e. the nature of mind, behaviour and being) and the best way this should be studied. A strong tradition in social psychology, inherited from general experimental psychology, has been *positivism*. As we have seen, psychologists who take this approach assume that the best way for social psychology to develop is to use the methods which have proved so successful in the physical sciences. They are generally concerned to deal only with those aspects of behaviour and experience which can be specified in some observable or quantifiable form. Their aim is to formulate hypotheses about the causal relationships between these observables and to test them – usually by means of experiment. Following Popper (1968), most psychologists would acknowledge that such testing is not a way of proving the 'truth' of the hypotheses (verification) but of testing for their possible falsity (falsification).

Positivists in psychology seem usually to assume that:

  (i) there is a definitive human nature to be investigated;

 (ii) behaviour and experience are causally determined;

(iii) the processes underlying behaviour and experience are not *fundamentally* different in principle from those of other sciences. The same methods for investigating them are therefore appropriate;

(iv) given time, psychologists will uncover the laws which govern the causal relationships concerned.

Such an approach is highly attractive. It would be encouraging (to many psychologists at least!) to think that psychology is capable of the kind of understanding, prediction and control that has been achieved in the physical sciences. The point has been made elsewhere in the course (see Unit 13, Block 5 and Paper 7 above) that social, economic and technological factors may shape our consciousness. Positivist assumptions are appropriate to our machine age. So much of the contemporary world is made up of objects which are clearly determined and are best understood by seeing them in terms of component elements which are interrelated. It is not surprising that there is a temptation to see human beings in a similar light.

However, as the preceding papers in this part of the Metablock have made clear, each of the assumptions listed above is open to dispute. It has been argued, for example, that social behaviour and experience are essentially constituted by meanings and that therefore the study of meanings is the key task for social psychology. If we accept this view, then we are confronted with a situation in which the subject-matter of social psychology is not easily quantifiable nor expressible in the form of observable events. Meanings are constructions which can be understood only by reference to other concepts and the shared conventions which underpin the use of these concepts (see *Freud and Psychoanalysis*, Chapter 11, for elucidation of this point).

Given this dependence on meanings: human nature, at the level of complex social behaviour and experience, can be regarded as localized and highly variable.

This 'nature' will vary from culture to culture (each representing a pattern of shared conventions and use of concepts) and, because of their different experiences, between individuals. It will also be open to continuous change and redefinition, not least because of our reflexive capacity. Defining a person in a particular way may serve to change how he behaves – either because, consciously or otherwise, he fulfills such expectations and comes to see himself as others describe him or because he deliberately reacts against this. Because of our capacity for self-reflection and, in contemporary society, our access to multiple ways of conceptualizing ourselves (in education, politics, religions etc.), human beings can be regarded as having some scope at least for self-definition and thus self-determination. If we accept this assumption of 'self-defining' man then it follows that the focus shifts onto individual differences. We need to know how and why this individual behaves and experiences as he does. We accept his uniqueness. The explanations which apply to others may not hold for him. Social psychology becomes a discipline more akin to natural history. We search for differences, patterns and underlying structures rather than fundamental cause-effect laws. It may well be this self-defining characteristic of human beings which explains the failure of psychology in practice, even after more than a hundred years of existence as a discipline, to produce any laws of behaviour which have any special power to predict an individual's behaviour in a real-life situation. It may also be why, at the end of an intensive endeavour to produce an account of scientific psychology now running to several volumes and with numerous eminent contributors, Sigmund Koch (1963) could only despair that the discipline could ever be regarded as a science.

This position then asserts that there *is* a fundamental difference between the subject-matter of social psychology and that of the natural sciences and that one cannot be reduced to the other. Nor are the goals, assumptions and methods of the positivist approach appropriate to the study of meanings. Chapter 14 of *Freud and Psychoanalysis* discusses this issue in relation to psychoanalysis and it is worth looking at this chapter in conjunction with this paper. Set out on pp. 145–6 are the broad principles for a *dialectical* psychology which would take into account the points raised above. Such a psychology would be concerned with '*processes* – the ways in which change comes about, and not the search for essences' (i.e. the fundamental unchanging nature of behaviour and experience). It would also be *holistic*. Working on the assumption that personal and social meaning patterns are interrelated and that each aspect can only properly be understood by relating it to others, it would be *integrative* in approach, concerned with the interplay of different forces underlying social behaviour and experience. Such an approach will be concerned with 'hermeneutic' understanding in the sense of eliciting and interpreting ways in which people make sense of and respond to their world. It would also be concerned with *possibilities* as well as the way people are. Shotter has expressed this:

> . . . [Psychology] will be a science of quite a different kind from that of physics and the other natural sciences with which we are familiar. It will lead to what I shall call a moral science: it will be concerned with, as Miller says, 'conceptions of what is humanly possible and what is humanly desirable'. In other words, it will be concerned not with seeking deeply into the inner workings of things and discovering their rock bottom, ultimate causes, but with our options as to how to live. And I feel justified in claiming that

such an enterprise can be called a scientific one as I take it that what distinguishes those activities we designate as 'scientific' ... is that in them we attempt to discover general principles by which we can transform ourselves from being victims to being masters of our fate.

(Shotter, 1975)

(How far a social psychology of this kind can be regarded as a science is an open question. Much depends on what for you constitutes a science. For a discussion of this issue in relation to psychoanalysis, see *Freud and Psychoanalysis*, Chapters 10, 11 and 14, especially pp.113–6 and pp.125–6. A similar line of argument could be mounted with regard to a dialectical or hermeneutic psychology.)

In the positivist tradition, the key criterion for assessing the worth of a theory is its predictive power. In practice, in psychology such prediction is almost invariably a statistical affair (i.e. given a sufficient number of observed events, we can predict that a significant number, though by no means all, will be in line with our hypotheses). Such predictions are usually also fairly closely tied to the conditions of the experimental situation. They are not necessarily generalizable to everyday life. Rarely, if ever, then has experimental social psychology come up with the means to allow us to predict precisely the behaviour of a specific individual in a specific natural setting. The criteria for assessing work in a dialectical and hermeneutic tradition are less clear-cut. (The problems of formulating and testing hypotheses based on a theory concerned with meanings is documented in detail in Chapter 10 of the set book *Freud and Psychoanalysis*.) The test of prediction is not easily applied. However, you may remember that in Paper 2 (Section 5) two principles were suggested as a way of assessing psychological theories in general – *power of differentiation* (the degree to which theories can provide detailed accounts of behaviour and experience) and *consistency* (the degree to which the propositions of an account provided by a theory fit together in consistent fashion). Both might be used to assess accounts of behaviour and experience of a hermeneutic kind. In the box below, Roger Sapsford suggests three further ways. His comments on his suggestions bring out the difficulties involved.

---

### Box 1  Three further ways of assessing social psychological theories by Roger Sapsford

As we have seen, *hermeneutic* psychology aims to describe and interpret the meanings of events and situations for their participants. I would also like to distinguish a related approach which we might call *critical* psychology. This aims to help people become aware of the determining influences upon their lives (for example, by laying bare the structures of social living and the norms which we take for granted) and, in this way, possibly putting them in a position to overcome such influences. As we have seen, the test of prediction cannot be used alone to assess the validity of accounts of a hermeneutic or a critical kind. How then can they be evaluated? In addition to applying the criteria of differentiation and consistency (which are discussed elsewhere), three further possible tests are described below. Although each is worth considering, they all ultimately lead to an absurdity. But they do serve to point up the problems of finding satisfactory criteria for evaluating accounts of this kind.

1  *The test of agreement*

The first version would be to regard the research subjects (or rather, participants) as the ultimate arbiters of what is true 'for them'. In other words, accounts of people's lives are considered to be more or less true to the extent that they themselves agree with them. One may readily see the strength of this approach, particularly for hermeneutic perspectives.

---

Given the notion (explored in Paper 7) that one may relevantly see people's 'worlds' as individually and personally constructed, then only the individuals can make entire sense of them.

However, if the psychologist is making any contribution at all to the process, he or she must be describing participants' lives to the participants in terms other than the ones they generally use – otherwise the research fails to widen conceptual horizons – and it seems to me that the participants could fail to agree without the psychologist necessarily being wrong. Participants' thinking might be subject to constraint; indeed, it might be precisely this constraint which the psychologist is trying to point out. Nonetheless, the test of agreement is seriously advanced by some social psychologists and other social scientists (see, e.g., Reason and Rowan, 1981; Fay, 1975).

### 2    *The test of consensus*

This perspective appeals to agreement among those best qualified to judge a theory's worth – the discipline, or the 'body of scientists' – and gets over the problems of the test of agreement by appealing only to those who have knowledge of and training in the concepts. (It also has the advantage of establishing some continuity with more positivistic approaches. The test of prediction is a special case of the test of consensus – one very good way of 'convincing the scientific community'.) The absurdity which this approach entails, however, is that a theory could not become 'true' until accepted by others – one could never say that the minority opinion was 'the right one'. Any new theorist would be advancing ideas which were not yet agreed and therefore wrong, presumably, until others had been persuaded of their truth – and persuaded on grounds other than by the test of consensus!

### 3    *The test of plausibility*

My own preference is for what one might call the test of plausibility: that a research conclusion is true to the extent that it makes sense *to the researcher* of all the evidence at his or her disposal. This seems to me the logical outcome of Kelly's view of man as scientist – that the researcher, like the man in the street, is primarily concerned with building and modifying theoretical perspectives to make the best possible sense of what he sees and experiences. (The test also reflects better *why* people do research, which is often to explore areas of their own lives and extend their own understanding.) I have to acknowledge, however, that the end-state of this test is even more absurd than the end-states of the other two. For *in itself* this test does not enable us to decide between conflicting accounts given by different researchers (unless you apply the dubious *ad hominem* argument that one researcher has 'a more developed understanding' than the other).

These suggestions, then, indicate the problems involved in finding satisfactory tests of hermeneutic and critical perspectives which try to deal with the experience of persons as whole and potentially undetermined beings. It is worth bearing in mind, however, that the working criterion of most day-to-day research will continue to be the test of prediction, because most of social psychology will still be about the causes of behaviour and how it may be changed. Any attempt to 'master our fate' must inevitably involve a thorough exploration of constraints on and factors underlying the ways in which we experience and behave.

Where does all this leave you the student? As with autonomy and determinism, how are you to regard what may well seem to be opposing positions? It may be that the two approaches (i.e. positivist and hermeneutic/critical psychologies) are not necessarily incompatible. As Roger Sapsford suggests in his final sentence, a psychology concerned with encouraging possibilities needs also to be concerned with causes and constraints. I would also like to suggest that another way of looking at this seeming dichotomy is in terms of level of analysis (see Paper 3). We may distinguish what we might term *process psychology* – that research and theory which concerns itself with the 'micro-processes' upon which behaviour and experience depend (perception, memory, thought and emotion), and *person psychology* that which concerns itself with the broader concerns of attitudes, relationships and the ways in which individuals perceive and plan their lives. Although it is not possible to draw a rigid line between these two kinds of psychology, this division may well be more profound than may at first appear. For it may well be that in process psychology we can rightly assume a 'fixed' model of the human being. The characteristics and principles of processes of memory, perceptual discrimination, simple learning are most probably explicable by general principles applicable across individuals. However, when it comes to the complex patterns of social behaviour and experience, we are forced to deal with the content generated by these processes, i.e. meaning, and this, as has been argued earlier, involves a wholly different set of principles which demand different aims and different methods in research.

Whether or not you find this suggestion makes sense or whether you prefer to emphasize a specifically positivist or specifically hermeneutic view, do bear in mind that even modern physics has come to regard its theories not as statements of truth but as *useful* ways of conceptualizing. As LeShan and Margenau have commented, 'We no longer search for what reality *is*, but rather for ways of usefully construing it; ways to define it that will help us achieve our goals' (p.213). You may find that the best approach in social psychology is to draw from whatever theory or perspective seems best fitted to your aims. Whether these be to make sense of your own behaviour or that of another person, or whether it is a specific practical aim like stopping smoking or changing someone's attitude, try to assess which theory or research study offers the most helpful guide for your ends. But be alert when you look at any theory to both the assumptions which appear to underpin it and your own assumptions in evaluating it. Bear in mind also the potential of theories to influence us – by thinking of ourselves in terms of what they presume we are. For psychological theories are not necessarily so much about what we are as what we may become. Again to quote Shotter (1975):

> If the living of our lives were not a task, if our form of life were given us in our biology, if we were not free agents, then we should not find the problem of what we are so crucial. We would simply live as we must ... However, experientially at least, determinism is not true: 'We are condemned to be free', says Sartre; we live lives full of uncertainty, and our freedom is a burden to us ... [However] there is no reason to suppose that the process by which we transformed ourselves from cave dwellers in the past to what we are now is at an end. Cultural progress is surely still possible, and a science called psychology can surely assist in making the future transformations of man more human ones, so that we can all in the future enhance one another's humanity.

(Shotter, 1975)

### References

KOCH, S. (ed.) (1963) *Psychology: a study of a science*, Vols 1–6, New York, McGraw-Hill.

LESHAN, L. and MARGENAU, H. (1983) *Einstein's space and Von Gogh's sky*, London, Harvester.

POPPER, K. (1968) *The logic of scientific discovery*, (2nd edition), London, Hutchinson.

SHOTTER, J. (1975) *Images of man in psychological research*, London, Methuen.

STEVENS, R. (1983) *Freud and psychoanalysis*, Milton Keynes, The Open University Press.

# PART IV – REVISION EXERCISES

*by Jane Henry*

## 1  Introduction

This part of the Metablock is in three sections: the first section outlines reasons why an active approach to revision is advisable and discusses what this consists of. You may well be familiar with these ideas and if you are good at exams you may want to skip this section. The second section offers some specific suggestions as to how you might go about revising D307. The third section discusses ways of notemaking. However, revision is a very personal business, so feel free to adopt approaches other than those presented here if this seems appropriate to you.

## 2  Active revision

Much of your time so far has probably been spent in attempts to take in and understand the course material. Assignments and exams call for a rather different skill, that of recalling and communicating ideas in your own words. This is much harder whatever the subject. In the extreme case of learning a foreign language, students typically find it relatively easy to understand a lot of the words but are hard put to string together even a few of them. The facility to communicate comes once the student starts actively trying to converse, not from passively reading or listening to conversation.

In exactly the same way, when revising for exams, you need to practice communicating ideas, not just passively familiarizing yourself with the course through reading. So, above all, your revision strategy should be active, this means asking and answering questions of the material you review and *reformulating ideas* in your own words, so that they are assimilated into your own construct system well enough for you to be able to recall them and apply them in the manner asked.

It is easy to be tempted by passive revision, i.e. re-reading the course material, underlining words in a haphazard fashion or taking unthinking notes that mean nothing second time around. Numerous studies have shown that unless active attempts are made to *recall material,* most of it is rapidly forgotten; in respect of lectures typical figures are 75 per cent in one week and 98 per cent in three weeks (Rowntree 1974). Hence a considerable proportion of your revision time should be spent actively recalling what you know, even if this means you do not have time to cover everything.

The D307 exam asks you to do more than merely recall a subject well enough to write an essay about it. You will be expected to apply that knowledge to the way the question is angled. This involves *reconstruing material* in a different way from that presented in the course and often comparing and contrasting information from two or more distinct areas. To do this, you need a really sound grasp of the systems of thought (theories, concepts and methods) presented in the course. Some suggestions as to how you could go about this are given later.

### 2.1  Exam Questions

The exam will have two sections and you will be expected to answer two questions from Part 1 and one from Part 2. Part 1 comprises block related questions and Part 2 an integration question that, like the final TMA, asks you, for example, to discuss and illustrate how a particular theme or key concept was used by the various theorists and researchers referred to in the course. This builds on your work for the final TMA.

It is worthwhile giving some thought to the kind of question which might come up, since part of the art of passing exams has to do with success in anticipating the *type* of question that will be asked. The Specimen Exam Paper should help here. The course team does not set out to be tricky and usually tries to ask questions they think are worth answering, such as questions about what they see as the key issues and main points. What are these you may ask? Well the course team has provided a lot of clues. The Metablock should prove invaluable in this respect and should be studied closely. For instance, Part III indicates course themes perceived by the course team as important. The Vade Mecum summarizes the content and purpose of each block and highlights links between different parts of the course. Block introductions, objectives, chapter headings and progress boxes pick out the majority of the main points for you.

The perennial question of 'How much detail do I need to know?' remains. In considering this issue it is worth bearing in mind what is required of you in the exam. You have to plan and write three essays in three hours. This normally only gives you time to offer a short introduction which comments on the subjects of the essay and your proposed treatment of it, then you move to the main part where you develop your argument through perhaps only four to six main points, supported with appropriate illustrations and examples, followed by a conclusion which summarizes your argument/ideas and comments on the wider implications placing the ideas in context. So you only have time to get down the bare essentials, illustrated by important details such as the best supporting evidence, an example or implication that allows you to demonstrate the point and show that you understand. If you have time, it can be useful to plan out answers to questions you think might come up.

## 3   Suggested exercises

So much for revision in general – what about D307 in particular? Well, first of all you obviously need some idea of what was in the course. You may be tempted to revise unit by unit, starting with Unit 1 and working steadily through the course. Research suggests that most students end up taking in more if they split this process up, beginning with an overview of the course, then an overview of the block or unit before attempting to fill in the detail, actively reviewing what is known at each stage.

### 3.1   Overview

You might like to begin by seeing just how much of the course you can remember before you start revising. Briefly try to answer the following questions, initially without referring back to the course:

1   What did the block *consist* of? What do you remember of the associated readings and assignments? How did the components interrelate?

2   What were the main *content* areas covered by the units in each block?

3   What do you see as the primary *purpose* of the block (or units, if they each have separate purposes)?

4   What is the *function* and place of the block (or unit) in the structure of the course?

5   What *links* can you see between the content of the block or unit and other parts of the course?

You probably found a lot of gaps, perhaps units you liked came back quite well and those you disliked were hard to recall. It would be worthwhile repeating this exercise using the Vade Mecum in Part II of the Metablock to help you fill in answers you missed first time round. The Vade Mecum is structured in such a way as to give an overview of each unit and to point out the links to the rest of the course – including the Reader, set books, Metablock papers and the projects. When you have done this exercise you should have an overview of the course and can start filling in the detail.

132

## 3.2 Content

The next step is to review the *content* of the course block by block and unit by unit. Once again there is a lot to be said for going for an overview first before filling in the detail. The block and unit introductions should orient you to the material and the chapter headings, objectives and progress boxes will give you a pretty good idea of the main points in the unit. You can use these to develop a framework and then go through the unit to make sure you understand what is being referred to, filling in the supporting material and important details.

The unit by unit approach is just one way of approaching the course, an alternative approach, which you may find deepens your understanding, is to think of the content of the course in terms of concepts, theories, methods and themes. Some suggestions as to how you might attempt to revise in this way follow in Sections 3.3–3.6 below. Do not get bogged down in trying to apply the exercises to every concept and theory etc, as few of them can be completed in a definitive way. Rather they are designed to set you thinking and to help you organize the course content in your mind.

## 3.3 Concepts

You could skim through each block or unit and list the primary concepts that are introduced. Then compare that list with that given at the back of each unit or block. Check that you know how each concept is being used and what it means. Where a concept has been taken up and developed in later units, link up what has been said about it. Note when and how concepts are used to mean different things by different schools or theorists. Then take a large sheet of paper and, where possible, attempt to organize the concepts you have listed into groups or hierarchies. For instance, in Figure 1 repression, reaction formation and projection

PSYCHOANALYTIC THEORY

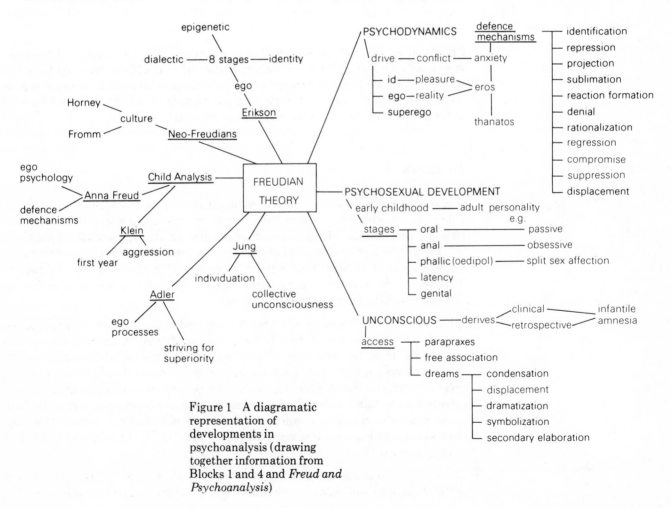

Figure 1  A diagramatic representation of developments in psychoanalysis (drawing together information from Blocks 1 and 4 and *Freud and Psychoanalysis*)

are all grouped as defence mechanisms, which in turn is placed under the more general heading of psychodynamics. Try to see what links and cross-references you can find between the concepts or groups of concepts you have listed, especially where their meaning overlaps, for example self and identity.

### 3.4 Theories

As regards *theories*: begin by compiling a list of the major theories or perspectives presented in the course (personal construct theory, psychodynamics, social learning theory etc.) and then attempt to compare them using the guidelines given in Paper 2 of Part III of the Metablock. This gives ten dimensions for contrasting theories and provides a worked example, which should help you apply the scheme to other theories. Where the information is provided, note how theorists' interests relate to their historical and cultural background and work experience. If you have time, you might like to turn your attention to the more specific and limited theories introduced and consider which are related, how far they can be subsumed under some of the general perspectives referred to above, and the extent to which they complement or contradict each other.

### 3.5 Methods

In the course you have encountered various research *methods* – observation, repertory grids, experiments, attitude scaling etc. Most of these are brought together in Paper 6 in Part III of the Metablock and in the *Introduction to the Projects* booklet. These papers offer a useful starting point as they review the main characteristics of each method discussed along with their advantages and disadvantages. To revise this area you could compile a list of the main methods used in the course, describing their features and variants. Then list their main advantages and disadvantages and note which studies and/or sections of the course particularly exemplify their use.

### 3.6 Themes

Finally, there are certain *themes* that run through the course, many of these are specifically discussed in the ten papers in Part III of the Metablock. By following up the references to these papers in the Vade Mecum you will be able to find the units which discuss and elaborate on these themes. Look for illustrations from different parts of the course not just one or two units.

## 4  Notes

Obviously, you need some means of reducing the course material into a manageable form. Making notes rather than merely underlining portions of the text will give you practice in putting out and reformulating ideas as well as taking them in; this will help you to remember and provide a written record for you to return to. New ideas often seem dull or hard to grasp until we have conceptual pegs to hang them on. Actively constructing notes will help this process and may even enliven bits of the course that seem dull to you.

When making notes, ensure you write legibly and make an effort to organize the material. Resist the temptation to jot down illegible notes in an undisciplined way. Done properly, note-making will force you to decide which are the main points and help clarify how they interrelate. Your notes should concentrate on these key points. Some people find the key points enough to bring important details back to mind, others find it necessary to add information to remind them of an example, relevant research or the psychologist(s) concerned. (For key theorists and researchers you may find Paper 1 in Part III of the Metablock useful in your revision.)

There are various ways of making notes and people vary as to the method they prefer. Conventional notes are the most common, these run vertically down the page, running on from one page to the next. Some people write summaries in prose, others produce outlines in note form. Research suggests that the latter are easier to revise from.

*Conventional notes*

I. MAIN POINT 1
   A. Sub section 1
      1. Point 1
      2. Point 2
      (e.g. . . .)
      evidence
   B. Sub section 2
      1. Point 1
      2. Point 2

II. MAIN POINT 2

A variant on this theme is to use a separate page (or large index card) for each point or area covered. This allows one to compare and contrast different areas more readily than conventional notes as the order in which they are stored can be interchanged easily.

Layout can be used to aid memory: with conventional notes you can use numbering systems, varied heading sizes and indenting to indicate hierarchy of ideas in much the same way as we do in the units. Symbols can also be useful – round brackets for examples and square ones for research, for instance.

Conventional notes, like the course itself (because it is written), suffer from the drawback that the material is necessarily presented in a linear, segmented way. The shortcomings of this restriction are apparent from the need to reintroduce the same themes, ideas, theories and theorists at various points in the course. The distinction between the areas covered by each unit or block and the structure imposed on the course is to some extent arbitrary as much of the subject matter in social psychology is interlinked, or at least has a bearing on other areas. As an antidote we have attempted, in the Metablock, to draw out the continuities, contrasts and relationships across the course.

Figure 2   A comparison of the stages of development propounded by Piaget, Freud and Erikson

|  |  | personality |
| cognitive development | psychosexual development | ego development |
| --- | --- | --- |
| (Piaget) | (Freud) | (Erikson) |
| sensory-motor phase | oral — passive / aggressive | oral-sensory (basic trust *vs.* mistrust) |
| concrete operations | anal | anal-muscular (autonomy *vs.* shame and doubt) |
|  | phallic | locomotor-genital (initiative *vs.* guilt) |
| formal operations | latency | latency (industry *vs.* inferiority) |
|  | genital | puberty and adolescence (identity *vs.* role confusion) |
|  |  | young adulthood (intimacy *vs.* isolation) |
|  |  | adulthood (generality *vs.* stagnation) |
|  |  | maturity (ego integrity *vs.* despair) |

(shift from egocentricity)

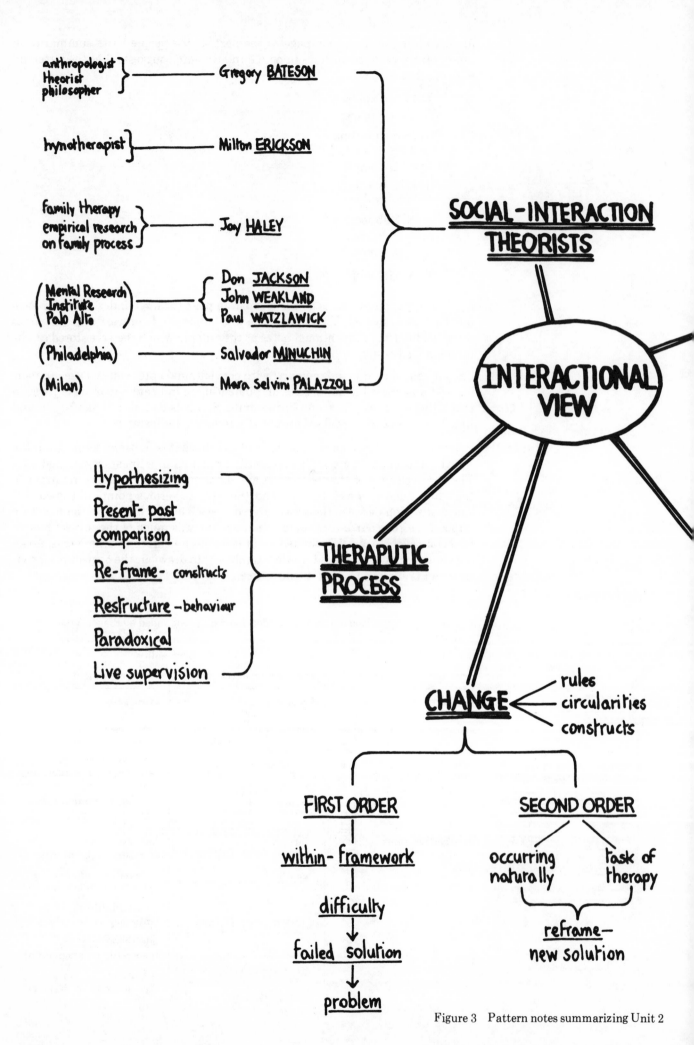

Figure 3   Pattern notes summarizing Unit 2

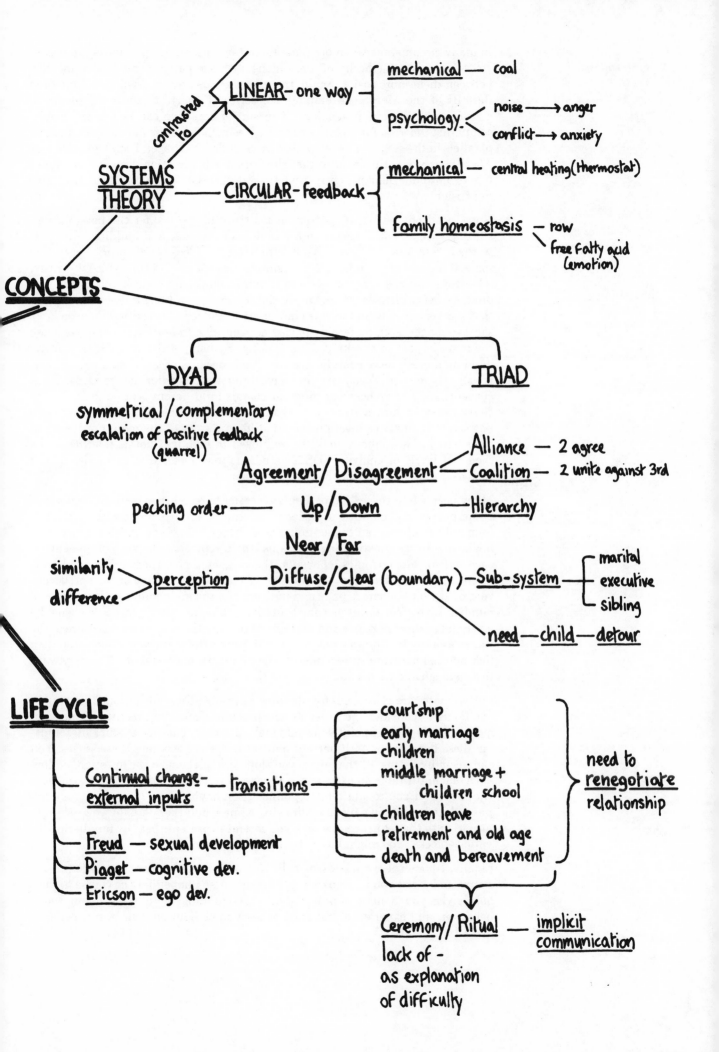

SYSTEMS THEORY

contrasted to

LINEAR – one way
- mechanical — coal
- psychology
  - noise ⟶ anger
  - conflict ⟶ anxiety

CIRCULAR – feedback
- mechanical — central heating (thermostat)
- Family homeostasis
  - row
  - free fatty acid (emotion)

CONCEPTS

DYAD

symmetrical / complementary
escalation of positive feedback (quarrel)

TRIAD

Agreement / Disagreement
- Alliance — 2 agree
- Coalition — 2 unite against 3rd

pecking order —— Up / Down —— Hierarchy

Near / Far

similarity / difference ⟶ perception —— Diffuse / Clear (boundary) — Sub-system
- marital
- executive
- sibling

need — child — detour

LIFE CYCLE

Continual change – external inputs —— transitions
- courtship
- early marriage
- children
- middle marriage + children school
- children leave
- retirement and old age
- death and bereavement

need to renegotiate relationship

Freud — sexual development
Piaget — cognitive dev.
Ericson — ego dev.

Ceremony / Ritual — implicit communication
lack of - as explanation of difficulty

In many circumstances a more diagrammatic representation of ideas can enable you to show the hierarchy of ideas along with the pattern and interconnection between them more easily. Again, there are various ways of doing this. Paper I in Part III of the Metablock employed a series of charts to show the historical development of social psychology. This sort of approach can be a useful way of comparing theories, for instance Figure 2 (see p.135) presents an attempt to show parallels in the stages of development propounded by Piaget, Freud and Erikson. These charts are still linear in that they run in one direction from left to right or top to bottom, though contrasting several theorists or areas along the same dimension.

Notes need not be linear, pattern notes (Buzan, 1982) offer the possibility of starting with a central theme in the middle of the page and building notes outwards in a number of directions. Figure 3 (see pp.136–7) offers a brief résumé of some of the key ideas in Unit 2, in a simple concept map of this type. Obviously, other formulations are possible and if you attempted this task you might well produce a very different map. One of the advantages of this form of notetaking is that it is very easy to add in extra information. Indeed they are best done on large sheets of paper (A3), preferably placed horizontally. In black and white you loose the main impact of this kind of notetaking. By using different colours, you can build up a much more complicated map that, because of layout and colour cues, is still easy to recall. You can either have different colours for each main area, e.g. concepts and life cycle or use different colours for different types of point – concepts, examples and evidence etc. Symbols or underlining in the same colour can be used to indicate connections across different areas of the map. For instance, the symbol of a rainbow, could be employed to highlight points relating to the theme of levels of analysis. (DS262 students may recall that extra visual cues such as the use of colour can aid verbal memory.)

Many people find these kind of diagrams easier to recall than conventional notes. Some people also claim it is easier to reformulate and reorder what you know from pattern notes than conventional notes which follow a definite sequence. You might like to try constructing diagrams which represent the key components of each unit or block (topics, concepts, theories, methods, themes etc.) and their interconnections. Detailed information about experiments can be noted conventionally on a separate page and indicated on the main map by a keyword and number. If you feel ambitious and find this technique useful, you could even take a very large sheet of paper and attempt to portray the shape and structure of the course as a whole. Add in what you consider to be the main components and then link up the important interconnections with arrows and symbols. You may want to do a rough and then a final version of these maps.

Pattern notes are also useful for planning essays. With a conventional linear plan one tends to consider the order in which you are going to present the material along with the type of point you could make. It is very easy to get stuck by confusing these two issues. With pattern notes it is easy to separate these stages. You can begin by listing all the points you think are relevant to the question, adding each one in turn like an extra spoke of a wheel but leaving enough space between the spokes for you to add related points. Then having done this you can encompass related points in a block by drawing a line round them, finally you turn your attention to the sequence in which you intend to present them by numbering the various blocks. You might like to try this in the exam.

Finally, I hope these suggestions help you assimilate the ideas presented in the course and assist you to prepare for the exam. Also I hope that the course has not only given you a more sophisticated understanding of thinking about social behaviour and experience, but shed at least some light on your own experience and relationships.